THE PLANTFINDER'S GUIDE TO

CACTI & OTHER SUCCULENTS

THE PLANTFINDER'S GUIDE TO

CACTI & OTHER SUCCULENTS

Keith Grantham & Paul Klaassen

PICTURE ACKNOWLEDGEMENTS

All photographs are by **Marie O'Hara**, except pages 12–13, 28–29, 34–35, 44–45, 70–71, 86–87, 101–102, 118–119, 134–135, 150–151 and 166–167 by **Karl Adamson**, and pages 24, 60 and 106 by **Keith Grantham**

Illustrations on pages 11, 49, 51, 52 and 53 by **Coral Mula**

NOTE: Throughout the book the time of year is given as a season to make the reference applicable to readers all over the world. In the northern hemisphere the seasons may be translated into months as follows:

Early winter	December	*Early spring*	March	*Early summer*	June	*Early autumn*	September
Midwinter	January	*Mid-spring*	April	*Midsummer*	July	*Mid-autumn*	October
Late winter	February	*Late spring*	May	*Late summer*	August	*Late autumn*	November

First published in the UK in 1999 by David & Charles Publishers,
Brunel House, Newton Abbot, Devon
ISBN 0 7153 0925 0
A catalogue record for this book is available from the British Library.

First published in North America in 1999 by Timber Press Inc.,
133 SW Second Avenue, Suite 450, Portland, Oregon 97204, USA
ISBN 0 88192 425 3
Cataloging-in-Publication data is on file with the Library of Congress.

Printed in the UK by Butler & Tanner Limited, Frome and London

Photographs page 1 *Ferocactus echidne*; page 2 *Echeveria glauca*; page 3 *Echinocereus brandegeei*

Contents

Preface

In recent years, reports on global warming have brought home the message that something in our climate is slowly changing. Add to this the often hectic pace of life today, and it is small wonder that there is a growing interest in plants that are specially adapted to survive times of drought and require relatively little time and attention. Although growing cacti and succulents is traditionally thought of as a greenhouse hobby, there is now an increasing interest in hardy types that can be grown in the garden.

Succulent plants have fascinated human beings since time immemorial. In their often arid native habitat many serve as a source of food and moisture for the native population, while many more provide the raw material for a range of useful items – from scouring pads to rope, and from medicine to poisons used in hunting. When the Europeans colonized much of the world hundred of years ago, the unusual forms and shapes of these plants intrigued the explorers who took samples home for further study. Many bcame and have remained popular houseplants, and there is infinite scope to indulge the collector:

- Cacti and other succulents can range from minute plants that hide from their natural enemies by mimicry, to large trees that dominate the often barren landscape.
- Many are grown for their colourful and attractive appearance and can be highly suitable as low-maintenance garden, conservatory or windowsill plants.
- Their flowers also range from the minuscule to the spectacular 30cm (12in) wide flowers *Selenicereus macdonaldiae*, which open at night, and tree-like inflorescence of *Agave* species.
- In shape, there are small, globular plants like the stemless members of the family Mesembryanthemaceae or the smaller cacti; mat-forming clumps; snake-like stems that sprawl or creep along the ground, as in *Stenocereus eruca*, or use tree trunks to climb to the forest canopy, as in many of the subtropical epiphytic plants; large rosettes; and telegraph pole-like statues that stand shimmering in the desert heat.

The 'golden barrel' cactus, *Echinocactus grusonii* – a favourite in many collections, but in habitat threatened with extinction.

- Their textures can be as smooth as a baby's bottom or soft and feathery, like *Mammillaria plumosa*, or hairy, like the leaves of *Kalanchoe beharensis* or the long white hair of the 'old man cactus', *Cephalocereus senilis*. Many have a fierce armoury with which to defend themselves against the attentions of hungry and thirsty animals, as in some of the *Euphorbia* species and, of course, cacti.

New interests develop as we travel further afield during our holidays and see exotic plants growing in their natural environment. Botanic gardens along the Mediterranean coast and on the Canary Islands after often the first experience northern Europeans have of seeing their houseplants planted out in a natural setting. Growing these plants at home then provides a living memory and souvenir of such happy times.

Collecting succulents is a familiar story, which often starts with the gift of a plant. Somehow, the strange shape or the paradox of fierce spines and delicate flowers enchants us. Cacti and other succulents with complementary or contrasting shapes and colours soon join that first plant in the semi-arid conditions of the centrally heated living room. There will be casualties, usually when our burgeoning interest leads us to give the plants too much care and attention in the form of extra water and food. This unhappy experience leads us to read up on cultivation – and the more we learn about our succulent friends, the greater our interest becomes and the greater the number of plants we collect. Soon the windowsill is full and a greenhouse is obtained. We're hooked.

We hope that this book will help and inspire both experienced growers and those who are new to the hobby, by providing advice on how to grow and propagate cacti and other succulents successfully, and by sharing some fascinating and often surprising facts that over the years have deepened our own interest. We hope to have clarified some myths and mysteries: Does a century plant really take 100 years to flower? Why do we find so many identical plants labelled with different names? And we look at how responsible propagation and cultivation can safeguard the continuation of species in the wild, while still meeting the demand for plants in our collections. Finally, the A–Z will help you to make an informed choice of which of these fascinating plants to grow.

Part One Introducing Succulent Plants

PLATE I
Globular cacti

Mammillaria woodsii

Rebutia canigueralii
f. crispata HS125

Mammillaria albilanata

Parodia mammulosa f. roseoluteus

Parodia magnifica

Mammillaria chionocephala

Turbinicarpus pseudopectinatus

Mammillaria discolor

Rebutia steinbachii f. *polymorpha*

Parodia mairanana f. *atra*
black-spined form

Rebutia mentosa f.
flavissima Lau 338

Parodia werdermanniana

Mammillaria hahniana

Mammillaria melanocentra f. *euthele*

2 History & Classification

The earliest fossil records for succulents go back some 24,000 years and were found in Peru – the dry environment that these plants have adapted to is not conducive to petrification. Bas-reliefs found at the Great Temple of Thutmose III (1501–1447 BC) at Karnak probably record the first botanical garden, containing many plants amassed during this Egyptian pharaoh's military exploits, and include the earliest pictorial record of a succulent plant, *Kalanchoe citrina*. They also depict many of the conventions of modern formal gardening, such as avenues, symmetrical beds, water features and buildings.

The earliest images of cacti are of those with hallucinogenic properties: *Echinopsis pachanoi* from Peru (c.1300 BC) and *Lophophora* species in Mexico dating back to around 300 BC.

SUCCULENTS IN CULTIVATION

Throughout history, the scientific interest of botanists and the horticultural interest in the cultivation of cacti and other succulents have been closely linked, often overlapping. Their cultivation in cool climates evolved along with advances in our ability to provide the right conditions: well-lit positions that could be kept frost free in winter and offer the plants some shelter from the high rainfall and humidity. Gordon Rowley's *The History of Succulent Plants* contains a copy of probably one of the earliest drawings of cacti growing in a glasshouse heated by hot water, dating back to 1828.

Their popularity in cultivation changes with fashion, but succulents continue to appear towards the top of the popular exotic plant 'hit parade' alongside orchids, palms and ferns, to name but a few 'competitors'. These shifting fashions also occur within the hobby: we have already commented on the recent increase and decline in the popularity of caudiciforms (see page 10). The issue of a monograph for a particular family or genus can influence fashions, as can different countries under exploration or colonization. Recently, new discoveries in nature have been a driving force, particularly where it is difficult for us to obtain these novelties for our collections, as is the case with the new species of *Aztekium, Mammillaria* and *Turbinicarpus* discovered in Mexico.

Plants from other lands

Whether collected on military or scientific expeditions, a succulent plant's adaptations to withstanding long periods of drought equip it ideally for transport during long journeys from its place of origin to its place of cultivation. Succulent plants enjoyed a spell of popularity following the discoveries of the Americas and from the long sea voyages around the Cape of Good Hope, while the first cacti to arrive in Europe were species of what are now called *Melocactus* from the Caribbean islands.

Plants such as the *Agave* and *Opuntia* species, brought back from the early explorations of the Americas, could be grown in the open in the Mediterranean climate of southern Europe and found their way into cultivation as ornamental garden plants. A flowering *Agave americana* is reported from the garden of the Bishop of Tornabonius in Pisa as early as 1583, less than 100 years after the discovery of America by Columbus. It is likely that the first plants brought home were merely souvenirs, unusual life forms from a New World. These created an interest for botanists first, and it was not until later, when plants became available in numbers, that their popularity in cultivation developed. Later, the botanical expeditions by von Humboldt and Bonpland specifically set out to discover and bring back samples of new species: their expedition during the early nineteenth century brought some 60,000 specimens back to Europe. The famous journeys by Charles Darwin during the 1830s gave us *Opuntia darwinii* and *O. galapageia*.

Cultivation in Europe

In northern Europe, success in cultivation depends on the ability to protect the plants from frost. Glass therefore plays an important role in the history of succulent cultivation. It was first known about in the second century BC, but was far too expensive for use in horticulture. Reports exist from the fourteenth century of flowers growing in south-facing glass pavilions in France, but it was probably not until the middle of the sixteenth century that the emergence of botanic gardens revived the

The lines on the leaves of *Aloe striata* make it impossible to confuse this species with others in the genus.

need for winter protection of tender exotics. Used initially for the cultivation of citrus fruit (in orangeries and citronières), a reference from 1611 indicates that the Bishop of Eichstatt had potted plant galleries protected by glass where he was able to flower and fruit the cactus *Opuntia tomentosa*.

It is known that the Romans produced the first 'central heating systems', dispersing the heat from underground stoves throughout a building; it is also known that they used this technique to force vegetables, fruit and flowers out of season. In the seventeenth century, heating was achieved by using the warmth retained in brick walls, resulting in the traditional lean-to greenhouse and conservatory, while mobile stoves on trolleys are also mentioned. The end of that century saw the completion of the first hothouse and of the largest orangery – 150m (488ft) long – at Versailles, as well as special rooms heated by underground stoves in England. The main problems were the poisonous fumes from the stoves and the small size of the glass sheets that were available. The invention of the pouring and rolling processes in glass manufacture in 1688, which produced larger sheets of much clearer glass, was a major advance. However, glass was still prohibitively expensive and in England was subject to a special tax until 1846.

By 1733, reports indicate that the fad for citrus fruits had begun to fade, while interest in tender exotic ornamental plants was on the increase. One hundred years later the quality of glass had improved again, but was used mainly to provide high-humidity conditions for tropical plants, rather than to exclude water for desert plants. Heating by steam provided the high humidity required by many tropical ferns and palms. Later, piped hot water or steam became the accepted form of heating, and the abolition of glass tax made glasshouses affordable for an ever-increasing number of gardeners.

During the nineteenth century, one of the largest collections of cacti was that of Prince Salm-Dyck near Dusseldorf in Germany, which by 1836 had grown to contain some 1,500 species and varieties of succulents, including cacti. Special expeditions were also arranged to obtain plants purely for cultivation, such as the two-month-long tour, mainly of German, Dutch, Belgian and French nurseries, by James Forbes, gardener to the Duke of Bedford at Woburn Abbey. The Botanical Garden at Leyden, founded in 1577, became the centre of distribution for material propagated from newly discovered plants. While many of these collections have disappeared,

a specimen of *Fockea capensis* collected by Francis Boos and George Scholl at the end of the eighteenth century is still on show at the Imperial Palace at Schoenbrunn, Austria, and is probably one of the longest-lived succulents still in cultivation.

Changing fashions

Succulents were often written about in the early gardening magazines, such as the *Gardener's Chronicle* in England and *Algemeine Gartenzeitung* in Germany, and featured in horticultural shows. After an initial interest in desert plants, the fashion changed to the epiphytic cacti of the subtropical forests and the many colourful flowered hybrids, which are still a specialist interest in a hobby that generally prefers to concentrate on true species found in nature. This popular interest enabled specialist nurseries to become established and participate in the collection and distribution of the plants in Europe, their catalogues providing a useful insight today into the plants that were available, while the more scientific botanical gardens also displayed many comprehensive cactus and succulent collections. Even newspapers covered the arrival of new-found treasures, such as a 324kg (713lb) specimen of *Echinocactus visnaga* (now *E. platyacanthus*) collected by Frederick Staines in Mexico in 1845 for the Royal Botanic Gardens at Kew, that required ten gardeners to lift and plant it in a large tub.

The first cactus boom peaked around 1840, to be replaced by foliage plants such as palms and ferns and a Victorian favourite, the aspidistra. Other peaks appear at the end of the nineteenth century, in the 1920s – which saw the formation of many national cactus and succulent societies – and again during the 1960s. Are we due to experience another increase in interest in cacti and other succulents soon?

CLASSIFICATION

Humans have developed communication to a fine art. We use languages, where objects and emotions have names. We also have a tendency to 'order', to 'pigeonhole'. Having given the 'thing' a name, we compare it to other, different (or similar) things which are called by different names. We try to establish their relationship with each other. We classify.

Early man used a primitive classification system for plants, distinguishing between those that were edible and those that were not, those that were harmful and those that were harmless. Studies have found that Mexican

Agave species and cacti have formed part of the human diet for at least 9,000 years; compilations of useful plants have existed for at least 5,000 years.

Aristotle (384–322 BC) and Theophrastus (370–287 BC) attempted written classifications of animals and plants that included members of the genera *Euphorbia, Sempervivum* and *Sedum*. Theophrastus used the word *Kaktos* for the artichoke (*Cynara*), but it was not until the seventeenth century that a formal classification system based on the natural affinities between organisms was proposed by John Ray. Swedish botanist Linnaeus (remembered by *Melocactus caroli-linnaei*) turned the concept of a classification unit proposed by Ray into today's species in *Systema Naturae* (1758) and proposed the binomial system of nomenclature, giving organisms a generic and a specific name. The international language between the scholars of the day was Latin (or latinized). Today, Latin is still the basis of most botanical names and crosses national language barriers, especially in writing. Pronunciation of these names is a different matter: British botanists and horticulturists commonly adopt the 'Traditional English' pronunciation, in contrast to the 'Reformed Academic' of classical scholars and many Europeans.

Classifying succulents

Using Latin as a single international language removes confusion caused by local names. For example, the name 'old man cactus' seems to be applied to any white and hairy cactus, including *Cephalocereus senilis, Echinocereus delaetii* and plants in the genera *Espostoa* and *Oreocereus*, while the name 'barrel cactus' is used for many species of *Echinocactus, Ferocactus* and *Sclerocactus*. It was Linnaeus who gave the name *Cactus* to a single genus consisting of 25 species.

During the middle of the nineteenth century, Alphonse de Candolle from Geneva examined and interpreted the existing methods of classification. Of the four system types, he gave greatest weight to the 'Natural' system, which is based on the natural affinities between living creatures. (The other three systems are the Artificial, based on a few arbitrarily selected characters; the Phenetic, based on as many characters as possible, but without evolutionary bias; and the Phyletic, again based on as many characters as possible, but weighted so as to reflect the supposed course of evolution.)

Candolle's classification of cacti in 1828 covered 164 species. This included *Mammillaria cornifera* and *M. radians*, now generally recognized as species of *Coryphantha*. Such

reviewing and renaming of species and genera has been ongoing and is commented on throughout this book.

In the twentieth century, the work of Americans Britton & Rose in *The Cactaceae* (1922) and the German Curt Backeberg in *Die Cactaceae* (1962) still act as valuable reference points for the naming of cacti, while Hermann Jacobsen's *Lexicon of Succulent Plants* (1970) serves the same purpose for the other succulents. Recent monographs for specific genera have updated our knowledge, while ongoing DNA analysis by David Pinkava and Robert Wallace, among others, can clarify some of the issues.

Labelling our plants

The dedicated cactus and succulent collector is keen to have accurate names on the labels for his or her plants. As already mentioned, and highlighted in the descriptions of the genera *Eriosyce* and *Rebutia* in the A–Z (see pages 108 and 156), the revision of these names is an ongoing process. The arguments swing back and forth between the 'lumpers', who point at the common features of what were once regarded as different species, and the 'splitters', who focus on the differences between plants and create new species for plants that differ from existing species only in small details. These reviews are often confusing to the hobbyists, who cannot understand or refuse to accept the latest revisions and re-label all their plants, and there can be great resistance to proposals to abandon old established names. As elsewhere in the animal and plant kingdoms, the Latin or latinized names of succulents are often derived from the following:

• People's names, to commemorate the person who discovered the plant for which a new species was established. Examples are *Aztekium hintonii*, named in honour of George S. Hinton, and the genus *Rebutia*, named after the French nurseryman Pierre Rebut (1830–1898).

• The area or place of origin, as in *Opuntia brasiliensis*, named after plants first found in Brazil (although the species is also found in Paraguay, Peru, Bolivia and Argentina). The genus *Copiapoa* is named after the town of Copiapoa in Chile, which lies almost centrally in its distribution area, while the genus *Sclerocactus* derives its name from the Greek *skleros*, meaning hard, dry, parched, which admirably describes the habitat of these cacti.

• Some feature of the plant such as size, spine characteristic or flower colour. Examples are *Carnegiea gigantea* (very large), *Discocactus heptacanthus* (seven spined) and *Echinocereus viridiflorus* (green flowered).

In the A–Z section of this book, the generic and specific names are used together with the name of the original author – the person who first described the taxon. If the original taxon has since been reclassified, the original author's name appears in brackets followed by the name of the author of the current classification. For example,

Echinocereus viridiflorus var. *davisii* (A.D. Houghton) W.T. Marshall

indicates that the plant was first described (as *Echinocereus davisii*) by Andrew Houghton, but was relegated to a variety of *E. viridiflorus* by Marshall.

Specific plants that have not (yet) been described or await formal identification within an existing species are often indicated by the genus name followed by 'sp.'. Many hobbyists use the same annotation for plants obtained without a label, pending identification.

In addition to the genus and species names, labels on succulent plant collections may also show a field collection number. These can be particularly useful when the specimens concerned have not yet been formally identified/classified. An example is plants seen in collections labelled SB 500, to identify a *Mammillaria* species that is related to *M. lasiacantha* and was collected by American Steve Brack. Similarly, the reference number LAU 88 is applied to an *Echinocereus* species characterized by the red colour of its young spines, which is now named as *E. rigidissimus* var. *rubispinus* but can still be found in collections under the name *E. pectinatus* var. *rubispinus*. Experienced growers will recognize LAU 88 and need not worry about the taxonomy. Field collection numbers serve another useful purpose in identifying plants from a particular population where certain differences with the type are so insignificant as not to justify a varietal or form name, but nevertheless still merit recognition.

Strictly speaking, field collection numbers should only be used for plants that have been vegetatively propagated, usually as cuttings, from the original plant(s) to which the number was allocated. This ensures that plants have consistent genetic properties. Seed lists frequently offer seed from plants with a field collection number, but the characteristics of the seedlings may not be identical to those of the original plant. We have to trust the field collector to select representative samples from a particular population.

Opuntia tunicata is so covered with shining silver sheathed spines that it glistens (see page 142).
(Overleaf) During the summer some succulents such as this *Senecio pyramidatus* may be grown outside in the flower border.

Part Two Growing Succulent Plants

Aztekium hintonii in habitat in Mexico, growing against sheer rock faces in gypsum.

Other desert areas are a result of the influence of ocean currents on land masses. As cold waters move from the Arctic and Antarctic regions toward the equator, they come into contact with the edges of the continents. Air currents cool as they move across cold water; they carry fog and mist but little rain. Such currents flow across the coastal regions of southern California, Baja California, South West Africa and Chile – although often shrouded in mist, these coastal plains are deserts. In particular, in the Atacama Desert in northern Chile and southern Peru rainfall may only occur once every ten to 30 years, making it one of the driest places on earth. Moisture is obtained from the sea fogs that daily shroud the vegetation, and this humidity reduces the great differences between night and day temperatures that are a feature of so many other deserts.

Mountain ranges influence the development of deserts by creating rain shadows. As moisture-laden winds flow upwards over the windward slopes, they cool and lose their moisture in the form of rain and snow. Dry air descending over the leeward slopes evaporates moisture from the soil. In North America, the Great Basin desert is a result of the rain shadow that is produced by the Sierra Nevada.

Other desert areas in the interiors of some continents have formed because the prevailing winds are far removed from large bodies of water and have lost much of their moisture by the time they reach those regions. Such deserts are the Gobi and Turkestan of Eurasia.

Human activity also causes the formation of new deserts. Man's need for wood in house construction and furniture manufacture has led to massive deforestation. Where tree roots once used to hold the soil in place and leaves provided shade and humus for the soil, now bare land is washed away by heavy rainfall on such a large scale that it has an impact on the region's – and the world's – climate.

Desert borders and chaparral

Many more cacti and other succulent plants live in the arid or semi-arid regions that border the desert. Here, the other vegetation, such as grasses and small bushes,

Variety in the family Crassulaceae: (front) *Dudleya hassei*; (centre) *Aeonium nobile* growing among *A. arborium* and *A. haworthii*.

PLATE II
Ceroid cacti 1

Oreocereus celsianus f. maximus

Pilosocereus
pachycladus f. azureus

Micranthocereus estevesii

Trichocereus scopulicola

Espostoa mirabilis

Cephalocereus senilis

4 Where to Grow Succulents

As we saw in Chapter 3, understanding a plant's natural habitat and the climatic conditions to which it is adapted is the key to successful cultivation. Here we examine the range of conditions in which succulents can be grown in the garden, greenhouse or conservatory, or simply on the windowsill. We also take a look at growing succulents for the show bench.

SUCCULENTS IN THE GARDEN

The term 'cold hardy' is commonly used for succulents that in habitat can withstand sub-zero temperatures for a significant amount of time. Usually, low humidity levels accompany these cold periods. Among the North American cacti, this includes plants such as species of *Opuntia*, *Echinocereus*, *Pediocactus* and *Sclerocactus*. From South America, there are again species of *Opuntia* as well as some *Cereus, Echinopsis, Rebutia* and *Gymnocalycium*. Other succulents that can be grown under these conditions include *Agave, Yucca, Sedum* and *Sempervivum* species.

To grow these plants in our gardens, we must ensure that their roots are never exposed to stagnant water for any length of time: a raised, sloping bed with excellent drainage, similar to an alpine garden, is essential. A position in full sun (in the northern hemisphere, south facing) that can be partially covered with plastic sheeting during wet spells in late autumn and early spring is ideal, so that any winter sunshine can raise temperatures above freezing. Prolonged periods of frost cause the greatest damage and it is advisable to cover plants with newspaper during the most extreme conditions. The soil should be low on humus and high in mineral content – humus retains moisture and provides ideal conditions for fungal attack, which is a killer. A dry stone wall, backfilled with suitable soil, provides an attractive feature in the garden and the gaps between the stones can be used to plant a selection of *Sedum, Sempervivum* and *Lewisia* species to add to the range of plants grown in the bed.

SUCCULENTS FOR GREENHOUSE OR CONSERVATORY

In the greenhouse, *you* take control of the climatic conditions. Without heating, the cold-hardy plants described above can be grown safely during the winter months and bedded outside when the likelihood of frost has passed. Large feature plants soon become difficult to move and are less suitable – many members of the South African family Mesembryanthemaceae are surprisingly hardy when kept dry and include a large number that are unlikely to outgrow their welcome.

Beware of high atmospheric humidity, which is a common feature of European winters, and provide good air circulation to reduce the risk of fungal attack. Provide some shading, especially during the first clear days of spring, when plants coming out of their winter rest can easily scorch, leaving ugly marks – or worse, become damaged at their central growing point. Again, good air circulation is essential to prevent scorching.

By providing extra heat, the range of plants that can be grown successfully increases. Heat can be provided in a number of ways. Electric fan heaters are to be preferred over the traditional paraffin heater, which produces a lot of water as part of the combustion process and can lead to condensation as moisture in the air meets the cold greenhouse glass and frames, causing drips to fall on the plants below. In contrast, fan heaters help to distribute the heat produced, ensuring improved air circulation, and often come with their own built-in thermostat, so that energy is used only when it is needed.

Most cacti and many of the other succulents can be grown successfully with minimum temperatures of 5°–10°C (40°–50°F). At the start of autumn, watering of cacti should be reduced, and stopped altogether halfway through autumn. Watering can be restarted during the first warm days of spring, but care must be taken to provide some extra heating to protect the plants from night frosts. Plants that originate nearer to the equator – which include *Pachypodium, Dorstenia, Euphorbia* and cacti such as *Melocactus, Discocactus, Uebelmannia*, most Brazilian ceroids and many subtropical epiphytic species – prefer higher minimum temperatures of around 15°C (60°F) and can then be watered occasionally during their rest period to prevent roots from dying back. Other succulents that require this extra heating during winter include many of the plants from Madagascar. Some plants can look distressingly shrivelled by early spring but it is amazing to see how they plump up after a couple of waterings.

Many people on their first visit to 'cactus country' are surprised to find that the plants they aim to give maximum sunlight at home actually prefer to grow in the shade of trees or small bushes, or almost hidden among desert grass. When the ultraviolet light elements that are present in sunlight hit the glass of the greenhouse, light energy converts to heat, and during the summer months temperatures in a small greenhouse can soar to 50°C (120°F).

First-time visitors are also surprised at the big drop in temperatures experienced during desert nights. Many succulents, including cacti, have adapted to these conditions by closing their stomata – the pores through which a plant exchanges oxygen and carbon dioxide with its environment – when temperatures are at their highest during the day, as yet another means of conserving moisture. Only when temperatures drop at night do the stomata open, allowing the plant to 'breathe'. The night temperature of a hot European summer's night does not often drop low enough for this to happen, so that the plant 'holds its breath' for weeks on end. It is therefore common for succulents to enter a second dormant period in their growing cycle during the warmest weather and care must be taken not to overwater them at this time.

Some plants retain their biological clock when they are moved from their native southern hemisphere habitat to cultivation in the northern hemisphere; these are noted in the A–Z and in the summary table on page 178. Many members of the family Mesembryanthemaceae continue to grow and flower during the South African spring and summer months from October through to the end of February, even when this happens to be autumn and winter, when low temperatures are the norm in their adopted greenhouse homes. Cacti tend to be easier in this respect and seem to regulate their dormancy in relation to the day length and temperatures.

SUCCULENTS FOR THE WINDOWSILL

Many cacti and other succulents will grow well on most windowsills. The aspect of the window is all-important. In the northern hemisphere, east-facing windows that receive the early-morning sunshine, gradually raising the temperature, are best. Plants on south- or west-facing windowsills will need some shading around midday

The spectacular inflorescence of *Agave shawii* races to the greenhouse roof. The plant dies once flowering has finished.

during the brightest, warmest days. It is also possible to select plants that require less light for north-facing windows. Plants used for indoor architecture, such as a tall *Cereus* or *Euphorbia* species, can survive for many years in a dark corner, but are unlikely to thrive and achieve the splendour of their counterparts in nature. Artificial plant lights can help, but are best used to supplement natural light rather than to replace it completely.

One difficulty with windowsill culture lies in providing plants with the period of winter dormancy that is usually triggered by lower temperatures. Maximum temperatures of 10°–15°C (50°–60°F) are best, but this can be uncomfortable for the human inhabitants, so that halls and bedrooms may be more suitable than living rooms during the winter period. Plants that do well include those found in habitats nearer the equator; most other succulents will survive, but may not flower as abundantly as they would after a proper rest period. As the plants never enter a complete state of dormancy, a light watering once a month during the winter is recommended.

Discocactus and *Melocactus* species require more warmth in winter and will not tolerate temperatures below 10°–15°C (50°–60°F). These two genera have been ignored by many amateurs as being too difficult to attempt to grow alongside the more common, hardier cacti such as *Mammillaria*, *Rebutia*, *Gymnocalycium* and *Echinocereus*. However, the smaller-growing species of *Discocactus* and *Melocactus* make ideal houseplants for modern living – a sunny spot on a windowsill in a centrally heated house is a perfect location.

In many ways, these particular cacti are much better suited to indoor culture than most others. They revel in warm sunshine, and whereas most other genera require a cool winter rest, *Discocactus* and *Melocactus* enjoy warmth all year round; their rest period is more in response to the shorter days and less intense sunlight of the winter months. In addition, with their symmetrical globular bodies, colourful spination and unique, distinctive cephalia, they are at all times ornamental plants – even when not in flower.

GROWING SUCCULENTS FOR THE SHOW BENCH

Sharing the delight that you take in your plants with others is a very satisfying experience. The annual show of any cactus or succulent group provides a shop window for the hobby, attracting more public interest and as a result more members than any other form of advertising.

People are amazed at the size to which the plants can grow and impressed when they see the various species in flower. They then want to know more about how to grow the plants themselves.

Showing can be great fun. The element of competition makes it more interesting and great friendly rivalry occurs. Even non-competitive displays, which are no less hard work, can be very rewarding and will encourage new enthusiasts to grow the wide range of succulent plants available.

When showing your plants, it is essential that they look their best. This starts with ensuring that they are in clean pots, neatly labelled, and show no signs of pests or diseases. If your aim is to produce specimens that can be entered for shows, it is even more important to establish the precise growing conditions for the species that you have selected in order to produce the very best plants you can.

Keys to success

Once you have decided to show some of your plants, make sure you obtain a show schedule as early as you can – firstly, to decide which classes to enter, and secondly, so that you can repot in good time where necessary.

When making your entries, it is vital that you enter your plants in the correct classes, so read the schedule again and doublecheck the conditions for each class. No one likes to have their treasures marked NAS (Not According to Schedule) because they are displayed in a pot of incorrect size, or because they have entered, say, a *Mammillaria* species in the *Notocactus* class.

At one time, the rarity of the plant displayed was a key factor that judges looked for, but this is no longer the case: well-grown plants are the criteria for the prizes. The art of showing is to make the exhibit attractive, to catch the judge's eye.

Once you have decided which classes to enter, you need to prepare your plants. Containers can be clay or plastic, plain or decorative, but above all else they must be clean. In some areas hard water can cause a lime deposit to form on clay pots, and this can be removed temporarily by washing them in warm water to which some vinegar has been added. Plastic pots can be wiped with a damp cloth. Topdressing is again essential, not only for aesthetic appeal but also to prevent rotting of the plant, but use a natural rather than a fancy-coloured grit.

The main factor is, of course, the plant. It must be free from cobwebs and pests, and should be in growth rather

Aporophyllum cv. 'Dawn', a showy hybrid between the genera *Aporocactus* and *Epiphyllum*, displays the pendent stems of the former and large flowers of the latter.

than dormant. This can present problems if the show is held at a time when a particular genus is dormant, for instance when a *Lithops* species is entered for a spring show. Trained judges will be aware of such complications and will allow for this in their scoring.

The final important step, which is often overlooked, is the transportation of the plants to the show. The day before the show the plants should be watered well to help prevent root disturbance, as a bumpy ride can cause plants to be shaken out of their pots. Pack the plants well in suitable boxes or trays using old newspapers or polystyrene, and ensure that they cannot move about and are protected from the spines of their neighbours, thereby preventing unsightly puncture marks.

CONTAINERS

First, ensure that pots and seed trays have drainage holes to allow excess water to drain away. Clay, glazed earthenware or plastic pots and bowls are those most often used; plants with long tap roots will require deep pots. Clay pots tend to dry out more quickly than plastic ones and this can lead to roots being concentrated along the edge of the pot rather than evenly throughout the soil.

Many plants do not like to grow in oversize pots. For cacti and most small, slow-growing succulents it is better to repot regularly, ensuring about 2cm (¾in) between the plant and the edge of the pot, than to plant them in too large a pot, where the volume of soil retains moisture for much longer than the roots prefer. Fast-growing succulents are not so sensitive to this and their roots will soon fill the available space: limiting the root development by planting in a small pot can create interesting bonsai subjects, but if you want to grow large specimens, a free root run is recommended.

SOIL MIX

Much has been written about the ideal soil composition for the cultivation of succulents, and widely divergent advice abounds. However, all agree that it is essential to provide a very open and porous mix in order to ensure superior drainage and root aeration – these plants hate to have 'wet feet' for any length of time. There are growers who strongly favour a loam-based compost, while some amazing results can also be found where plants are grown in a soil-less, peat-based compost. For many species, it is best to avoid composts with a high humus content, as this retains moisture longer and is a favourite breeding ground for bacteria and fungi which the plants would not normally encounter in nature.

In the A–Z, unless otherwise indicated, we assume that the plants can be grown in a 'standard cactus or succulent compost'. This term is used for either loam- or peat-based compost, depending on individual preference, with the addition of grit to facilitate drainage. Pumice and perlite are other good additives that help to prevent the soil becoming waterlogged. Sand, on the other hand, is not usually coarse enough to provide good drainage, and if obtained from seaside beaches (which is, in any case, often forbidden by local authorities) will contain too much salt. You may have to experiment with the proportions to suit your requirements, but keep the need for excellent drainage and good aeration uppermost in your mind. Many growers use mixes starting from 4 parts peat or loam to 1 part grit, through to 1:1 mixtures for very water-sensitive specimens. Many garden centres offer 'cactus compost' and these mixes are certainly worth a try for convenience in your experiments.

The following observations should help you decide on the correct compost mix for you.

Peat-based compost
Advantages
• Slightly acidic, which is useful if you need to use hard water for your plants. Many succulents prefer a slightly acidic soil to an alkaline one.
• Light in weight, so useful in hanging baskets, for plants displayed on shelves and for specimens that are transported frequently.
• With a typical pH value in the range 5.5–6.5, more minerals are available to the plants in a usable form than at a lower or higher pH value.
Disadvantages
• Favoured by the sciara fly (mushroom fly, fungus gnat) as a place to lay its eggs. The larvae develop in the soil and feed on roots and young seedlings. Covering the soil with a topdressing will reduce this problem.
• Difficult to rewet once it has dried out. This can be overcome by adding a few drops of washing-up liquid as a wetting agent.
• Using peat is not environmentally friendly. Our use of it for horticulture is greater than the rate at which nature replaces it, and the bogs that are mined to obtain peat are the habitat of many forms of wildlife that only survive in these natural conditions.
• Tends to break down over time, so that regular repotting is required.

Loam-based compost or garden ('native') soil
Advantages
• Often a better source of minerals than peat and slightly alkaline. Many North American and Mexican cacti grow naturally in alkaline soils.
• Does not deteriorate as fast as peat-based compost but can compact badly.
Disadvantages
• Can be unpredictable in quality and harbour a range of pests and diseases.

Trichocaulon flavum – the Latin word *flavum* means pale to greenish yellow and is used to indicate the colour of the small flowers, which have a faint, unpleasant odour.

6 Propagating Succulents

So many succulent plants are threatened with extinction that their propagation is an important aspect of the hobby. The popular methods used are to raise plants from seed or take cuttings. In addition, grafting plants can greatly reduce the age at which they will flower, increase the number of flowers and increase the number of offsets produced.

For very rare plants, micropropagation can be used to take cells from the growing point of the plant and grow these in laboratory conditions into 'proper' plants. Using this technique, *Mammillaria hernandezii* was grown during the 1980s in sufficient numbers to satisfy demand for the plant in the UK, thus reducing the threat of extinction through over-collection of plants in their natural habitat. The main disadvantage of this and other methods of vegetative reproduction is that the gene pool of plants in cultivation is limited.

Raising plants from seed, on the other hand, produces specimens where the genes of both parents are represented in the new plant, thus providing a range of variability within the species. However, unless great care is taken to prevent the introduction of 'foreign' pollen by insects visiting the plants, unintentional hybrids can result.

While these can be attractive, most enthusiasts prefer to raise their plants from well-documented seed. Where habitat seed is legally available, the opportunity for hybridization to occur has been reduced by nature through biological mechanisms such as differing flowering times, by adaptation to pollination by specific insects for plants growing side by side, or through geographic separation.

RAISING PLANTS FROM SEED

Raising plants from seed is one of the most rewarding and best ways of producing new plants. For the majority of species this is not too difficult, while others certainly present something of a challenge and require considerably more skill.

For some species, raising plants from seed is the only means of natural propagation. This applies particularly to those cacti and other succulents that do not offset freely, such as *Ariocarpus* and *Lithops* species.

Harvesting seed

Many plants are self-fertile and after the flowering season will produce fruits containing viable seed – the fruits themselves can sometimes provide as attractive a flash of colour as the flowers. A good example is *Mammillaria schwarzii*, where the small, pale cream-coloured flowers are followed by masses of bright red fruits that contrast nicely with the whitish spination.

Different plants have developed different mechanisms for releasing and distributing their seed. When ripe, some fruits dry and split, either longitudinally or transversally, and allow their seed to drop on to the soil or to be carried away by insects such as ants. Other plants, such as *Mammillaria* species, produce berry-like fruits that in nature are eaten by birds and small rodents – if you wish to produce seed from your plants, beware of ants and rodents that can carry away the seeds before you have a chance to harvest them.

Seed can be harvested by collecting the fruits and putting them and a quantity of water through a liquidizer. Viable seed will sink to the bottom of the vessel, so that the mixture of water and pulp can be decanted. The seed is then dried and can be stored until you are ready to sow it, which can be done any time from midwinter to late spring or early summer.

In general, it is best to obtain seed as fresh as possible as over a period of time it can lose its viability. As always, there are exceptions: seed of *Sclerocactus* and *Pediocactus* species, for example, can be stored for several years in cool, dry conditions.

Scarification

In habitat, the scattered seed acts as a natural seed bank that is activated by the optimum conditions. During this period the seed is exposed to extremes in temperature and moisture, and some species appear to rely on this scarification before germination occurs. In cultivation, growers who are too impatient to allow nature to take its course can carefully wear down the hard seed coat (testa) using sandpaper, exposure to acid or by breaking the

Mammillaria geminispina cristate. Cristate growth can occur in most succulents, creating unusual and fascinating shapes.

Seedlings of *Gymnocalycium horstii* and *Rebutia spinosissima f. hoffmannii*. After germination, the seedlings can be pricked out and repotted, leaving sufficient room for the plants to grow.

testa carefully in the hilum area with a pin or sharp razor blade. Genera for which this is necessary are *Echinocactus*, *Pediocactus*, *Opuntia* and *Sclerocactus*.

Sowing seed

Before sowing, collected seed should be cleaned by removing any fruit remains, and can then be dusted lightly with a fungicide to prevent damping off, which is caused by fungi.

Seeds can be sown in either a soil-less or a loam-based compost with added grit. Individual growers prefer a range of different seed compost mixtures, but all agree that it is essential for it to be free draining. Some growers prefer to sterilize the soil, to kill off fungi and insect larvae or eggs that can pose a threat to young seedlings. It is best to use the same type of compost as that in which the seedlings will ultimately be grown, so that there is no need for them to adjust to a different

medium later when they are potted on.

A variety of containers may be used; if only small numbers of plants are required, individual pots are ideal. Water the compost thoroughly and sow the seeds on top, then cover them with a thin layer of grit to reduce the risk of attack by sciara flies, whose grubs can quickly devour young seedlings. This can be a problem, particularly if a peat-based compost is used.

Place the pots in a propagator or inside a closed plastic bag, depending on the time of the year – if sowing seed during the winter months, a propagator is essential, but in late spring or early summer extra heat is often unnecessary. The best temperature for germinating the seed is a steady 20°C (70°F).

Guard against the soil drying out completely: young, newly germinated seedlings have not yet developed many of the features that enable mature plants to survive droughts. Adding a copper-based fungicide, such as Cheshunt compound or Chinosol, to the water both before and after germination can prevent damping off, although some growers feel that this practice inhibits the germination process itself.

Transplanting

After germination, which usually takes place within a month of sowing, some seedlings make rapid growth and will need to be transplanted, or 'pricked out', while others can stay in the same pot until the following year, depending on the conditions and when the seed was sown. For this reason, it is best to use separate containers for each species.

Transplanting the young seedlings for the first time can be delayed until they are snugly packed, filling the pot. When the soil is quite dry, repot the whole clump into a wider container, shaking off just some of the old compost to avoid damaging the tender root tissues. Once established, the plants will push themselves apart with no noticeable damage: seedlings appear to grow better in close quarters. Prepare the new container by adding compost on the bottom and sides, and leave a space in the centre which is the same size as the clump of seedlings. Gently work the soil mix around the clump to blend the composts.

Keys to success

When germinating seeds of cacti and other succulents, there are two golden rules:
• Never let the seedlings dry out completely.
• Never throw away the seed unless you are *absolutely certain* it will not germinate.

ROOTING CUTTINGS AND OFFSETS

The easiest way to propagate cacti and other succulents is from offsets and cuttings – it requires no special equipment and is successful in most cases. The advantage of this form of vegetative reproduction in cultivation is that the genetic make-up of the plants produced is always identical to that of the parent plant.

The best time to take cuttings is during the plant's growing season, which is frequently in spring or early summer. This does not apply in all cases, especially with members of the family Mesembryanthemaceae, and the summary table on page 178 provides general guidance for this.

Cuttings can be taken from the plant's leaves, stem or roots. In many *Opuntia* species, the fruits can also be treated as stem cuttings. Leaf cuttings can be taken from plants in the family Crassulaceae, such as *Echeveria*, *Graptopetalum* and some *Kalanchoe* species. *Haworthia* species can also be propagated by this method.

Stem cuttings

Stem cuttings can be taken from most branching, shrubby succulent plants and from stem succulents, including the cacti – particularly the ceroid and epiphytic types.

A cutting 5–8cm (2–3in) long will carry its own weight without being supported. However, there are exceptions: for example, many succulents are dwarf

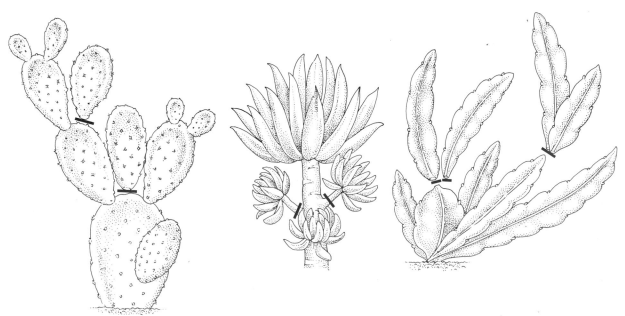

Cuttings of cacti and succulents should be taken in such a way as to produce the smallest possible area of cut surface. Left to right: *Opuntia*; *Dudleya*; *Epiphyllum*.

plants that may never reach these proportions. At the other end of the scale, the purpose of taking a cutting may be to prevent a tall-growing cactus from hitting the roof of the greenhouse, when it is possible to cut off the top part of the stem and treat it like a cutting – which may be several metres in length (or, equally, just a few centimetres). In the species where flowers appear only on mature growth, the aged cells in the cutting can produce flowers on plants no taller than an 'adolescent' seedling. The base of the plant is left in the ground and will usually produce several new stems from areoles just below the cut surface (see illustration opposite).

If rot attacks a plant, it is usually at the base where it is in closest contact with stagnant moisture in the soil. It is often possible to cut the plant higher up the stem, taking off slices until clean, healthy tissue is reached. The remaining top part of the plant can then be treated as a cutting.

Offsets

Some plants readily produce offsets, which are lateral off-shoots or branches that often form roots while still attached to the mother plant. Many globular cacti, such as *Mammillaria* and *Rebutia* species, produce offsets to form large clumps or mats, while in the tall ceroid cacti the offsets form arms or branches, as in the arms of the saguaro cactus (*Carnegiea gigantea*). Examples among the other succulents include *Conophytum*, *Euphorbia* and *Stapelia* species, to name just a few.

Sometimes, a plant may develop abnormalities in the apical growing point, giving rise to cristate or monstrose forms. In cacti, some monstrose forms produce offsets at every areole, although the typical habit for the species is to form solitary plants. It is possible to induce offsets by removing or causing damage to the central growing point: this is a common procedure in commercial culti-vation, where the number of plants that can be produced, rather than the aesthetic value of a single plant, are the main consideration. Damaging the growing point in stem succulents is similar to pruning, for example in roses and fuchsias, where this encourages the plant to form branches that make a full, attractive bush. In nature, this often happens when grazing cattle or goats remove the top part of a cactus growing in grass.

Some cactus genera form cladodes or joints: these are secondary stems that are sometimes flattened, as in the pads of *Opuntia* species, or leaf-like, as in the green stems of *Epiphyllum* species. Such cladodes are easily removed

and will often produce roots readily. In habitat, the joints of the cholla or chain *Opuntia* are easily detached by passing animals (including humans), and may be carried in this way for some distance before dropping on to the soil, where they can root and form a new stand.

Root cuttings

Root cuttings are appropriate for many caudiciforms and plants that naturally produce stolons – in which the tip of the root develops into a new plant where it breaks the soil surface – such as species of *Agave*, *Pelargonium* and *Sansevieria*, and some cacti. Short sections of root are sim-ply cut off and planted to encourage this natural process.

Method

The method of taking offsets and cuttings is similar for most succulents. Always use a sharp knife, preferably sterilized by dipping in a strong disinfectant such as methylated spirit – never pull offsets from the mother plant, as this can cause serious damage. After the cuttings have been taken, the cut surface should be left to dry and form a callus before planting. This is the plant's natural reaction when it is wounded; the callus consists of a thin layer of parenchyma cells that prevent infection of inter-nal tissues by external agents such as bacteria and fungi, and is the area where root cells can develop.

Once the cuttings have dried, they can be placed in their rooting medium. Use a compost that is low in organic material – perhaps a slightly moist mixture of perlite and sharp sand, or the standard compost for cacti and succulents described earlier – with a thick top layer of grit in which the base of the cuttings should be placed, as direct contact with the soil during the early stages of rooting can increase the risk of fungal infection. Once roots have formed, they will soon find the soil in order to take up water and nutrients. Rooting hormone can be used to assist in the production of roots, but opin-ions vary on its effectiveness. Root cuttings should be covered with a thin layer of grit.

Cuttings must be protected from excessive dehydra-tion until they have formed roots and can take up moisture, so are kept in a light, warm position but not exposed to full sun. It is not usually necessary to cover the cuttings: succulents already have a thick epidermis to reduce water loss, although in very dry climates plants can be rooted in a propagator. Some species root very easily, while others can take up to a year or even longer; as with seed germination, patience is a virtue.

Taking a stem cutting (left to right): Remove the top of the stem and allow the cut surface to dry for some days; then place on slightly moist soil. Offsets will be produced on the old stem, close to the cut surface; each offset can be removed and rooted.

Plants that 'bleed' latex when cut are generally a little more difficult to propagate from cuttings, and this is especially true of many members of the family Euphorbiaceae. Dipping the cut end into water and spraying the cut surface on the mother plant with water can arrest the flow of latex.

Cuttings of *Euphorbia* species are best taken during early to midsummer, to give the plants some time to settle before winter. The trickier species come from east Africa and, like many difficult cacti, are often grafted.

GRAFTING

This method of propagation has a number of objectives:
• To propagate plants which are difficult to cultivate on their own roots.
• To speed up growth. Brian Lamb describes grafting a two-year-old seedling of *Oreocereus ritteri*. At eight years of age, the grafted plant (six years after grafting) measured 70cm (28in) long and had two branches, each 25cm (10in) long and 12.5cm (5in) in diameter; rooted seedlings from the same batch measured 7.5–12.5cm (3–5in) in length and 3.75cm (1½in) in diameter.
• To promote earlier flowering. Lamb's grafted *Oreocereus ritteri* seedling flowered at ten years old, instead of the 50 years it would take on its own roots.
• To increase flowering.
• To increase seed production. In Lamb's grafted *Oreocereus ritteri*, for example, seed can be produced for an additional 40 years!
• To enable plants to survive which would not normally do so on their own roots – for example, *Gymnocalycium mihanovichii* var. *friedrichiae* cv. 'Hibotan', which has no chlorophyll to enable it to photosynthesize.
• To propagate the many cristate, variegated or monstrous forms that are very difficult or impossible to grow on their own roots.
• To rescue diseased plants.

The main objection to grafting is that plants can become 'blown up' and unnatural in appearance.

Tools and equipment

To undertake grafting, you will need some specific tools and equipment:
• Two razor-sharp stainless steel knives with 10–12cm (4–5in) long blades
• Jar containing methylated spirit, to disinfect the knives
• Scissors/cutters to remove spines
• Elastic bands
• Paper tissues

Flat grafting

In this method, which is used in the majority of cases, two plants are cross-sectioned. When the cut surfaces are brought together, several vascular bundles will come into contact and the surrounding cambium layers grow together. Usually, the central fibrovascular bundles will also unite if they are of similar diameter. The scion and stock (the upper and lower plants in the graft) must usually belong to the same plant family.

1 Dip the knives in a disinfectant such as methylated spirit before each cut and wipe dry with a tissue.

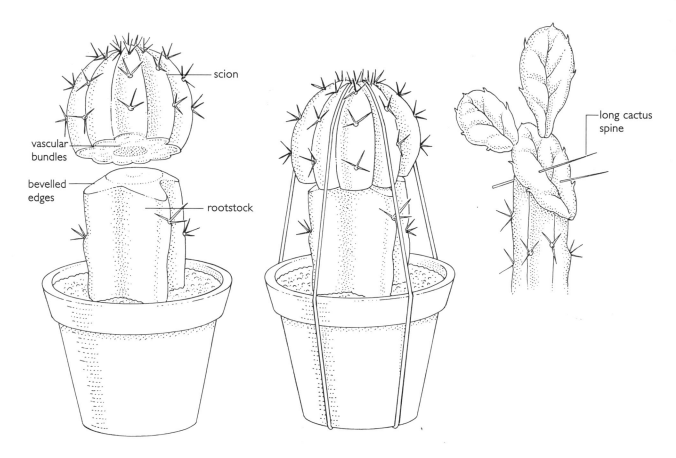

scion

vascular bundles

bevelled edges

rootstock

long cactus spine

Grafting (left to right): Prepare the scion and rootstock by two horizontal cuts, then bevel back the edges at 45 degrees. Using two elastic bands, keep the scion in place on top of the rootstock for about a week. Angled grafts can increase the surface of contact between scion and rootstock.

2 Cut the rootstock about 3–4cm (1¼–1½in) above soil level with one clean stroke. Then bevel back the edges at 45 degrees.

3 Prepare the scion in a similar manner, removing any spines near the cut surface.

4 Cut a 1mm (1/16in) thick slice off both the stock and the scion, and gently push the scion on to the stock, using a circular motion to squeeze out mucilage, air bubbles and sap, and ensuring that the vascular bundles are best matched.

5 Secure the scion on top of the stock using two elastic bands.

6 Place the freshly grafted plants in a warm, semi-shaded position for seven to 14 days.

Variations

Some variations on this method are necessary to suit specific plants. Young cactus seedlings can be grafted on to *Pereskiopsis* a few days after germination. Due to the small size of the scion, there is no need for elastic bands to keep scion and stock together.

Some people prefer a 45-degree angled cut to a flat cut. This increases the surface area where the vascular bundles can join.

Instead of an elastic band to hold the two parts together, a clothes peg is used with a thin stock, while for thicker stock a long cactus spine, dipped in methylated spirit, can be used to pin the scion to the stock. Metal pins should not be used.

Another variation is to make a V-shaped cut in the first horizontally cut surface of the stock. The flat cut surface of the scion can then be trimmed into a wedge shape to fit the V cut. Again, this increases the surface area where vascular bundles can join.

Rootstocks

Suitable rootstocks for grafting cacti and succulents are listed opposite.

Grafted cact (left to right): *Eriosyce laui, Geohintonia mexicana, Mammillaria tezontle* and *Copiapoa laui.* These rare and relatively recently discovered cacti were grafted soon after germination and in under a year have reached flowering size.

Semi-hardy rootstocks for cacti

Echinopsis macrogona	
Echinopsis pachanoi, E. spachiana,	
E. schickendantzii	Prone to suckers
Harrissia jusbertii, H. guelichii	For *Toumeya, Escobaria,* *Mammillaria* and *Parodia* species
Cereus hildemannianus	

Non-hardy rootstocks for cacti

Myrtillocactus geometrizans	
Hylocereus triangularis, H. trigonus	
Pereskiopsis diguetti f. velutina	Ideal for seedlings

Rootstocks for other succulents

Euphorbia canariensis, E. ingens	For the Euphorbiaceae
Cereopegia woodii	For the Asclepiadaceae
Pachypodium lameri	For all Madagascan *Pachypodium* species and *P. namaquenum*
Oleander	For *Adenium* species

Many species of *Opuntia* also make a good stock. Take a vigorous pad, at least one year old, from a species such as *O. triacantha,* and cut it vertically into strips 1.5–3cm (½–1¼in) wide. Dry the strips for two to three weeks, then root in the usual way (see page 50). Once rooted, they can be used as stock, particularly for cristate forms.

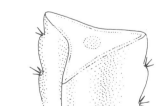  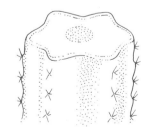

Rootstocks (left to right): *Harrisia Jusbertii, Hylocereus* (*H. triangularis* or *H. trigonus*), *Echinopsis* (*Trichocereus*) *spachiana* and *Echinopsis* (*Trichocereus*) *pachanoi.*

Part Four Conservation

By 1930 the moth was breeding naturally in Australia, and by 1933 some 90 per cent of the prickly pear plants had been eradicated. Nevertheless, the near takeover of eastern Australia by *Opuntia* cacti indicates the plants' competitive ability and their extremely high capacity for biomass production.

As with many interactions in nature, there is often a balance and in the long term many such systems adjust into some accommodation, sometimes being cyclical in each population, but out of phase. *Opuntia* plants still grow in Australia, the moth comes and goes, and private collectors do not appear to have experienced problems.

An impressive specimen of *Aztekium hintonii* in habitat in Nuevo Leon, Mexico, growing on almost vertical cliff faces.

THE INTERNATIONAL ORGANIZATION FOR SUCCULENT PLANT RESEARCH (IOS)

The aim of this organization is to co-ordinate succulent plant research throughout the world and conservation of the succulent flora forms an important aspect of its work.

Started at a meeting held in Zurich in 1950 by a group of the most prominent names in the cactus and succulent world, preparations are currently underway to make the fiftieth anniversary, in the year 2000, a memorable one. The IOS holds a congress at two-year intervals in various countries throughout the world and produces an annual bulletin and *Repertorium*, which lists all new taxa of succulents along with place of publication and a classified index of new literature. Membership is open to all botanists or enthusiastic amateurs.

Below, Keith Grantham relates his experiences at the 1995 IOS inter-congress meeting, held in San Miguel de Allende in central Mexico, where he was able to join in with one of the projects, undertaking group studies of plant populations for CITES, the organization that monitors the Convention on International Trade in Endangered Species:

On 23 September we set off for the small town of Tula and visited the type locality of *Turbinicarpus ysabelae* (the type locality of a plant is the place where grow the specimens upon which the first descriptions of that species are based).

Here we performed a site survey that consisted of finding those plants, some 50 in number, that had been tagged during a previous visit three years earlier. Each of these plants had been marked on a grid map and, when found, was checked against a register, measured and photographed. Each plant is identified by a unique number that is inscribed on an aluminium tag hammered into the ground by the side of the plant.

On this occasion, my task was to take the measurements of the plants' height and diameter, to record these in the register and compare them against the previous records to see if the plants had grown. Secondly, we looked for signs of regeneration – of seedlings to indicate a thriving population. All the plants recorded three years earlier were still there but had grown very little. There were no signs of regeneration.

I also visited the type localities of other cacti, including *Turbinicarpus saueri*, *T. subterraneus* and *Obregonia denegrii*, to check the plants tagged on earlier visits, and the wonderful site of the then newly discovered *Geohintonia mexicana* and *Aztekium hintonii*. At some of these sites, a more expensive method of tagging was used. Using a hypodermic syringe, an electronic microchip was injected into the plant body and this then emits a permanent signal of the plant's identification number that can be read easily on a hand-held meter.

Both systems are very worthwhile in helping us to understand the survival of threatened species in their natural habitat. However, they cannot remove the threat posed by unscrupulous collectors or urbanization, and time will tell if these plants remain in nature for the enjoyment of future generations.

CONSERVATION BEGINS AT HOME

After mowing the lawn, Mr Jones looked back over the smooth green sward. Just a few particularly tenacious dandelions that kept reappearing right in the centre of the lawn spoilt the otherwise perfect picture. Fortunately, he had a herbicide spray in the shed that would deal with this menace once and for all.

Having applied the chemicals, it was time for coffee on the patio and a relaxed read of the Sunday papers, where one of the supplements featured an article about Mr Jones's favourite succulent plants. He became mildly irritated when he read that farmers in Brazil were cutting down his beloved *Melocactus* and *Pilosocereus* to replace them with grazing ground for their cattle. Why could this wanton destruction not be stopped by the government? After all, the Mexican government had been so successful in protecting their endangered flora that it was now almost impossible to obtain the new species that had recently been discovered in that country. A smile appeared on his face as he looked over the lawn to his greenhouse, where a single field-collected *Turbinicarpus alonsoi* was showing off its flowers. It had not been cheap to obtain this from a foreign nursery, but at least his collection of that genus was again complete.

Mr Jones turned to the exotic holiday section in the supplement and asked himself if he should take his wife along on the planned holiday to Madagascar. She might not be impressed with the local shopping facilities and would no doubt complain about the mosquitoes that had kept them awake on a previous holiday to South Africa. Still, the extra suitcase would enable him to bring back some more plants and cuttings of species that were nearly impossible to obtain at reasonable prices back home.

Next, there was a gardening feature and a report of the latest edition of the *Red Book*, listing the newly reported endangered species. Oh, and a photo of a dandelion with very similar pointy leaves to the one that he had just zapped in his lawn, probably an advert for the herbicide spray he had used. But no: it seemed that this plant was now also included in the *Red Book* and was only known to grow in a small field half a mile from his home. What a coincidence, he would write a letter to the editor to inform them that it also grew in his garden – or rather, had grown …

(Overleaf) *Mammillaria* group of the series *Lasiacantha* including *Mammillaria plumosa*, *M. schiedeana*, *M. laui*, *M.l.* var. subducta, *M.l.* var. dasyacantha and *M. carmanea*.

Part Five A Choice of Plants

the strong sunlight to which most species are exposed in habitat. Dense spination offers further protection from the sunlight for the epidermis and discourages many animals from feeding on the plants. However, this strategy is only partially effective and we have seen cattle in the USA feeding on the most ferociously spined *Opuntia* species, sometimes in preference to non-spiny vegetation.

The hooked spines on many offset-producing cacti also play a role in vegetative reproduction. The offsets, often already equipped with roots, are easily detached from the mother plants as their spines hook on to the hair or fur of passing animals. Later the offsets drop off and, provided they land in a favourable position, establish themselves quickly in their new territory.

The flowers of cacti are often large and showy but do not last for more than a few days, as they represent a major loss of water to the plant. They often occur singly rather than in clusters of several flowers. The perianth (floral tube) does not have clearly differentiated sepals and petals, but rather consists of a series of bracts (modified leaves), which gradually grade into sepals and finally into showy petals. The flowers have many stamens; the ovary is inferior and fused to the perianth.

The fruits are often brightly coloured and fleshy, and are an important source of food and moisture to both humans and other animals in their native habitat. Some of these can now be found on the exotic fruit shelves in European supermarkets.

Because cacti can survive with little care and exhibit bizarre forms, they are popular for home cultivation. The collection of plants from habitat to satisfy demand for these houseplants is often wrongly regarded as the main threat of extinction that faces many cacti species. Chapter 7 is devoted to the subject of conservation, with the aim of dispelling some of the myths.

Most of the 135 genera are found in cultivation, where the small, slow-growing species are most popular for windowsill and small greenhouse cultivation and are grown for their variety of shapes, colours and spines. The larger species are much more popular where the climate allows them to be grown outside as feature plants in landscape gardens. Typical cactus shapes include the tall telegraph-pole-like ceroids, of which the saguaro *Carnegiea gigantea* is probably best known from western movies; globular plants such as members of the genus

The large flowers of 'baby's toes' (*Fenestraria aurantiaca*) are typical of the family Mesembryanthemaceae.

Mammillaria; and the *Opuntia* species, consisting of spherical, cylindrical or flat pads.

There is also a large group that contains the widely grown Christmas cactus (*Schlumbergera truncata/russelliana*) which naturally occur as epiphytes – plants that grow on others for anchorage but, unlike parasites, without taking their food from them. These subtropical rainforest plants do not fit the popular image of cacti as squat or tall, fleshy plants of desert regions. Examination of their stems, however, reveals the presence of the cactus family's unique organ, the areole, and their flowers display the typical cactus features.

Many groups of plants that are unrelated to cacti have also adapted to survive in arid regions and often resemble cacti in appearance. These offer examples of parallel evolution: unrelated organisms subjected to similar environmental stresses often evolve similar anatomical and functional characteristics (see page 11).

A total of 65 different genera are described in more detail in the A–Z.

ASTERACEAE

Also known as the daisy family, with composite flowers including such well-known plants as aster, burdock, daisy, edelweiss, fleabane, lettuce, marigold, sunflower and the desert sagebrush, this is one of the largest families in the plant kingdom.

Two genera, *Othonna* and *Senecio*, are included in the A–Z, where we have assumed that the 40 species identified by C. Jeffrey (1986) as *Kleinia* are now part of the genus *Senecio*. A fourth genus, *Notomia*, also includes some interesting succulents. Most of the succulents come from South Africa but some occur in the Canary Islands, Mexico, Madagascar and Yemen. The most popular with succulent growers are the *Othonna* species, although in some cases they can be difficult. They are winter growers in the northern hemisphere, so in summer require a dry rest period.

CRASSULACEAE

This family comprises some 33 genera and 1,500 species of succulent shrubs, herbs and sometimes treelets, found often in arid regions and more rarely in moist habitats in Eurasia, the Americas and Australia, but not in the western Pacific. Nine genera are described fully in the A–Z.

The representative genus in the family is *Sedum* or stonecrop. Two European species, cultivated in rock gardens and flower borders and grown extensively in the USA, are the mossy stonecrop, *S. acre*, a low, creeping evergreen with golden flowers, and the live-forever or garden orpine, *S. telephium*, an erect perennial with reddish blossoms. Both plants spread from cultivation and are widely naturalized in North America.

CUCURBITACEAE

The cucumber family contains many unusual succulent plants. Found throughout the world, mainly in tropical regions, they often have a large caudex and are usually deciduous plants grown for their bizarre shapes rather than their small, yellowish, dioecious flowers. Most plants do not require high temperatures during the winter months and if given plenty of root room by bedding out, they soon make very large plants.

The genera most often seen in cultivation are *Cephalopentandra* (which is described in more detail in the A–Z), *Corallocarpus*, *Dendrosicyos*, *Gerrardanthus*, *Ibervilla*, *Kedrostis*, *Neolsomitre*, *Seyriga*, *Xerosicyos* and *Zygosicyos*. Most of the cucurbits are easy to grow, the exceptions being *Cephalopentandra* and *Dendrosicyos*.

DIDIERACEAE

This family has four genera – *Alluaudiopsis*, *Alluaudia*, *Decaryia* and *Didierea* – comprising 12 species found only in Madagascar. Any of them can be grafted on to species of *Pereskiopsis*, a genus in the family Cactaceae, and this indicates the affinity between the two families. The Didiereaceae are therefore sometimes referred to as the Old World cacti.

The main attraction of these plants is the combination of wonderful spination with attractive foliage. They require an absolute minimum winter temperature of 10°C (50°F). Some members of the family are a challenge to grow or propagate. An example is *Decaryia madagascariensis*, which is best grafted on to *Alluaudia procera* or on to a *Pereskiopsis* species. The other genus that can be challenging is *Alluaudiopsis*, with both species – *A. fiherenensis* and *A. marnieriana* – being thin stemmed and not easy to propagate. All these plants require plenty of water during their growing season. The genus *Alluaudia* is described in more detail in the A–Z.

DIOSCORACEAE

Although there are some 600 species in this family, divided over eight genera, only five – all in the genus *Dioscorea* – are desirable in a collection of succulent plants. These are examined in more detail in the A–Z.

DRACAENACEAE

This is a small family comprising just two genera, *Dracaena* and *Sansevieria*, that between them account for some 130 species. Until recently, both genera were included in the family Agavaceae. Both are described in the A–Z.

EUPHORBIACEAE

Many members of the family Euphorbiaceae, the spurges, that grow in dry parts of Africa where cacti are not found, exhibit leafless, spiny, fleshy stems and provide an excellent example of parallel evolution with cacti.

The family contains many genera that cover some 8,000 species, some of which are succulents, including the genus *Euphorbia*. They occur primarily in the tropics, but representatives are found throughout the world except in polar and mountainous areas. The plants range from small geophytes and annual herbs to large trees, and the genus *Euphorbia* contains many common North American weeds. Members of this family often have milky latex, which in some species is irritating to the skin and can be fatal to livestock. Rubber is derived from the latex of several members of the family, most importantly *Hevea brasiliensis,* the para rubber tree.

The floral whorl in members of the family is usually inconspicuous, but the flowers are often grouped together in dense clusters that sit on top of large, coloured leaves, or bracts, which serve the petals' function of attracting pollinators. With its brightly coloured bracts, *Euphorbia pulcherrima,* the poinsettia, a Mexican member of the family, makes an attractive and popular Christmas decoration.

The genera *Monadenium* and *Pedilanthus*, as well as *Euphorbia*, are described in more detail in the A–Z.

FOUQUIERIACEAE

This small family of small trees or shrubs is native to the desert regions of Mexico and the southwestern United States. There are just two genera: *Fouquieria* (described in the A–Z), with 11 species, and *Idria*, which is a monotypic genus.

GERANIACEAE

The family Geraniaceae contains 11 genera and about 750 species of mostly temperate herbs or shrubs. The representative genus, *Geranium*, commonly called cranesbill because the fruit bears a long 'beak' formed from the persistent style, contains about 250 species, many of which are cultivated.

The family Geraniaceae includes several genera containing plants that are of interest to the succulent enthusiast – *Erodium, Masonia, Pelargonium* and *Sarcocoulon* – with most of these coming from South Africa.

MESEMBRYANTHEMACEAE

The family Mesembryanthemaceae is South Africa's largest succulent plant family, comprising about 120 different genera and 1,800 species, even after a recent split that saw all non-succulent genera moved into the family Aizoaceae, so that now only the succulent plants remain. The entire family is currently under revision and many changes are expected. The name mesembryanthemum is connected to the Greek word *mesembria*, meaning midday, and *anthemon*, meaning flower.

MORACEAE

This family includes such plants as the banyan, bo tree, breadfruit, cannabis, fig, hemp, hop, mulberry and ricepaper tree. Two of the 37 genera – *Dorstenia* and *Ficus* – are associated with succulents and are decribed in more detail in the A–Z.

PASSIFLORACEAE

The common name of passionflower is used both for this family and for its principal genus, *Passiflora*. The flowers are usually perfect, generally having a five-parted calyx and five-parted corolla. All species have a conspicuous crown of filaments springing from the throat of the tube formed by the base of the calyx and the corolla.

The family contains about 530 species, most of which are climbing plants, such as the passion vine (*Passiflora incarnata*) of the southern USA, which reaches heights up to 9m (30ft); the bell apple or water lemon (*P. laurifolia*) of the West Indies, a species of passionflower with an edible fruit; and its close relative, the giant granadilla (*P. quadrangularis*), which is native to Jamaica and South America. The pulp, or aril, surrounding each seed of the giant granadilla is used to flavour drinks and icecream.

The succulent members of the family are found in the genus *Adenia*, which is described in detail in the A–Z.

PEDALIACEAE

This small and unusual family, with its asymmetric flowers and variously formed fruit, contains over 12 genera which are all found in Africa, Madagascar and Asia. The genera most commonly grown by collectors of succulent plants are *Pterodiscus, Sesamothomnus* and *Uncarina*.

Plate IV
Mesembryanthemaceae

Lithops julii subsp. julii C64

Lithops optica var. rubra

Lithops bella

Frithia pulchra

Lithops lesliei var. albinica

Faucaria tuberculosa

Argroderma ovale

Dinteranthus pole-evansii

Lapidaria margratiphora

Conophytum obcondellum

Conophytum taylorianum

Conophytum marginatum

Conophytum uviforme

Gibbaeum cryptopodium

Conophytum albescens

Conophytum bilobum

9 A–Z of Cacti & Other Succulents

From the 19 plant families described in Chapter 8, we have selected specific genera and species that demonstrate the wide variety of forms of cacti and other succulents, their horticultural uses – as garden, greenhouse and houseplants – their specific cultivation needs and their standing in terms of conservation issues. In addition, we have chosen plants that we like and grow ourselves (Paul mainly the cacti and Keith the other succulents) – the biggest challenge has been the limited space available to write about them. One family in particular, the Cactaceae, is looked at in more detail and provides roughly half the genera featured in the A–Z.

The table on page 178 provides general guidance on growing and flowering times, minimum temperatures and methods of propagation. Remember that particular taxa often occupy a very specific niche in nature with a very limited distribution, but that in total these plants can be found just about anywhere in the world with the exception of the two poles. Our experience of growing

Acanthocalycium spiniflorum – both the genus and species names refer to the characteristic spiny flower tube.

them in cultivation is limited to the UK and Holland, although Keith in particular has travelled widely and seen many of the plants in their native habitat. We hope that this book will be enjoyed in many countries by people who again will experience many different climates, so that specific statements about when a plant is likely to be in growth need to be adjusted by the reader to reflect local conditions.

The same applies to our recommendations for minimum temperatures. These are based on our experience of the cold and humid British winters: in habitat, plants can often experience much lower temperatures combined with very low humidity. We strongly encourage those who have been 'hooked' and want to build a small collection of cacti and other succulents to join a local club or society. The experiences of others in your area in growing these plants will be invaluable, and you will also have the opportunity to swap plants.

You will soon learn that there are probably as many different methods of growing a particular plant well as there are members in your club. All we can do is offer advice on what has worked for us and highlight some of the key factors that are shared by many of these different approaches. Do not be afraid to experiment. Many of the plants described are easy to propagate, so that it is possible to have several specimens on the go at once in order to try out different conditions. If a plant is described as 'cold hardy', it might still be a good idea to keep one in the protection of the greenhouse and to experiment with a spare plant.

ACANTHOCALYCIUM Backeberg

Cactaceae

A genus of slow-growing, globular to short cylindrical cacti from northern Argentina, with close affinities to *Echinopsis* and included in that genus by some people. The name indicates the spiny flower tube that is characteristic of the genus.

Over the years, some 14 species have been described. The current view is that there is only one good one, *Acanthocalycium spiniflorum*, which takes in the old names *A. klimpelianum*, *A. peitscherianum* and *A. violaceum*. Another group, with predominantly glaucous body colour and yellow flowers, has already been moved to *Echinopsis* as synonyms of *E. thionantha: A. aurantiacum, A. glaucum, A. catamarcense, A. thionanthum, A. brevispinum, A. ferrarii, A. griseum* and *A. variiflorum.*

Acanthocalycium spiniflorum Schumann

Both the generic and specific name indicate the spiny receptacle and pericarp scales that are characteristic of the genus. Now that this species is considered to include three other old names, there is some scope for variability. The flowers are wide funnel-form, and in addition to the spiny characteristics already mentioned, have a wool ring or hymen at the base of the receptacle. Plants that have all three of these features are included in the genus, separated from others that exhibit only one or two of them, such as some species of *Pyrrhocactus* (now *Eriosyce*), *Rebutia* and *Parodia*. The flower colour can vary from white to pink-mauve or pale violet.

ADENIA Forsk.

Passifloraceae

This is the only genus in the family Passifloraceae that can be considered under the heading of succulents and it is found in Africa, Madagascar, Indonesia and Malaysia. The main reason for growing *Adenia* species is their attractive caudex, as the flowers are usually small and greenish to yellow in colour, although they often have an appealing perfume and attractive fruits.

The genus can be divided into two groups:
1 Climbers, with tendrils and small to medium-sized tubers, from Malaysia.
2 Larger species from eastern and southern Africa.

As usual, there are some exceptions – of species that are low, erect plants that are without tendrils but produce large tubers.

In cultivation, *Adenia* species need to be kept warm. When propagating from seed or cuttings, it takes a long time for the plant to form the desirable caudex.

Adenia aculeata Forsk.

A particularly attractive species from Somalia that has a stem randomly studded with black prickles. The leaves vary from slightly lobed to deeply dissected. It can be propagated easily from seed.

Adenia glauca Schinz

This plant is a native of the Transvaal in South Africa, where it grows in crevices among the rocks – it is one of the smallest-growing species in the genus. The rounded caudex has a large tap root and the plants are monoecious, with the male and female flowers (both yellowish

green) carried on the same plant. The flowers are very strongly perfumed and just a couple of open blooms will scent the entire greenhouse.

Adenia globosa Engler

A species from Tanzania, Kenya and Somalia that has an extraordinary wart-covered, hard, lumpish green caudex, which in habitat can grow to a diameter of 2.5m (8ft). A thicket of interlacing, fiercely spined branches that bear tiny deciduous leaves covers the stem, but there are no tendrils – these are modified into spines.

There are two associated species that are sometimes regarded merely as varieties of *A. globosa. A. ballyi* from Somalia looks almost the same but has larger fruit and flowers. *A. pseudo-globosa* differs from the type only in minor morphological features, but has a different habitat range: it comes from Kenya, and grows at a higher altitude of 1,900m (6,200ft).

Adenia goetzei Wild

This species is a member of the *A. huillensis* group that also includes *A. wilmsii, A. erecta, A. huillensis, A. malangeana, A. ovata* and *A. tisserantii,* all of which are low and erect in growth habit and without tendrils sprouting from their tubers. The mainly veined-leaved plants have pale yellow flowers and are found in southern Tanzania. Extra care should be taken not to overwater them.

ADENIUM Roem. & Schult.

Apocynaceae

Adenium species are distributed from the Arabian peninsula through to Kenya and Tanzania and are also found in Namibia, but do not occur in Madagascar. They are stem succulents with thickened tuberous stems and thick branches that carry spirally arranged leaves. Unlike in species of *Pachypodium*, another closely related genus in the family Apocynaceae, there are no spines or thorns. The showy flowers are large, funnel-shaped, pale pink to red in colour, and are often produced in great numbers. In recent years, many hybrids have been produced with flower colours ranging from dark red to a pure white, which is not normally found in this genus.

The plants must be grown in a heated greenhouse but also make good plants for the windowsill. They have a long tap root that requires a deep pot (sometimes known as a 'long tom'). All need plenty of water in hot weather during the growing season to produce the maximum number of flowers, but are very prone to rotting if kept wet in cool weather. If kept warm (15°C/60°F) in winter, watering can be continued and the plants will

Adenium obesum is frequently offered for sale under the name 'desert rose', although not a member of the family Rosaceae.

then not shed their leaves. Feeding with a houseplant fertilizer at this time will increase the duration of the flowering period.

Take care when handling these plants: the milky sap that oozes out when they are cut is very poisonous, especially in *Adenium oleifolium*, although in very low doses it provides a useful antidote in the treatment of snakebites.

There is some controversy regarding the correct number of species in the genus. While Plazier describes five – *A. boehmianum, A. multiflorum, A. obesum, A. oleifolium* and *A. swazicum* – others argue that there is only one, variable, species, *A. obesum*, with the other names included as subspecies.

Adenium boehmianum Schinz.

The milky sap of this plant is very poisonous – members of the Hotentot tribe use it as arrow poison in hunting. The plant comes from Damaaland in Namibia, where it reaches a height of 1.5–2m (5–6ft). The large, leathery leaves are 10–14cm (4–5½in) long and approximately

6cm (2½in) wide. The flowers, which appear before or at the same time as the leaves, range from pink to deep purple in colour and have an attractive darker throat.

Adenium obesum (Forsk.) Roem. & v. Schult.

This is probably the species most commonly seen in cultivation. It is distributed over a wide area from Yemen and Uganda to Mozambique, Kenya and Tanzania, where it can reach a height of 2m (6ft). The thick, fleshy stem has short branches that carry spiralling leaves at their tips. The inflorescence is made up of two to ten pink flowers.

A. o. subsp. *swazicum* has its distribution area restricted to the eastern veld of the Transvaal and neighbouring areas such as Natal and Swaziland. The dark, narrowly oblong leaves are borne on numerous branches that arise from a thick, carrot-shaped tuber. The flowers are star-shaped and vary in colour from bright pink to light purple. Flowers and leaves appear at the same time.

Adenium oleifolium Stapf

This species has been recorded from the far north-western Transvaal near Thabazimbi. Unlike *A. obesum* subsp. *swazicum* or *A. multiflorum*, this species has very short branches, and in most cases the entire caudex is hidden underground. The flowers are light pink, tinged with white. The milky sap is very poisonous.

AEONIUM Webb & Berth.

Crassulaceae

Aeonium species are found mainly on the Canary Islands, but they also occur along the Mediterranean coast of north Africa, Ethiopia and Yemen, and on the other Atlantic island groups, the Azores and Madeira. They are mostly succulent shrubs with woody, branching stems that often have aerial roots. The leaves are arranged in rosettes at the ends of the stems, like Old World versions of the Mexican *Echeveria* species. There are also some small, stemless species that form rosettes close to the ground. The flowers are carried on large, pyramidal, dichotomously branched racemes and come in white, yellow, pink and red, depending on the species.

The plants can be grown outdoors during the milder months, but should be protected from frosts during winter. They are mostly winter growing, from early autumn until mid-spring, with flowers produced during the second half of this period. Many are monocarpic, but young rosettes are often formed around the flowering stem and the plants are also readily propagated from seed.

Aeonium nobile Praeg.

Native to the island of La Palma in the Canary Islands,

this short-stemmed plant has rosettes which can reach a diameter of 50cm (20in). These consist of large, fleshy leaves, olive-green in colour, that each grow up to 30cm (12in) long and 20cm (8in) wide. The flowers are scarlet and are carried on a large inflorescence. After flowering the plant dies, and as it does not produce offsets, it is worth pollinating the flowers to obtain seed and thus retain a specimen in your collection. This species is not difficult to grow in cultivation.

AGAVE Linnaeus

Agavaceae

The name *Agave* means noble, and if size is taken to be a sign of nobility, it is an apt one to apply to many of the species. These plants have been known for hundreds of years, but the creation of a separate family is a fairly recent (1985) event; it comprises the genera *Agave, Furcraea, Hesperaloe, Manfreda, Yucca, Polianthes* and *Prochnyanthes*. Other related genera – *Nolina, Dasylirion, Beaucarnea* and *Calibanus* – were at the same time transferred to the family Nolinaceae.

Agaves are usually stemless plants (although there are some species that form a trunk) with numerous large, thick and fleshy leaves that can store considerable quantities of water and are arranged in a spiral to form an attractive rosette. The leaves are spiked, particularly at the tips, and grow to a length of about 2m (6ft). Most species are monocarpic – that is, they usually flower only once, generally when the plant is between ten and 25 years old. Shortly before it flowers, a long stem arises from a woody caudex or from the short, erect rootstock, and grows rapidly upwards to a height of up to 12m (40ft). The numerous tubular flowers are arranged in either a raceme or a panicle. *Agave stricta* is one of the few exceptions, where the rosette lives on after flowering.

Fortunately, many species form offsets around the base of the old rosette that can be propagated to replace the dead plant; rhizomes or suckers also often develop into new plants, which can also be raised from seed. Contrary to the implied meaning of the common name 'century plant', the usual lifespan is from eight to 25 years. All members of the genus are known as 'maguey' in Mexico.

Many species of *Agave* are of economic importance. *A. sisalana*, or sisal, is native to the West Indies but is now also grown commercially in Mexico, Madagascar and Eurasia. Its leaves contain fibres up to 1.5m (5ft) in length that are used to make rope. Species such as *A. chrysoglossa* and *A. parviflora* are known as soap plants or amoles, as their tissues yield a pulp that produces a lather when wet and is used as soap.

The sap of some species is fermented to obtain a drink called pulque, which can be distilled to make a colourless liquor, mescal. The mescal industry started in 1950 in the Oaxaca valley, with *A. angustifolia*. Similarly, the sap of *A. tequilana* is the source of tequila and is produced from the meristem and leaf bases of the plant. When the plant is mature and ready to flower, the short, broad stem with the attached leaf bases is cut and carried to large steaming ovens and cooked for up to 48 hours. During the boiling, the raw starches are converted to sugars that are allowed to ferment to form alcohol, and this is then distilled. Unlike tequila, pulque is flavoured with herbs, roots and bark, and forms a regular part of the almost meatless diet of many of the poor Indians. For visitors to this part of the world it is an essential alternative to drinking the local water, as this can produce unpleasant stomach problems.

Agave are often confused with *Aloe* species. Unlike aloes, agaves have many fibres in their leaves, as can be seen when a mature leaf is broken. In agaves, the leaves develop in a sheath in the middle of the rosette and unfurl, often leaving an imprint in the underside of the next leaf, while in aloes the new leaves grow out from the centre of a rosette. You can pour water into the middle of an aloe – you cannot do this with an agave.

Agaves can be grown in loam-based or soil-less compost. Several species from the USA are quite hardy and can be grown in a sunny greenhouse, without heat. If repotted regularly they soon grow to become large, handsome specimens and eventually need to be planted out in the garden in a sheltered position, with some protection from excess moisture and frost during cold spells in winter. The hardiest species include those from Arizona (*A. parryi*), New Mexico (*A. neomexicana*) and Utah (*A. utahensis*). If planted at an angle, say on a slope of a landscaped rock garden, rainwater will not collect at the centre of the rosette – the part of the plant that is most likely to rot. If the long-term weather forecast is very severe, the plants are best covered with sacking while the conditions last.

Agave americana Linnaeus

This is one of the largest-growing species, with rosettes that can reach 3–4m (10–12ft) in diameter, freely forming stoloniferous offsets to cover a large area. The leaves are about 20cm (8in) wide and 2.5m (8ft) long. A stem that can reach a height of 8m (25ft) holds the yellow-green flowers aloft. Beginners in the hobby of collecting succulent plants often start on a windowsill or in a small greenhouse with a little offset of this plant, that is passed on years later when it has outgrown its welcome.

This is a very easy plant to grow, and there are a number of interesting varieties. *A. a.* var. *marginata* has yellow-margined leaves, *A. a.* var. *striata* alternate green and yellow lines on the leaves, and *A. a.* var. *medio-picta* a broad median yellow band.

Agave celsii Hook

By contrast, this is one of the smaller, clumping species that will make a welcome addition to any subtropical rockery. The rosettes of bluish green to red-tinged leaves rarely exceed 45cm (18in) in diameter.

Agave parryi is quite a hardy plant, at times covered under snow in its natural habitat in Arizona.

Agave desertii Engelmann

As its name suggests, this species is found in desert regions, mainly in California but also in Arizona and Sonora. It is caespitose and about 40–80cm (16–32in) in diameter, with light grey leaves that are 3–6cm (1¼–2½in) wide and about 15–40cm (6–16in) long. The chrome-yellow flowers are borne on a stem that can reach a height of 2–7m (6–22ft). This plant was included in the diet of the local Native Americans and is important to the wildlife of these extreme desert regions. The birds and insects visit the flowers for nectar, small rodents live among the fiercely armed rosettes and feed on the leaves and seeds, while Bighorn sheep eat the flowering shoots.

Agave parryi Engelmann

This is another beautiful species, as demonstrated on the cover of this book. It is easy to grow, with grey leaves and

orange-yellow flowers. Its native habitat is in the mountains of northern Arizona and New Mexico, where the densely leafed rosette may reach a diameter of 1m (3ft).

Agave parviflora Torr.

By contrast, this is one of the smallest-growing species and also one of the most attractive. As a bonus, it is easy to grow in cultivation where, propagated easily from seed, it soon makes an attractive plant. It is found in several locations in Sonora and Chihuahua in Mexico and in Arizona. The mature rosette is about 18cm (7in) in diameter and may be single or produce offsets. The slender leaves are dark green with white margins and white marginal threads. The flower spike is a modest 60–100cm (24–36in) tall and has pale yellow flowers.

ALLUAUDIA Drake

Didiereaceae

There are only six species in this genus – *Alluaudia ascendens, A. comosa, A. dumosa, A. humbertii, A. montagnaci* and *A. procera* – all of which have succulent trunks that in habitat in Madagascar can reach a height of 15m (50ft). The most attractive of the species is *A. montagnacii*.

These are easy succulents to cultivate if kept warm. Like so many of the plants that are native to Madagascar, they should be grown in a heated greenhouse.

Alluaudia ascendens (Drake) Drake

This plant occurs along the southernmost coastal strip of Madagascar. The tall, tapering stem can reach a height of 15m (50ft) or more and branches at the top, creating a tree-like appearance. It is covered from the base to the top in spirally arranged strong spines and paired leaves turned on edge. The spines are 1–3cm (½–1¼in) long and almost white, while the bark is a dull greenish brown. The leaves are egg- to heart-shaped with a conspicuous notch at the apex, and are some 2cm (¾in) long and up to 1cm (½in) wide. The white to reddish flowers appear at the top of the branches and are up to 12cm (5in) long.

If grown in a pot, the plant tends to produce offsets from the base that can be removed and grown on as cuttings to make new plants.

Alluaudia comosa Drake

This easily recognized shrub, from the coastal calcareous Mahafaly plateau area in south and southwest Madagascar, produces numerous thorny twigs from the main succulent stem. The plant can reach a height of 2m (6ft). One or sometimes two obovate to suborbicular fleshy green leaves, around 1.5cm (½in) long and nearly as wide, emerge from below the round-based thorns, which are 3.5cm (1½in) long. The small white flowers appear in groups.

ALOE Linnaeus

Aloeceae

This genus of more than 450 species is mainly native to southern Africa, the Arabian peninsula and Madagascar. At a glance, the plants initially resemble their New World cousins in the genus *Agave*, although the two genera belong to different families. Generally, aloes are smaller than agaves and the dwarf species can even be grown on the windowsill. As a bonus, aloes flower annually, and will do so for many years.

During the growing season, the numerous tiny leaves of *Alluaudia ascendens* mask the fierce spines.

This rare 4m (12ft) tall *Aloe helenae* is one of the tree aloes that are rarely seen in cultivation.

The plants usually have short stems with fleshy, lanceolate leaves crowded in rosettes at the end of them, but there are some dwarf species that remain small, such as the 'grass aloes', while others can grow to become massive trees. The inflorescence consists of a raceme of varying length and usually carries numerous dense clusters of red to yellow, sometimes greenish, tubular flowers. Species vary in height from several centimetres to more than 9m (28ft) and can be cultivated as garden and tub plants, if they are protected from frost. Several species are used in medicine and are of commercial importance. The use of *Aloe barbadensis* in the treatment of skin ailments and in the cosmetics industry is well known. Other species are used to prepare purgatives, treatments for toothache and rheumatism, and the flowers of *A. ferox* contain a sweet liquid which is narcotic.

Unlike some agaves, aloes do not tolerate temperatures below freezing and a higher minimum winter temperature is recommended. Their biological clock remains that of the southern hemisphere, so that plants will want to grow during the winter months in North America and in Europe.

Aloe calcairiophila Reynolds

This delightful little species has white flowers that are only 1cm (½in) long. The roots are cylindric, not fusiform. Plants produce suckers from the base and at the axils of the lowest leaves, forming small, dense groups that can be cut off and used for propagation. The leaves are long and narrow and have long, pointed white 'teeth'.

In habitat this species grows on limestone hills south of Ambatofindrahana on the island of Madagascar, where it was first discovered by B. Descoings in 1960. Unlike most aloes, it can be difficult in cultivation. For the best results, some gypsum should be added to the compost.

Aloe dichotoma Linnaeus

In habitat in Namaqualand and Bushmanland, this distinctive tree aloe can reach a height of 10m (30ft). It has smooth branches, but the bark on the trunk forms large golden brown scales. The blue-green leaves are borne in relatively small, terminal rosettes and the flowers are yellow. The common name 'kokerboom' means 'quiver tree', as the local people used to make their quivers from the hollowed stem. This species grows easily from seed and even as a seedling is very attractive. *A. ramosissima* is closely related and is a smaller, more bushy plant.

Aloe helenae P. Danguy

This large tree aloe is found on the island of Madagascar near fort Dauphin (now called Tolanaro) on the track to Vinanibe, where it grows among bush in sandy soil. It can reach a height of 4m (12ft), when the stem will measure some 20cm (8in) across with a large rosette up to 1m (36in) in diameter. The old dried leaves remain attached to the stem and provide some protection against the sun. The numerous yellowish flowers emerge from scarlet buds.

The counterpart of this species in South Africa is *A. thraskii*, discovered by Decary, who named it after his wife. The flowers are lemon-yellow to orange in colour.

It is obvious from the arrangements of the leaves why *Aloe polyphylla* is also known as the 'spiral aloe'.

Aloe saundersiae (Reynolds) Reynolds

Unlike the tree aloes described above, this is the smallest of all known species and belongs to a group known as the grass aloes. These are small, more or less stemless plants, easily recognized by the long, narrow, grasslike leaves that are only slightly succulent. The upper leaf surfaces are usually unmarked, while the lower surfaces may have whitish spots. The small flowers are dull pink to red in colour and have brown tips.

The plant's habitat is a mountaintop north of the Nkandhla Forest in Zululand, where it grows at an altitude of 1,700m (5,500ft). It was first collected in 1931 by Lady Saunders and was named in her honour.

The cultivation of this species is not particularly difficult, but it is a good idea to keep some young plants propagated from cuttings, as mature plants have a nasty habit of dying back, particularly when they are grown in full sun.

APOROCACTUS Lemaire

Cactaceae

Still recognized as a genus in its own right in the CITES *Cactaceae Checklist* (1992), *Aporocactus* was included in *Disocactus* by Barthlott and it is likely that another old and familiar name, in use since 1860, will disappear when the next IOS review of succulent plant names is published.

In habitat, these epiphytes from Mexico live in the forks of branches, where a little humus collects to retain water. In cultivation, they make an attractive display in a large hanging basket that will do well both indoors or, during the summer months, outside. A minimum winter temperature of 10°C (50°F) will produce an abundance of attractive flowers in spring, although the plants will survive almost freezing temperatures if kept dry. The flowers are up to 10cm (4in) long and range from orange, through red, to pink. When in full growth the plants require ample water, and even during winter they will appreciate an occasional light watering or the tips of the stems will die back. They are good plants for beginners and will live happily indoors in a bright position.

The common name of 'rat's-tail cactus' derives from the thin (2cm/¾in diameter) stems that can reach up to 2m (6ft) in length. In the botanical name, the Greek *aporos* means tangled, indicating the somewhat untidy appearance of a mature plant, which will benefit from an annual pruning to remove old, marked stems. This encourages the growth of strong young stems from the base of the plant that will produce flowers the following year. Propagation is easy from stem cuttings taken during spring and early summer.

Aporocactus flagelliformis (Linnaeus) Lemaire

The 'rat's-tail cactus' is one of the earliest known cacti, first described as *Cactus flagelliformis* by Carl von Linne (Carolus Linnaeus) in his *Species Plantarum* of 1753. Today, *A. flagriformis* and *A. leptophis* are regarded as synonymous with this species.

The plants are easy to grow and are easily propagated by taking cuttings of strong young stems during spring.

There is only one other species included in the genus, *A. martianus* (syn. *A. conzattii*), which is more robust in appearance, but there are some interesting intergeneric hybrids (*Aporophyllum*) of plants crossed with *Epiphyllum* hybrids, and these produce much larger flowers with a wide variation in colour. Propagation is easy from cuttings that soon root.

ARGYRODERMA N.E. Brown

Mesembryanthemaceae

The name *Argyroderma* comes from the Greek words *argyros*, meaning silver, and *derma*, meaning skin. H. Here, in *The Genera of the Mesembryanthemaceae* (1971), lists 48 species, while Dyer in *The Genera of South African Flowering Plants* (1975) records 50. Heidi Hartman suggests that her further studies of the genus could reduce this number to ten. All of these stemless succulents come from the Cape Province in South Africa, where they grow either above ground or partly sunken into the soil.

Many members of the family are remarkably cold hardy when kept absolutely dry and grown in a bed rather than in pots. *Argyroderma* is just one genus that has been reported to take temperatures down to −1°C (30°F), along with others that include the species *Aloinopsis malherbi* and *Cephalophyllum alstonii,* most *Cheiridopsis* and some *Dintheranthus* species, *Faucaria, Pleiospilos* (but not *P. nelii*), *Ruschia* and *Titanopsis calcarea.*

Argyroderma roseum Schwantes

Also seen in collections under the name *A. delaetii*, this is one of the most beautiful species in the genus. The plant has one or two shoots with two to four leaves joined halfway up. The leaves are 3.5cm (1½in) long and 4cm (1½in) wide, and are flat on the upper side but convex on the lower; the lower side is more or less drawn over the upper side, resulting in a chin-like appearance. They are blue-green to white in colour. The old dried-up leaves remain around the base of the stem and should not be removed. The flowers are violet-rose in colour with limp petals overhanging the plant.

This plant is easily raised from seed and presents few problems in cultivation. Take care not to water too early in the growing season and also not to overwater, as if the plant takes up too much water split bodies may occur.

ARIOCARPUS Scheidweiler

Cactaceae

This genus of cacti from the Chihuahua desert in northern Mexico and the bordering state of Texas has adapted to the extremely harsh environment by mimicry and hiding from the elements. In habitat, the flattened round body hardly emerges above the ground, which makes the plants difficult to find until they flower in autumn. Growing in silt flats, they are at times completely covered with water for a few days, before the extreme dry conditions return. Water is stored underground in a large tap root, which in cultivation is prone to rot. On top of the tap root grows a rosette of large tubercles that appear almost flush with the soil. These resemble triangular leaves, short or long, grey or green, and their surface is either smooth or deeply fissured. The upper surface especially is thickened like armour plate. Spines are present only in very young plants.

Flowers are formed on young tubercles, on the growth of the current season. They appear near the apex of the stem, at the base of the obscure, hair-covered upper side of the tubercle in an area distant from the vestige (if any) of the spine-bearing part of the areole. The flowers, which open during the day and last for several days, are 2–5cm (¾–2in) in diameter and saucer- to bell-shaped. The floral tube above the ovary is obconical in shape and white or magenta in colour. The fruit is a greenish to red or reddish purple berry that ultimately turns brown: the genus name comes from the Greek and means 'with fruit similar to that of the whitebeam tree'.

These are very slow-growing plants; the majority of mature specimens seen are 6–12.5cm (2½–5in) in diameter, while some may take 80 years to reach a width of 30cm (12in). They only offset sparingly late in life, but many can be raised from seed and then reward your patience by flowering at between eight and 15 years of age. In cultivation, growth can be increased dramatically by grafting the plants. Unless they are then grown 'hard', young plants will readily offset and produce flowers much earlier. Under the right conditions, it is possible to graft a seedling within days of germination and force it into flower in under a year. This greatly increases the amount of seed that can be made available commercially.

All eight *Ariocarpus* species are threatened with extinction in habitat. Often there are only a few relatively small populations found in a limited area, with humans and their livestock posing the biggest threat. For example, goatherds dig up *A. agavoides* and eat the juicy plant flesh as sweets. In 1840, the German botanist Wilhelm Karwinsky von Karwin (1780–1855) brought the first three plants to Europe. One of these was bought by Prince Kotschoubey, after whom *A. kotschoubeyanus* was named by French botanist Charles A. Lemaire (1801–1871). Prince Kotschoubey paid 1,000 francs for his specimen, another was sold for $200. Due to the popularity of the plant in Europe, many mature specimens were dug up and exported during the earlier part of the twentieth century. Conservation laws in Mexico have since been tightened to such an extent that it is now illegal to obtain even seed from habitat plants.

Grafting the plants and increasing their number to satisfy collectors' demand is therefore a good strategy to reduce the pressure on habitat material, even though a grafted plant will not display the typical physical characteristics of its Mexican cousins.

Ariocarpus agavoides (Castaneda) E.F. Anderson
When he first described this species, Castaneda proposed a new genus, *Neogomesia*, for this small, virtually spineless plant from the edge of the Chihuahuan desert in the Mexican state of Tamaulipas. It is only known from three sites within an area of 2sq km (¾sq mile) and it is thought that only some 12,000 specimens exist in the wild. The sites are close to 'civilization' and despite current numbers the plant has been listed as endangered.

The long, divergent, slightly pointed areoles make a small rosette up to 8cm (3in) in diameter that has given the plant its name: *agavoides* means like an agave. The woolly areoles are positioned some distance from the end of the tubercle. If given a sunny place in the greenhouse, the magenta flowers, 4cm (1½in) long and across, will appear from early to late autumn and are followed by pinkish red to reddish purple fruits. The fleshy roots are very sensitive to excess moisture and easily rot if the soil is not well drained.

Ariocarpus scaphirostris Boedeker
This small, spineless cactus barely rises above ground and could easily be mistaken for a small *Agave* species, with its long, pointed tubercles forming rosettes that are partially buried in the flaky grey limestone in which it grows. Plants more than 7cm (3in) in diameter are rare, even in cultivation. In the wild, until recently plants were only known from one valley in the Mexican state of Nuevo Leon, where collectors have stripped several sites that have been monitored by conservationists, and all mature plants offered for sale in the cactus trade were field collected. Many did not survive the shock of transplantation to their new environment.

The bright magenta flowers are 3–4cm (1¼–1½in) in diameter and must be cross fertilized in order to produce the greenish fruit. This species and the recently discovered *A. bravoanus* would benefit greatly from intensive artificial propagation so that the commercial demand from collectors can be met without risk to habitat plants.

ARROJADOA Britton & Rose
Cactaceae
This genus was named in honour of Dr Miguel Arrojado Lisboa, superintendent of the central Brazilian railways at

the time that Britton & Rose described the genus in *The Cactaceae* in 1922.

Native to southern Brazil, these are shrubby, upright or recumbent, columnar plants, often thin stemmed and usually only sparingly branched. At maturity they vary in height, with *Arrojadoa dinae* remaining at a modest 30cm (12in) while *A. rhodantha* can reach a height of over 1m (3ft). Plants remain shorter when treated as bonsai, grown in small pots that restrict their root spread. As their habitat suggests, these cacti are not hardy.

The stems of *Arrojadoa* species are shiny green and armed with numerous sharp, fine spines. Mature stems produce an apical cephalium that usually consists of numerous long red or brown bristles and white wool. The cephalic stem tip is often noticeably swollen, especially in *A. penicillata*. Unlike in *Discocactus* and *Melocactus* species, the cephalium is not terminal, but instead the subsequent new growth appears through it. The old cephalia can continue to produce flowers and fruit for one or two more seasons.

Production of the cephalium indicates that the plant has reached maturity and is ready to flower. The flowers are diurnal, fleshy and waxy in texture, and often shocking pink in colour. They emerge from the cephalium at midday, during spring and summer for most of the species.

In cultivation, the flowers usually require manual pollination using a fine paintbrush to produce the fruit, which is a top-shaped, juicy berry that is soon ejected from the cephalium.

The plants are readily propagated from seed, although the usual method is from cuttings that root easily. There are nine species from which to choose: *A. albiflora, A. aureispina, A. beateae, A. dinae, A. eriocaulis, A. horstiana, A. multiflora, A. penicillata* and *A. rhodantha*.

Arrojadoa dinae Buining & Brederoo

This is a much sought-after species, due to its small size and compact, branching habit. It is ideally suited to windowsill culture and can easily be maintained in an 8cm (3in) pot, where it will grow to a height of 30cm (12in). It flowers prolifically over a long period during winter and early spring, producing red and orange multicoloured blooms that are followed by a substantial crop of large, distinctive, mahogany-coloured fruits.

ASTROPHYTUM Lemaire

Cactaceae

This is a small genus of only four species from Mexico and just across the border in the southern USA, particularly in Texas. The name *Astrophytum* means star plant, because of the small number of well-defined ribs that give the plants a star-shaped appearance. They are easily recognized by the white woolly patches on their skin, a feature found only in this genus and in the South American *Uebelmannia*. These white-flecked plants readily produce their yellow flowers, some of which have a red throat. There are also forms where the flecks have all but disappeared (f. *nudum*).

In addition to the species described below, there is *Astrophytum capricorne* with long soft, twisting spines, and *A. ornatum* with five to 11 strong, straw-yellow spines that become brown with age. The different species readily cross, producing some interesting cultivars which are often seen for sale, identified by the first letters of their parents' specific name, for example *A. ASCAP* is a hybrid of *A. asterias* and *A. capricorne*.

After flowering, the floral remains are retained on a semi-fleshy fruit that is covered with dry scales and dense, felty hair, eventually splitting in various ways to release the large, helmet-shaped seeds. The edge is curved over the deep cavity of the hilum. The seed coat is shiny, dark brown and almost smooth, and the seeds germinate quickly after sowing.

The genus has been linked to *Echinocactus* and was included by Buxbaum as the only North American species in his South American group of Notocacteae, because of the small woolly patches on the epidermis that are found only in *Astrophytum* and *Uebelmannia*. *Echinocactus* species are usually larger plants than *Astrophytum* and have many ribs, but the principal difference is that *Astrophytum* flowers do not possess spiky scales.

Astrophytum asterias (Zuccarini) Lemaire

This is probably the most difficult member of the genus in cultivation, either drying up through lack of water, or rotting when the roots have been kept too wet or when grown in a peat-based compost. Grafted plants have a greater life expectancy, but lose the characteristic flat shape that gives the plant its common name of 'sea urchin cactus'. Its habitat is in southern Texas and the bordering Mexican states of Nuevo Leon and Tamaulipas.

This plant has no obvious spines and the areoles are instead adorned with tufts of wool. When grown well in the sunniest part of the greenhouse and given regular doses of low-nitrogen fertilizer, the plant produces its straw-yellow flowers – which have a brownish to carmine-red throat – throughout late spring and

Ornate by name *and* appearance, the density of the white flecks on *Astrophytum ornatum* can vary greatly.

summer. To err on the cautious side, keep winter temperatures above 10°C (50°F).

This species is often used as one of the parents of hybrid crosses with other *Astrophytum* species. There are some very attractive and sought-after forms that originate from selective breeding in Japan, which are now also available from specialist nurseries in Europe and go by exotic names such as 'Super Kabuto'.

Astrophytum myriostigma Lemaire
This is another attractive plant and much easier to grow than *A. asterias*. In cultivation it forms a short, cylindrical plant, eventually reaching some 30cm (12in) in height and 20cm (8in) in diameter. It should be watered freely during the summer, with a little low-nitrogen fertilizer added every two weeks. In habitat, there are three distinct forms: those from the Mexican state of San Luis Potosi are broad rather than tall when young, while those from Jaumave tend to be tall rather than broad; the third is a distinct columnar form with its habitat in between the other two.

Four-ribbed plants, which give rise to the species' popular name of 'bishop's hat', are the most sought after, often to disappoint their owner by developing an extra rib or two later in life. There are usually no spines, with dense white, woolly flocking covering the epidermis. The yellow flowers do not have the red throat found in many of the other species but possess an abundance of stigmata, *myrio* meaning countless. Stems remain solitary, so that seed provides the only means of propagation. To produce the multi-headed plants that can be found in cultivation, offsets can be induced by damaging the original single growing point. There is a monstrose form that offsets profusely from every areole, but this form is rather difficult in cultivation and is usually grafted.

AUSTROCACTUS Britton & Rose
Cactaceae
All six of the species in this genus (*Austrocactus bertinii, A. dusenii, A. hibernus, A. patagonicus, A. philippii* and *A. spiniflorus*) present quite a challenge when cultivated in European conditions and are difficult to find on offer, except from specialist nurseries and then often only as grafted plants. Their native habitat is Patagonia in southern Argentina and southern Chile, and this is an indication of the origin of the name: *austro* means southern. These strongly spined, columnar plants remain quite small and are therefore unlikely to outgrow a collection where space is limited.

For these cacti, it is best to add extra grit to the compost and to allow it to dry out completely before watering again. They can withstand low winter temperatures and have a second dormant phase during the summer when temperatures are at their highest. Most casualties occur when watering is continued during these dormant stages. The plants need plenty of light to develop their mature spination and flowers, which are large and last for several days, closing at night.

Austrocactus bertinii (Cells) Britton & Rose
This plant was first collected in 1855 by E. Cels, but died; it was found again in 1861 by Captain Bertin, after whom the plant is named, on the Patagonian coast near Comodore Rivadavia in southern Argentina. The short, columnar stem may reach 40cm (16in) in height, and the plant's most distinguishing feature is the magnificent yellowish central spines that can reach a length of 6cm (2½in) and may be hooked or straight. The pinkish yellow flowers have a red style and stigma and have been reported to grow to as much as 10cm (4in) across.

Austrocactus patagonicus (Weber) Backeberg
The soft, fleshy body of this plant can be up to 50cm (20in) tall and will then have a diameter of 8cm (3in)

with nine to 12 notched ribs. The one to four strong, horn-coloured central spines are up to 4cm (1½in) long and are sometimes hooked, while the shorter white radial spines are always straight. Those fortunate enough to have discovered how to grow this plant may be rewarded by flowers 5cm (2in) across, whitish to pink-white in colour with a violet-red stigma.

AZTEKIUM Boedeker

Cactaceae

This is a genus of extremely slow-growing, globular plants that seldom exceed 5cm (2in) in diameter, from the state of Nuevo Leon in Mexico. Until recently *Aztekium ritteri*, first described in 1929, was the only species. The discovery of *A. hintonii* in 1992 caused some excitement, as many hobbyists wanted to own this new species that occurs only in a limited area.

The plants' wrinkly, ribbed, almost spineless appearance is unlike that of any other cactus and they are therefore much sought after. However, they are difficult to grow, requiring a very free-draining compost and infrequent watering. The seed is among the smallest in the family Cactaceae, and as the seedlings are very slow growing they are often grafted within weeks of germination. Grafted plants are much greener and offset much more readily than plants grown on their own roots.

Aztekium hintonii Glass & Fitzmaurice

This plant, together with *Geohintonia mexicana*, caused quite a stir in the cactus world when they were discovered in 1992. Both were found by and named after George S. Hinton, owner of a large ranch in the Mexican state of Nuevo Leon who now looks after the herbarium of his grandfather, George Boole Hinton, who in 1930 started the Hinton collection of Mexican plants. George B.'s son, James C., continued the collection, aiming to represent the total flora of Nuevo Leon. Today, it is rumoured that there are at least another 50 undescribed plant species from different genera growing in the collection.

These plant discoveries occurred at a time when the Mexican government had tightened its laws concerning the collection and export of native plants, so that it became impossible to meet the collectors' demand for these highly desirable plants outside Mexico without breaking the law (see Chapter 7).

Like the other species in the genus, these plants are very slow to grow on their own roots. Grafted young seedlings can be forced on to produce their deep pink to magenta flowers, 1–3cm (½–1¼in) across, within five months of germination, producing more seed to increase the numbers of plants available to collectors throughout the world. While the weathered appearance of habitat-collected plants reflects the harsh conditions they endure, the cultivated seedlings are very pretty, with white-haired tufts on areoles adorning the ribs.

Aztekium ritteri (Boedeker) Boedeker

Originally described as *Echinocactus ritteri*, Boedeker created the new genus of *Aztekium* to accommodate this strange plant. In nature, it survives in only one isolated valley in the Mexican state of Nuevo Leon, in an area no larger than 50sq km (20sq miles). Here the plants grow in cracks in the gypsum or limestone rocks on the sides of steep cliffs, where mosses and lichens provide a nursery bed for young seedlings.

Because of their slow growth, plants in cultivation are often grafted, when they can offset profusely and produce an abundance of delicate white flowers, with pinkish outer perianth parts, that readily set fruit, to provide large quantities of very tiny seeds.

BIJLIA N.E. Brown

Mesembryanthemaceae

This genus from Cape Province in South Africa is named in honour of Mrs D. van der Bijl. Originally the genus was considered monotypic but now a new species – *Bijlia dilatata* (H.E.K. Hartman) – has been discovered.

Bijlia cana N.E. Brown

The tufted growth of this plant consists of four to six thickened, semi-cylindrical or triangular leaves in a rosette. These are about 3cm (1¼in) long and up to 1.5cm (½in) across at the base, widening and then tapering, with the keeled end drawn forwards over the tip to form a chin. The colour is pale grey-green and the surface smooth. The flowers are yellow and 3.5cm (1½in) in diameter.

The plant presents no problems in cultivation provided that the growing period from mid-autumn to mid-spring is recognized and the plant is allowed to rest outside this.

BLOSSFELDIA Werdermann

Cactaceae

These miniature cacti from South America (from Jujuy to Catamarca in northern Argentina and Tarija, Chuquisaca and Potosi in Bolivia) are reputedly the smallest plants in the family Cactaceae, with stems no

This tiny *Blossfeldia liliputana* has been grafted in an attempt to rescue it from the fungus that has marked the stem.

more than 1.5cm (½in) in diameter. The pale yellow flowers are huge by comparison, again to 1.5cm (½in) across, so that a plant which has several buds opening simultaneously is completely hidden beneath the flowers.

The small, clustering bodies look like smooth little balls: there are no ribs or spines, just woolly tufts appearing at each areole. The plants offset freely, to form clumps that look particularly attractive when in flower.

Blossfeldia liliputana Werdermann

The five other names that are still seen in collections – *B. atroviridis, B. campaniflora, B. fechseri, B. minima* and *B. pedicellata* – are all regarded as synonymous with this species. *B. minima* is the smallest form, with stems rarely more than 0.5cm (¼in) in diameter.

The plants are more suited to the experienced grower, and then, certainly when grown in European climates, do best on a graft.

BRACHYSTELMA R. Brown

Asclepiadaceae

The name of this genus is derived from the Greek word *brachys*, meaning short, and *stelma*, meaning column. The plants are found in South Africa, Namibia and Ethiopia, and are closely related to the genera *Ceropegia* and *Riocruxia*. These are dwarf perennial herbs that often form large tubers or fusiform roots. There are no succulent stems or leaves, but their interest is due to their close affinity with the genus *Ceropegia*, where many species have evolved a completely succulent habit. The naming of species and forms can be problematic, as many display a great variability from habitat to habitat and even within single populations.

These plants are not easy to grow in cultivation and great care must be taken not to overwater, as this will cause the roots to rot. A very open compost is recommended. Keep a lookout for red spider mite, which seems to have a particular liking for all three of the related genera.

Brachystelma barberae Harv. ex Hook

This species is found in a wide area from the eastern Cape in South Africa to Zimbabwe and is probably the most profuse flowering species in the genus. The second part of the name honours Mrs Mary Barber (née Bowker) of Grahamstown, who in 1866 was the first to make a painting of the plant that was discovered by her brother, Henry.

This perennial dwarf herb is one of the most spectacular species due to the size and shape of its numerous red-brown flowers that resemble a bird cage – and which, regrettably, have a particularly foul-smelling odour. They appear from a short stalk arising from a comparatively large, flat tuber which can grow to 20cm (8in) in diameter and, like that of many other species, is eaten by the natives of the Transkei, where it was first found. In other species, this use as a source of food has dangerously reduced the number of plants that remain in the wild. For example, *B. perditum* may never have been discovered if Roy Bayliss had not observed herd boys in Lesotho preparing a meal of the tubers. However, for

Brachystelma barberae produces the most spectacular flowers of the genus, but unfortunately also one of the worst smells.

PLATE V
Cactus flowers

Opuntia lindheimeri

Epiphyllum cv.
'Chelford Night'

Cleistocactus
varispinus

Opuntia
paraguayensis

Echinopsis
bruchii

Opuntia
durangensis

Rebutia
pygmaea

Rebutia
muscula

Rebutia
spegazziniana

Echinopsis
hertrichiana f.
binghamiana

Rebutia arenacea
f. candiae

Aporophyllum cv.
'Pink Duchess'

Echinocereus
scheeri

Echinocereus pentalophus

Epiphyllum cv. cooperi × peacocki

Opuntia erectoclada

Pereskia grandifolia

Epiphyllum cv. 'Clementine'

Epiphyllum cv. 'Jennifer Ann'

Epiphyllum cooperi

Epiphyllum cv. 'Plumwood'

B. barberae this appears not to be the case, possibly due to the fact that it is claimed to have a better than average seed production.

BURSERA Jacquin ex Linnaeus

Burseraceae

Many plants in this genus are grown for their caudex. Although in nature they can become trees, if grown in shallow pots they make a wonderful bonsai subject with very small, inconspicuous flowers and leaves that when brushed give off a strong aromatic odour.

Bursera species are generally not difficult to cultivate. As they do not require high winter temperatures, they will grow happily alongside many cacti in a cool greenhouse. Germination from seed is relatively poor, but fortunately the plants are readily propagated from cuttings.

Bursera microphylla A. Gray

Native to Arizona, Baja California and Sonora, this species has a thickened main stem from which arise branches that are 1–8m (3–25ft) in height. The tissue of the cortex contains a resinous latex, copal, used commercially in varnishes and lacquers, and the pinnate leaves have a strong aromatic odour when brushed. The flowers are very small and are yellow in colour. Native Americans use the plant as incense in their churches.

CARNEGIEA Britton & Rose

Cactaceae

This is a monotypic genus.

Carnegiea gigantea Britton & Rose

More commonly referred to as 'saguaro', this giant from the Arizona and Mexican Sonora Desert leaves a lasting memory with those who have seen it in its natural habitat. Many tourists take home seed of the plant as a souvenir and find that it germinates readily but that growth is slow, producing an unspectacular pot plant. It will take some 20 years for the seedlings to reach 60cm (24in) in height and around 70 years before the plant will form the characteristic arms. By then, it will have outgrown most greenhouses. If the climate suits (they do not survive periods of continuous frost), these plants can make an impressive display when grown in a cactus garden.

Due to work undertaken in 1990 to enlarge Lake Pleasant, northwest of Phoenix, Arizona, the federal Bureau of Reclamation offered saguaros to people willing to remove them from the land to be flooded. Within a few weeks, more than 4,000 applications had been received. As these plants can exceed 20m (70ft) in height,

and at that height will weigh in excess of nine tonnes, this must have been quite an evacuation. Even at 5m (15ft), the plant will tip the scales at two tonnes. Yet, cactus rustling is big business in Arizona, where these giants can fetch $15,000 or more each. Most of the weight is water, collected by roots that radiate away from the plant to a distance similar to its height. Although a typical desert plant, one of the threats to its existence in habitat is a change in the local climate, which is becoming even drier. During the summer rainy season, plants have been known to increase in diameter from 75cm (30in) to 120cm (48in), building up a water store to help them survive droughts.

The saguaro plays an important part in the ecology of the Sonora Desert. Bees, bats and the western white-winged dove feed on its nectar and distribute its pollen. Later, the doves and other birds and rodents return to feed on the fruit. Humans, too, collect the fruit, pitahayas – a Spanish word applied to the edible fruit of any ceroid cactus or to the cactus itself – and turn it into jam and wine. Several species of woodpecker, most of all the Gila woodpecker, find the soft tissue an easy place to build a nest. After the brood has flown, other birds – including the small elf owl – use the cavity, while still others, such as the red-tailed hawk, build their nests in the elbows where the arms poke out of the stem. The wood of the plant is used in the building of rafters for the adobe houses and for fencing, and its importance is reflected in the choice of the saguaro blossom as the state flower of Arizona.

Saguaros can live in excess of 200 years. It is ironic that these giants can fall victim to a species of tiny fruit fly, *Drosophilla*, and a small pyralid moth which feeds on the brownish, oily sap that seeps out of wounds when the plant is injured. These insects are the carriers of a bacterium that will quickly kill the plant. Saguaros also succumb to frost, and a week of sub-zero temperatures will kill the old and the weak.

CARPOBROTUS N.E. Brown

Mesembryanthemaceae

These plants are widely spread throughout the world, with 23 species in South Africa from Clanwilliam through the Cape Province to Natal, one each in Chile and the USA (California), and four from Australasia, including Tasmania and New Zealand. The name *Carpobrotus* comes from the Greek words *karpos*, meaning fruit, and *brota*, meaning edible.

These little shrubs have long, prostrate branches and can be planted out in spring. The large, sabre-shaped leaves are triangular and united at the base. Large red or purple, sometimes yellow flowers occur singly on stalks from mid-spring to late autumn and are up to 6cm (2½in) in diameter.

Carpobrotus edulis L. Bolus

Originally from the Cape Province and Natal in South Africa, this plant was introduced and grows as naturalized in Australia, Europe and California. It has branches up to 1m (3ft) in length with triangular, spreading green leaves that are 8–12cm (3–5in) long and up to 1.5cm (½in) thick, with a slightly serrated keel. The flowers are red or yellow in colour. This species in particular is known for its edible fruits.

Now firmly established on the cliffs of the mainland of southwest England and in the Channel Islands, this species was deliberately planted out on the Scilly Isles by Augustus Smith in the mid-1800s together with marram grass, to stabilize the sand dunes and prevent the wind from blowing in sand that covered crops and penetrated houses. It also managed to 'island hop' without man's intervention, distributed by seagulls that use it in building their nests.

The plant is therefore quite suitable for cultivation in areas with a mild climate that experience only light frosts in winter.

CEPHALOCEREUS Pfeiffer

Cactaceae

Taxonomic opinion seems to change as often as the Paris fashion scene. At one stage, this genus embraced most tropical and subtropical ceroids that produce flowers from a distinct area on the stem, the cephalium (meaning head): *Arrojadoa, Austrocephalocereus, Backebergia, Buiningia, Coleocephalocereus, Espostoopsis, Haseltonia, Micranthocereus, Mitrocereus, Neobuxbaumia, Neodawsonia, Pilosocereus, Pseudopilocereus, Stephanocereus* and *Subpilocereus*.

The characteristic cephalium, an area at the top or side of the stem with extremely dense spination from which the flowers are produced, gives rise to the name of this genus. The CITES *Cactaceae Checklist* (1992) retains only five good species: *Cephalocereus apicicephalium, C. columnatrajani, C. nizandensis, C. senilis* and *C. totolapensis*. Most of the other species have been moved to the genus

A mature stem of *Cephalocereus senilis*, offsetting at the base with, to the left, a seedling that is about ten years old.

Pilosocereus, while some of the former genera (*Arrojadoa, Coleocephalocereus, Espostoopsis, Micranthocereus, Neobuxbaumia* and *Stephanocereus*) are retained.

As a group, the plants display a variety of spinations and body colours. Spines can vary both in colour – from pure white to yellow and brown – and in texture – from long and woolly to short and stiff – while body colours range from light to dark green to azure blue. In cultivation, winter temperatures should be kept above 10°C (50°F) to reflect their tropical and subtropical habitat and to avoid the stems becoming badly marked. At these temperatures, a light watering can be given once a month throughout winter.

Cephalocereus senilis (Haworth) Pfeiffer

Known as the 'old man cactus' because of its long white hair, this is a popular plant seen in many collections and on windowsills. As a young plant it is quite easy to grow, provided the minimum temperature recommendations are observed and a well-drained compost is used, and plants can be watered quite freely during the growing

season. Later in life, they become more sensitive to overwatering and then easily lose their roots. The plants do best in a very gritty, loam-based mixture with temperatures kept above 7°C (45°F). The white flowers are not produced until plants reach a height of around 6m (20ft), so are grown primarily for their hairy spination. Hidden below the white hair, they have a green body and sharp yellow spines.

In habitat, in the Mexican states of Hidalgo and Guanajuata, *C. senilis* dominates the otherwise barren desert landscape, making impressive stands of individual stems that can reach heights of 15m (50ft) but are only 45cm (18in) in diameter. Such giant specimens are in excess of 200 years old.

CEPHALOPENTANDRA Chiov.

Cucurbitaceae

This is a monotypic genus.

Cephalopentandra ecirrhosa Chiov.

Although this caudiciform from Ethiopia, Kenya and Uganda has been around for a few years, it is only recently that it has come to the forefront due to seed now becoming readily available, from which it grows easily. The caudex has a curiously pimpled surface, from which first a rosette of green leaves appears, and later, vine-like growth with long grey foliage. The caudex can reach up to 30cm (12in) in height and diameter, and at that size has a conical shape along with its irregular texture. The flowers are cream coloured and 4cm (2½in) across – large for a cucurbit – and as with all species in this family, male and female plants are required to produce seed. After flowering, attractive orange fruits 4cm (2½in) long and 2.5cm (1in) across appear on female plants. Care must be taken to avoid overwatering.

CEROPEGIA Linnaeus

Asclepiadaceae

Like the two closely related genera *Brachystelma* and *Riocreuxias*, these are popular plants, both in cultivation for their highly intricate flower structures, and in the wild, where they feature in the diet of the local tribesmen and of wild animals such as baboons, porcupines and many insects and rodents.

There are some 160 different species that are found in temperate zones from the Canary Islands in the west, throughout Africa into India and the Far East, to New Guinea and northern Australia. The type species, *Ceropegia candelabrum*, comes from Sri Lanka (formerly

Cephalopentandra ecirrhosa. This three-year-old seedling has reached the 6cm (2½in) pot size.

Ceylon) and India. In classification, vegetative characteristics such as the size and shape of leaves are often neglected, as they can differ widely depending on the conditions under which the plants are grown, and plants in the wild can differ significantly in appearance from those in cultivation. Instead, attention focuses on the floral structures.

Many species present some challenge in cultivation, where they require a well-drained, light, sandy soil with a little decayed compost, and careful watering – too much water will cause rot, while the plants will also suffer if too little is provided.

Ceropegia conrathii Schltr.

This species was named after Paul Conrath, a manager of a dynamite factory at Modderfontein, near Johannesburg, early in the twentieth century. After a promising botanical start, collecting other plants in that area, he returned to Eastern Europe and was not heard of again. *C. conrathii* can be found near Pretoria and extends as far north as Botswana and possibly Zimbabwe. The plant is a dwarf herb with a perennial tuberous rootstock from which one or more stems arise annually. The numerous greenish yellow flowers initially appear together with the annual leaves, but in mature plants the depressed centre of the caudex becomes crowded with buds that, with regular watering, produce a spectacular ball of flowers. The blooms have connate tips, which join to form a cage-like structure above the tube. A musty smell from the flower attracts numerous small pollinating insects.

In cultivation, this species is one of the easiest in the genus to grow. The caudex should be buried to protect it from full sun. During winter dormancy, the plant should be kept completely dry. Plants can be propagated from cuttings 6cm (2½in) long, taken from the tips of the annual growth. Planted immediately in a moist compost and kept in humid conditions, these cuttings will root within one to two weeks. Within a further month a small pea-sized caudex will have developed, and the cuttings can be persuaded to carry on growing throughout the winter by continued watering and increasing the temperature to around 15°C (60°F).

Ceropegia woodii Schltr.

This is another relatively easy species to grow, as evidenced by the many plants found on windowsills and in hanging baskets throughout the world. It has wiry stems with small, heart-shaped leaves and tiny purple flowers. Those collectors who want to grow the more challenging species have noted its vigorous growth, as these can

Cleistocactus hyalacanthus f. *jujuyensis* is another white-spined plant that is often confused with *Cleistocactus strausii*.

be grafted on this plant's bulbous rootstock. Aerial tubers appearing on the vine-like stems can be propagated as cuttings. The species is named after Medley Wood, founder and director of the Natal Herbarium in Durban, South Africa. Again, there is some variability, with variegated and completely green-, purple- or grey-leaved forms, and forms with climbing rather than hanging stems.

CLEISTOCACTUS Lemaire

Cactaceae

These slender, long-stemmed, densely spined plants branch from the base and grow either upright or sprawling, when they can become difficult to control. The stems of some are sufficiently slender for the plants to be grown in a hanging basket.

The current concept for the genus includes plants formerly found in *Borzicactus, Loxanthocereus, Seticereus, Maritimocereus, Bolivicereus, Cephalocleistocactus, Akersia, Winteria, Seticleistocactus, Winterocereus, Hildewintera* and *Borzicactella*. The CITES *Cactaceae Checklist* (1992) shows the number of names reduced to 30 accepted and a further 19 provisionally accepted species, all from southern Brazil and southern Peru to the north of Argentina,

taking in Bolivia, Paraguay and Uruguay. The plants will usually flower when they reach a height of 30–60cm (12–24in). The zygomorphic flowers seldom fully open (cleistogamous) and give the genus its name – from the Greek *cleistos*, meaning closed. Although many cleistogamous flowers are self-pollinating, this appears not to be the case with species of *Cleistocactus,* as the pollen is often produced before the stigma is able to receive it. Consequently, if self-pollination occurs it must be from pollen of flowers higher up the stem that falls down on the ripened stigma of flowers at lower levels.

The plants grow well in a peat-based compost, and if they are not potted on regularly the main stem often stops growing and produces offsets.

Cleistocactus strausii (Heese) Backeberg

This is the name seen on the cleistocacti most often found in collections and nurseries, where it is frequently used incorrectly for any of the densely white-spined species. The 'true' *C. strausii* has upright stems, up to 10cm (4in) thick, that can grow to a height of up to 3m (10ft) and straight, deep carmine-red flowers up to 9cm (3½in) long that contrast nicely with the white spination. Each areole has up to four pale yellow, downward-pointing spines, which are slightly longer than the 40 or so softer white spines that can reach up to 2cm (¾in) in length.

This vigorous plant needs a good loam-based compost and regular potting on. It branches from the base, and when the clump becomes too large, stems that are taken out root readily after the cut surface has first been allowed to callus over.

Other white-spined species are *C. brookeae* (syn. *C. wendlandiorum*), with slender stems only 3cm (1¼in) in diameter and S-shaped flowers that are orange to vermilion in colour, and *C. ritteri*, with slender yellow flowers that protrude from a silky white cephalium.

CONOPHYTUM N.E. Brown

Mesembryanthemaceae

The name of this genus is derived from the Greek words *konus*, meaning cone, and *phyton*, meaning plant. It was a very large genus with numerous species until Steven Hammer's review in *The Genus Conophytum, A Conograph* (1993), that reduced the numbers to a rational amount. This genus is one of the most popular with

The 'true' *Cleistocactus strausii* — the straight, deep carmine-red flowers never open fully (cleistogamous).

hobbyists, as a complete collection can be housed in a relatively small greenhouse.

Conophytum species are endemic to Namibia, where they grow in Namaqualand, the Karoo, Little Karro, Clanwilliam and Van-Rhynsdorp districts, mainly in rock crevices that protect the plants from both animals and the intense sun. The plants remain very small (the genus includes the smallest plants found in the family Mesembryanthemaceae) and are stemless or develop short stems with age. The fleshy body consists of two leaves that are fused into one, with merely a tiny cleft at the top. They often divide, forming small clumps. The flowers arise from between the lobes or from the cleft, in colours ranging from shades of pink, red and magenta to pale yellow and white. Hammer divided the genus into nine diurnal and six nocturnal flowering sections. The night-flowering plants often have a delightful perfume to attract the moths that are the main pollinators.

Cultivation of most *Conophytum* species is easy, with only a few exceptions. Raised from seed, the plants quickly form small clumps. Propagation from stem cuttings, taken a few millimetres below the heads, is best carried out from late summer to early autumn. During the resting period, from early spring to early summer they should be lightly shaded, as the small-bodied species can burn and die. Misting will help to reduce this problem. Unlike many other genera in the family Mesembryanthemaceae, *Conophytum* are not usually cold hardy. The following are some of the newer, rarer species and present more of a challenge to grow.

Conophytum angelicae (Dinter & Schwantes) N.E. Brown

A member of the section *Costata*, this species was named in honour of Angelika Rusch, wife of Ernst Rusch. There are two subspecies: *C. a.* subsp. *angelicae,* a round-bodied plant from the area between Witsand and Pofadder, and *C. a.* subsp. *tetragonum,* the remarkable 'square form' from the Richtersveld. The reddish brown to pale orange flowers are nocturnal and powerfully scented.

Conophytum reconditum A.R. Mitchell

This little gem was discovered in 1981 by Antony Mitchell. The plant is caespitose, mat forming and fragile, with lateral roots. The sheath consists of small, persistent, flask-shaped bodies that are warted down the sides. The flowers are white.

Conophytum stephanii Schwantes

A species named by Dr Schwantes to honour Paul Stephan, who was in charge of the succulents at the

Conophytum pearsonii is one of the easiest conophytus to grow and flower in cultivation. An ideal plant for beginners.

Hamburg Botanic garden, where he assisted the good doctor. This member of the section *Barbata* is one of the most sought after by collectors, the 1cm (½in) diameter hairy plant bodies forming low, slightly convex mats to 5cm (2in) in diameter.

There are two subspecies. *C. s.* subsp. *stephanie*, from the Steinkopf area, has a whitish, densely papillate sheath and olive-green or reddish brown epidermis. The name of the other, *C. s.* subsp. *abductum*, means taken away, as collectors have repeatedly stripped its habitat in the hills east of Port Nolloth. Its nocturnal flowers are brownish yellow to bronze.

COPIAPOA Britton & Rose

Cactaceae

Many members of cactus societies will have attended slide presentations or seen photographs of extensive, dense clumps of these plants taken by those fortunate enough to have visited their habitat, an 800km (500 mile) stretch of exposed coastal deserts in northern Chile, where mists coming in from the sea provide the only moisture during years of drought. The annual rainfall for the area is almost non-existent, not seasonal and sometimes associated with El Niño, an irregular phenomenon that has a great impact on the climate of the Pacific Basin. However, humidity levels are high for a typical desert area, so the evaporation rate experienced by the plants is low and temperature variations are less dramatic, with temperatures fluctuating within the range 18°–27°C (65°–80°F). The centre of this area is the small mining town of Copiapoa, from which the genus derives its name. Plants reported in the nineteenth century from Peru are now 'true' Chileans, as the borders between the two countries have changed.

Grown from both seed and cuttings in cultivation, many species are extremely slow growing and are unlikely to produce flowers for many years. Other, small-growing species like *Copiapoa humilis* and *C. hypogea* can produce the characteristic yellow flowers at three to five years of age. Here we used the names according to the 1998 monograph on the genus by Graham Charles.

Copiapoa cinerea (Philippi) Britton & Rose

In habitat, this variable species (as evidenced by the large number of old names that have been reduced to synonymy) forms the most impressive of the clumps that are often the only visible forms of life in an almost lunar-like desolate landscape. Given the scarcity of water, the volume of these plants must indicate their age of many hundreds of years.

Copiapoa cinerea var. krainziana (Ritter) Slaba

This is one of the larger-growing species, popular because of its attractive dense spination that can vary from pure white and quite woolly to light brown and bristle-like.

It is rare for this species to flower in European cultivation. It is only found in the San Ramon Valley, where the humidity in the atmosphere encourages algae to grow on the plants, staining the spines a dark grey to black. It is a shame to see this very distinctive plant lost into synonymy, but study of these plants in habitat seems to confirm this new combination.

Copiapoa humilis (Philippi) P. C. Hutchison

This is a small-growing, free-flowering species. The yellow flowers contrast beautifully with the dark brown, globular stems that with age build into large clumps. This plant is closely related to *C. hypogea*, also from the province of Antofagasta.

CORYPHANTHA (Engelmann) Lemaire
Cactaceae

A thorough review of this genus is needed in order to rationalize the many species that are still recognized. The name is derived from the Greek words *coryphe*, meaning crown, and *anthos*, meaning flower. The common name is 'beehive cactus', from the shape of the stem of some of the larger, solitary species. The tubercled, globular to short columnar plants often form large clumps and in the main produce yellow flowers. They are characterized by a furrow along the tubercle that runs from the areole more or less to the axil. The flowers are formed at the base of the furrow, in the axil of the tubercle. Many species have nectar-producing glands here, and the sugary sap from these can cause the formation of a black fungus/sooty mould that can give the plant an unsightly appearance. This problem can be prevented by rinsing off the nectar at regular intervals and by using a fungicide. The typical fruit is greenish in colour and contains light brown, smooth seeds.

There is an affinity with other genera of tubercled, globular North American cacti such as *Mammillaria* and *Escobaria*. In fact, many still regard *Escobaria* as a subgenus of *Coryphantha*, for those plants with fringed flower petals and pitted seeds.

The characteristic yellow flowers of *Copiapoa humilis* var. *tenuissima* appear on plants that are three to five years old.

The plants can be grown without too many problems in a bright, sunny greenhouse, rather than on the windowsill. As a rough guide, the denser the spination, the less water the plants require. They should be kept dry during winter when most can tolerate nocturnal frosts, although it may be wiser to set the thermostat to a minimum of 5°C (40°F).

Coryphantha elephantidens (Lemaire) Lemaire

This is one of the larger-growing species, sometimes reaching 20cm (8in) across, with conspicuously large tubercles. The other unusual feature is the flower colour, which ranges from pink to carmine with a brownish sheen and a red throat. The blooms can be up to 6cm (2½in) across. Their habitat is in Michoacan, Mexico.

Coryphantha palmeri Britton & Rose

This clump-forming species has smallish, individual globular stems up to 8cm (3in) in diameter, with white radial spines and one hooked central spine that curves downwards. The yellow flowers are up to 4cm (1½in) long. This is another Mexican species, from the states of Durango, Zacatecas and Coahuila.

CRASSULA Linnaeus

Crassulaceae

There are over 300 species in the genus *Crassula*, mostly native to South Africa but with a few found in South America and Australia. This large genus has been divided into seven sections – *Tillaeoideae, Stellatae, Tuberosae, Crassula, Sphaeritis, Globulea* and *Pyramidalis* – based on the shape of the flower.

Nearly all the species are easy to grow in cultivation and flower freely. Some plants grow to the size of small shrubs but the majority remain small, forming almost stemless rosettes or little shrublets consisting of slender-branched stems. Many are cold hardy; they need a moderate amount of water all year round, which is reduced for a few weeks after flowering. The plants can be propagated from seed, offsets or stem cuttings. In an unheated greenhouse, they will flower in mid- to late winter.

Crassula arborescens (Mill.) Willd.

This is a member of Section 2: *Stellatae*, indicating a star-shaped flower, and in its native habitat of the Cape Province in South Africa will grow to become a shrub up to 2m (6ft) tall. The broad leaves are grey-green with red edges and reddish dots on the upper surface. The flowers are pinkish white, up to 2cm (¾in) in diameter and usually occur in late winter. This species can also be grown as a houseplant of easy culture.

Crassula perfoliata Linnaeus

This is a member of Section 4: *Crassula* and grows into a large shrubby plant up to 1m (3ft) tall. The plants are among the largest and most striking examples in the genus with large, pointed leaves that are a beautiful grey-green colour and have a velvety texture. In their South African habitat, the first two varieties flower in early summer (early to late winter in the northern hemisphere): *C. p.* var. *perfoliata* has white flowers and *C. p.* var. *miniata* red (*miniata* means vermilion, not miniature). *C. p.* var. *heterotricha* also has white flowers but blooms in early winter (late spring to late summer in the northern hemisphere), while the red-flowered *C. p.* var. *falcata* is another early summer-flowering plant.

As with some other *Crassula* species, *C. perfoliata* can suffer from a fungus that leaves rust-coloured spots on the leaves. These can be prevented by regular spraying with a fungicide, but once they have appeared, they cannot be removed. The plants can withstand very low temperatures in the winter if kept dry.

DIDYMAOTUS N.E. Brown

Mesembryanthemaceae

The name of this monotypic genus is derived from the Greek words *didymos*, meaning double, and *aotus*, meaning flower. It occurs in the Ceres Karroo in South Africa.

Didymaotus lapidiformis (Marl.) N.E. Brown

The species name is derived from the Latin and means formed like stone. The plants consist of a pair of very succulent, stemless leaves, flattened on the upper parts and keeled underneath. They are about 5cm (2in) long and 3cm (1½in) across. The surface is rough and greyish or green in colour. The flowers are white with a pinkish to red centre and appear on both sides of the base of the shoot rather than from the centre of the plant.

This is one of the most difficult plants to grow in cultivation in Europe, presumably due to the lack of available light.

DIOSCOREA Engelman

Dioscoreaceae

Many of the species in this genus are perhaps better known under their old genus name of *Testudinaria*. Originally, the genus *Dioscorea* was used for plants with underground tubers, while *Testudinaria* species displayed their caudex above ground. Currently, these two genera have been merged into *Dioscorea*.

Plants in this genus are generally known as the 'elephant's foot' in Mexico and 'Hottentot bread' in South Africa, due to the caudex which is entirely exposed above soil level – in habitat, this can be massive. To the collector of succulent plants, in particular caudiciforms, this genus has only four species that are desirable in cultivation: *D. macrostachya* from Mexico, and *D. glauca*, *D. elephantipes* and *D. silvatica* from South Africa.

The flowers of all species are dioecious and not very showy – the main reason for growing them is the beautifully patterned caudex of mature plants (especially so in *D. elephantipes*, with its prominent, many-angled, corky tubercles that appear to have been hand carved by a master craftsman).

The plants are not difficult to grow and do not require high winter temperatures, but care must be taken not to allow the soil to dry out, even during the resting period. They are slow growing, taking a considerable time to become specimen plants. The growing season varies, some species growing during the summer while the majority leave it until autumn to produce an untidy vine from the segmented caudex. When in growth, the plants can be watered generously. Once the growing season is over, the vine dies off and watering should be reduced. Continue to water sparingly during the dormant period, because these are difficult plants to re-establish once the roots have been allowed to dry out altogether.

Dioscorea elephantipes (l'Her.) Engler

This plant was first described as *Tamas elephantipes* by l'Her in 1788. However, in 1824 the then monotypic genus *Testudinaria* (Lindl.) was created for this species, but by 1827 it had been transferred to the genus *Dioscorea* as a very special yam. Nevertheless, some authorities, notably Jacobsen, still uphold *Testudinaria* as a genus and plants are found in collections and nurseries under either name.

D. elephantipes is well known for its medical properties and for many years was imported in huge quantities, as it contains diosgenin from which cortisone was manufactured. Today, cortisone can be produced synthetically, without the need to remove plants from their habitat. The Hottentots gouge pieces out of the caudex and bake them in the embers of their fires to eat like bread, hence the common name.

In cultivation, growth starts towards late autumn with small, insignificant flowers appearing about a month later. The foliage dies back around late spring.

DISCOCACTUS Pfeiffer

Cactaceae

Requiring higher winter temperatures than most cacti, these flat-globular (*disco* means like a disc) plants from Brazil are often offered for sale only by specialist nurseries. They are at all times very ornamental plants – even when not in flower – with their symmetrical globular bodies, colourful spination and unique, distinctive cephalia. Although they will survive short spells at 10°C (50°F), it is safer to provide a minimum temperature of 15°C (60°F).

Mature plants are usually solitary, although there are some exceptions that cluster freely (*Discocactus buenekeri*, *D. araneispinus*, *D. boomianus*), and they usually have shiny green, prominently ribbed or tubercled stems. They vary in size at maturity from about 5cm (2in) in diameter (*D. horstii*) to over 20cm (8in) (*D. pseudoinsignis*). Most species are armed with strong, colourful spines.

At maturity, the plants produce an apical cephalium, usually consisting of brown to black bristles and copious white wool, from which the flowers are produced. Cephalium-producing plants vary in age according to eventual mature size. The smaller-growing species, such as *D. buenekeri*, *D. horstii*, *D. araneispinus* and *D. boomianus*, can produce cephalia within two to four years from seed. The larger-growing species often take many years.

The flowers of *Discocactus* are nocturnal, usually white in colour and sometimes tinged with green or light brown. In some species, particularly *D. buenekeri* and *D. placentiformis*, they are extremely fragrant. When the plants are in flower their aroma is intoxicating, filling a small greenhouse or surrounding area with a scent reminiscent of gardenias. The flowers are borne in clusters – as many as 12 on a single plant – on and off from late spring to early autumn.

The flower buds remain hidden in the woolly cephalium and then suddenly, one morning, start to push through. By mid-afternoon they are fully developed and protrude from the cephalium, ready to burst into full bloom shortly after dusk. They remain fully open throughout the night, but wilt rapidly before sunrise.

The fruit is usually an elongated, fleshy, whitish to pale green pod (but dark red in *D. araneispinus* and *D. boomianus*) that soon splits longitudinally, revealing the shiny black seeds that are difficult to extract as they are held by the mucilaginous wall of the fruit.

Another peculiarity of *Discocactus* species is the tenacity with which the fruit is secured in the cephalium (unlike, for instance, *Melocactus*, where the fruit is readily expelled by cephalic pressure). To extract the fruit before it dries and spills its seeds into the cephalium, run a pair of forceps along the side of the fruit and extract it with a gentle twisting motion, being careful to avoid pulling a significant tuft of wool from the cephalium.

The plants are readily propagated from seed, and accept the same general treatment as most other seedling cacti – with the caveat that low temperatures are not well tolerated. The clustering species are easily propagated from offsets, which are readily detached from the mother plant and come equipped with their own root system.

Discocactus buenekeri Abraham

This is a true miniature, and can be successfully grown to maturity – and maintained – in a 7cm (2¾in) pot. It grows rapidly and easily, soon producing a multitude of offsets that develop healthy root bundles while still attached to the mother plant. These are easily detached and potted up, while the mother plant continues to produce offsets. It is very free flowering, and the large, frilled white flowers are very strongly perfumed.

Other species recommended for windowsill cultivation (that will form a cephalium, flower and fruit in 8cm/3¼in pots) include *D. araneispinus*, *D. boomianus*, *D. horstii* and *D. placentiformis*.

DORSTENIA Linnaeus

Moraceae

The genus *Dorstenia*, named after the German botanist Theodor Dorster, who was born in the late fifteenth century, contains about 180 species of mainly herbaceous plants from the tropical rainforests of Africa, Madagascar, Yemen and America. There are about 20 succulent

This *Dorstenia* species from South Yemen is a member of the *foetida* complex, which are among the easier ones to grow.

species. The flowers are monoecious and very small; both male and female flowers are crowded together on a flat, saucer-shaped receptacle known as the hypathodium, a type of pseudoanthium. The shape of the saucer is a significant characteristic in determining the different species.

In cultivation, the best results are obtained when plants receive plenty of heat and moisture, and temperatures during winter should be kept above 10°C (50°F). The flower is like a fig turned inside out, and the saucer is covered in many flowers, each producing a single seed which is shot away from the plant when ripe, leaving a little raised pimple (a sign that the seed has gone) rather than the seed pod. Propagation is mainly from seed.

Dorstenia crispa Engler

From Kenya and Somaliland, the glossy brown stems of these plants can reach a height of 40cm (16in) and a diameter of 3cm (1¼in). The long, slender leaves that occur on the ends of the main stem and branches are about 8cm (3in) long and have serrated margins. The scars left by the old leaves make an attractive pattern.

Dorstenia ellenbeckiana Engler

This species was first described by Engler in 1902 and until recently remained almost unknown to collectors of succulents. The original description, freely translated from the Latin and German, describes the plants as 'having a small underground caudex, with many leaves', the hypathodium being slightly hairy and rust coloured. The plant is found at Arussi-Galla near Burkar in the Galla Highlands in Ethiopia, growing among rocks at an altitude of about 1,200m (3,900ft).

In cultivation, this is not a difficult plant to grow. It needs plenty of water during the growing season.

Dorstenia foetida (Forsk.) Schweinf.

This species occurs over a wide area in Yemen, where it is found growing in association with many other succulents such as *Euphorbia*, *Aloe* and *Commiphora* species. The plant consists of a flattened, greyish green main stem reaching 15cm (6in) across and about 3cm (1¼in) high when mature, with numerous short, thick branches up to 5cm (2in) in length. The leaves are very similar to those of *D. crispa*, but are considerably smaller.

Dorstenia gigas Schweinf.

This, the largest-growing species in the genus (*gigas* means giant), is found on the island of Socotra in the Indian Ocean between Yemen and Somalia. For many years, the endemic plants from Socotra were difficult to obtain in cultivation, as a large Russian naval base on the island discouraged visitors.

The plant forms a small tree, up to 2.5m (8ft) in height and 0.5-1.5m (1½-5ft) thick at the base. The dark leaves are carried on the tips of the short branches and in mature plants can reach a length of 15cm (6in) and a width of 3cm (1¼in). In habitat, *D. gigas* grows on the vertical faces of cliffs. In cultivation, the plant can take a considerable amount of water during its summer growing period. In autumn, the leaves turn brown and still look attractive until they drop off for the winter rest.

Dorstenia hildebrandtii Engler

This species comes from northern Kenya, where it grows in the same area *as Pyrenacanthe malvifolia*. It is a variable species linked to a dozen or more synonymous names; there are two varieties – *D. h.* var. *hildebrandtii* and *D. h.* var. *schlechteri* – and each of these has different forms based on the shape of the inflorescence. Their habitat is usually shady, in wet places near streams or even as epiphytes on trees, between mosses and humus on wet ground in very light soil. They occur in tropical East Africa: Kenya, Tanzania, Uganda, Zaire, Rwanda, Burundi and Mozambique.

This species is a much quicker grower than the others described, and unlike them does not have a definite resting period. It forms a swollen, reddish green caudex at its base, with a tall, thinner main stem extending from it which is green speckled with red. The leaves are formed in clusters at the growing tip of the main stem and on the tiny branches.

In cultivation, the plants thrive in half shade, well watered in the summer and occasionally during winter as they are not deciduous, if temperatures are kept above 10°C (50°F). In full sun, growth stops and the plants shed their foliage so that only some apically arranged leaves remain. With age, both varieties of *D. hildebrandtii* may become straggly, so keep them in small containers. The plants can be prone to rot if kept too cold and wet during the winter months.

DRACAENA Vand. ex Linnaeus

Dracaenaceae

Dracaena species – the name means female dragon – are native to Africa and make popular houseplants. Many are only borderline succulent, with slightly succulent stems.

Dracaena draco Linnaeus

This is perhaps the best-known species, the famous 'dragon tree' found on the Canary Island of Tenerife and recently also in the Anti-Atlas mountains in Morocco. Fossil remains have been found dating back some 200 million years, when this species had a much wider distribution. There is also a similar species, *D cinnabari*, from the island of Socotra.

There are reports of a specimen of *D. draco* that reached 25m (80ft) in height with a succulent stem up to 26m (83ft) in circumference! It was said to be more than 600 years old, but unfortunately died during a hurricane in 1867. The name dragon tree comes from the red resin – 'dragon's blood' – that used to be added to varnish to give it extra colour.

In mild Mediterranean climates this species can be planted outside, but closer to the poles it will need to be protected against frost and excessive moisture, so is probably best brought in for the winter period.

DUDLEYA Britton & Rose
Crassulaceae

This genus from Mexico and the southern USA was first described by Britton & Rose in 1903 and named in honour of Professor W.R. Dudley of Stanford University. Most of the species have silver-coloured leaves, and there are close relationships with the genus *Echeveria*, with a number of hybrids between the two. (In fact, the plants in the genus *Dudleya* were at one time included under *Cotyledon* and *Echeveria*.) Plants of both genera are grown for the range of colours presented by the attractive rosettes of succulent leaves.

Although the plants closely resemble echeverias, they differ in flower structure and their cultivation requirements are opposite. Echeverias are summer-growing plants, resting in winter, while *Dudleya* species rest in summer and grow in autumn and winter. If this rule is followed, they are not difficult to grow successfully in cultivation. Unlike in echeverias, the dead leaves persist for some time, so do not be in a hurry to remove them as this can damage the plant.

Dudleya species are relatively slow growers. If grown with a free root run, dividing clumps can increase the number of plants. Pot-grown plants are propagated by taking stem cuttings. Best grown in a heated greenhouse, in mild climates they can also be planted out in the rockery.

Dudleya brittonii D. A. Johansen

This species is one of the most beautiful of all with its large, normally single, pure white rosette that can reach from 15cm (6in) to as much as 40cm (16in) across. The rosette has an upright bowl shape and retains this throughout the life of the plant, with the old dead leaves persisting in the upper stem. The stem can be up to 50cm (20in) long and 6cm (2½in) in diameter on old

plants. The white leaves are covered with a chalky pulverulence that easily rubs off if the plant is touched. The flower colour is usually pink or red. This species grows along the coast of Baja California, where its white leaves contrast strongly with the dark cliffs.

Dudleya hassei Rose

This species is found on the islands of Santa Catalina and Guadalupe, off the coast of Baja California. Its stems are about 1.25cm (½in) thick and up to 38cm (15in) tall, usually branching almost at once to form clumps up to

Dudleya brittonii – the chalky white, farinose covering of the attractive rosette leaves rubs off easily, marking the plant.

The flower stalk emerges from between the delicately striped leaves of this *Dudleya* hybrid.

1m (3ft) in diameter. Stems often drop the oldest dead leaves and have a dull, brownish red colour for the lower part nearest the root; nearer the top, the old leaves remain on the stem, just below the many rosettes, which are quite upright. The twisted, dead leaves are a pale pinkish colour. The lower stems are usually branched, and flowers are white. This is an easy plant to grow and there are several horticultural forms propagated by nurseries. It can be grown in either full sun or partial shade.

ECHEVERIA De Candolle
Crassulaceae

The genus *Echeveria* is perhaps the most popular of all in the Crassulaceae family, with over 140 species. Found from southern Texas in North America southwards, the main habitats are in Mexico, but there are also some 20 species from South America. Here they grow at altitudes of 2,000–4,300m (6,500–14,000ft), with *Echeveria chiclensis* holding the altitude record, growing high in the Peruvian Andes. Plants are readily crossed with those from other genera, such as *Dudleya,* giving rise to plants known as × *Dudleveria,* × *Graptoveria* (*Graptopetalum*), × *Pachyveria* (*Pachyphytum*) and × *Sedeveria* (*Sedum*).

Echeverias have been in cultivation all over the world since the discovery of *E. coccinea* in 1790. Their attraction lies in the remarkable variety of leaf colour and form displayed by the genus, rather than in their flowers, which are generally on the small side and can be red, orange, purple or yellow, the latter being the most attractive. However, *E. harmsii* is a firm favourite species with florists and is sold in quantity as a houseplant. It forms a small, branched subshrub with flowers that are usually solitary and 3cm (1¼in) long – easily the largest in the genus – and bright scarlet with a lighter tip. The old name for this plant was *Oliveranthus elegans.*

Some species are easy to grow while others are much more demanding of time and cultivation skills. In cultivation, echeverias suffer from the same pests as all other cacti and succulents – mealy bugs in particular seem especially fond of them. Constant vigilance is needed to keep the collection clean, and as soon as the bugs are found they should be picked off before they have a chance to multiply. All dead leaves should be removed, as they make an ideal breeding ground.

Many species and hybrids can be planted out in the open, provided that during winter they are given some protection from excess moisture and frost. Propagation is from seed, and stem or leaf cuttings.

Many hybrids have been created during the last 100 years and these include some of the best colour and leaf forms found in the genus. They are usually easier to grow than the species.

Echeveria glauca Bak.
This is a freely offsetting, stemless plant with purplish blue leaves and red flowers. It comes from two localities: Distrito Federal and Santa Fe Valley, both in Mexico. It is almost hardy if kept dry in winter and is very popular in public parks, where it is used in formal displays. An ideal beginner's plant, *E. glauca* is easy to propagate from offsets.

Echeveria lindsayana E. Walther
This species from Chihuahua in Mexico, discovered in 1972, is certainly one of the most attractive of all echeverias. It forms a stemless rosette, about 15cm (6in) in diameter, of succulent leaves that are white with deep rose edges. The flowers that appear in mid-spring are shaped like small bells, light red on the outside and yellow inside, and are carried on stems about 50cm (20in) long. Unfortunately, it is not easy to propagate this plant from leaf cuttings.

ECHINOCACTUS Link & Otto
Cactaceae

There has been some confusion about the exact nature of this genus, the name of which is derived from the Greek *echino*, meaning hedgehog. When it was first described in 1827, Link & Otto listed 14 species, 12 of which have since been referred to *Melocactus*. For a time the genus was seemingly used for any globular cactus found in North or South America that did not bear a cephalium. Karl Schumann recognized 138 species in 1898, while in total more than 1,000 species names have been used. Today the CITES *Cactaceae Checklist* (1992) recognizes only six species: *Echinocactus grusonii, E. horizonthalonius, E. parryi, E. platyacanthus, E. polycephalus* and *E. texensis*.

Echinocactus grusonii Hildmann

It has been argued that this, the most common species of the genus, is really a *Ferocactus* species. Although very common in cultivation, both as young seedlings on windowsills and, where the climate permits, as feature plants in landscaped gardens, the plant is threatened with extinction in the wild since its type location in Mexico became submerged following the construction of the Rio Moctezuma hydroelectric dam.

In Europe, the combination of cold and humidity can leave ugly marks on the epidermis, so it is recommended that you aim for a minimum temperature of 10°C (50°F) – and yet I have seen plants in Arizona on the Mexican border endure −5°C (20°F) with not a mark on them. In the summer months it can take plenty of water and will grow at a steady rate, making a golden barrel 1.2m (4ft) tall and 1m (3ft) across after some 40 years, provided that the roots are not restricted in a pot. The plant needs to reach a diameter of 35cm (14in) and be grown in full sun before a ring of golden yellow flowers, each some 4cm (2½in) across, appears from the woolly apical centre of the plant.

Echinocactus polycephalus Engelmann & Bigelow

Unlike *E. grusonii*, this species and its smaller-growing variety *E. p.* var. *xeranthemoides* can present significant difficulties in European cultivation, unless grafted soon after germination. Mature plants in habitat have impressive dense and fierce spination that turns a deep red when moist, and form large clumps of 20–30 heads, each up to 70cm (28in) in height. The species is distributed throughout the southwestern USA (Nevada, Utah, western Arizona and southern California) and into Mexico (northern Sonora), while *E. p.* var. *xeranthemoides* is only found on the Kanab Plateau on the borders of Utah and Arizona. It is not the cold but the combination of low temperatures with high humidity that is fatal.

This species grows much better in a high-mineral soil than in a peat-based compost, but is notoriously difficult to cultivate outside its natural habitat – even plants that have been salvaged from land-development projects have problems re-establishing when transplanted to local gardens. They are also difficult to raise from seed, but those that germinate and survive the first year generally have a better chance of survival than specimens transplanted from the wild. Their growth rate is very, very slow and it will take many years for a plant to reach mature flowering size.

ECHINOCEREUS Engelmann
Cactaceae

This is a genus of interesting cacti from the western USA and northern and central Mexico, varying in shape from globular, through short columnar to pencil-thin stems. Most have large, bright flowers, but unfortunately in many species these leave ugly scars where the bud has burst through the epidermis. Most of the species are found in great abundance, while some, including *Echinocereus ferreirianus, E. knippelianus* and *E. pulchellus*, are threatened with extinction.

There is a great variety in size, from often solitary, thumb-sized plants such as *E. viridiflorus* var. *davisii* from Marathon, Brewster County in Texas, through plants with robust stems that can reach 1m (3ft) high and form large clumps several metres across, to the species formerly included in the genus *Wilcoxia* which have thin stems that can reach 2m (6ft).

In the greenhouse, it is the variety in spination, both in colour and in length, that is the main attraction. Plants include the fiercely spined *E. brandegeei*; the white-woolly *E. longisetus* var. *delaetii*, which was thought to be a *Cephalocereus* species when it was first discovered by Guerke in 1909; the densely pectinate-spined plants in the *Reichenbachii* group, where the spines completely conceal the epidermis and protect it from intense sunlight; and finally the predominantly green and sometimes almost spineless species and forms such as *E. knippelianus*.

The spination can vary with the amount of sunlight to which the plants are exposed. For example, in habitat *E. triglochidiatus* var. *triglochidiatus* favours shaded locations at the base of a tree, on the east or north side (in the northern hemisphere) where the soil is often slightly damper and more acidic. These plants are often dark green and

PLATE VI
Succulent flowers

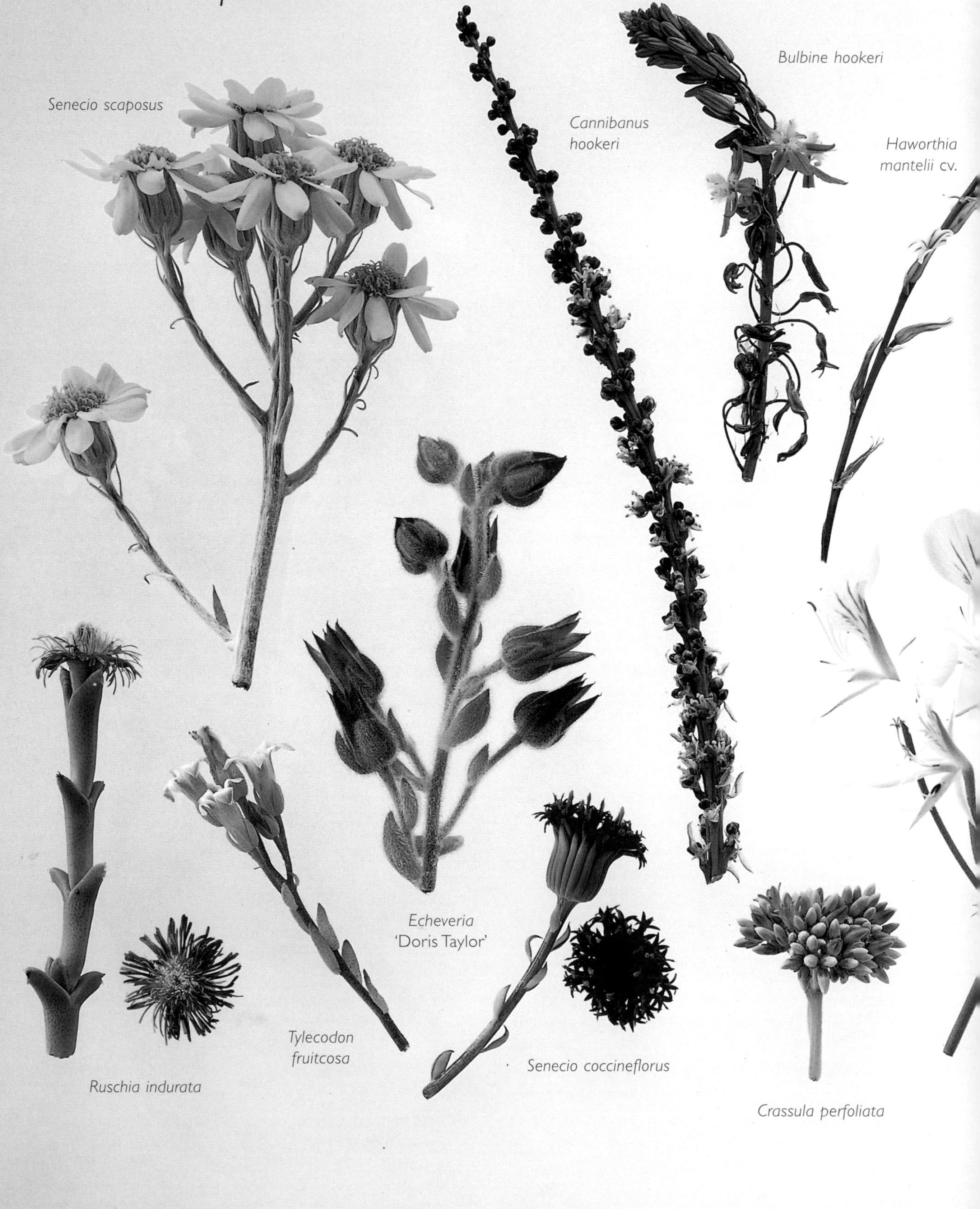

Senecio scaposus

Cannibanus
hookeri

Bulbine hookeri

Haworthia
mantelii cv.

Echeveria
'Doris Taylor'

Tylecodon
fruitcosa

Senecio coccineflorus

Crassula perfoliata

Ruschia indurata

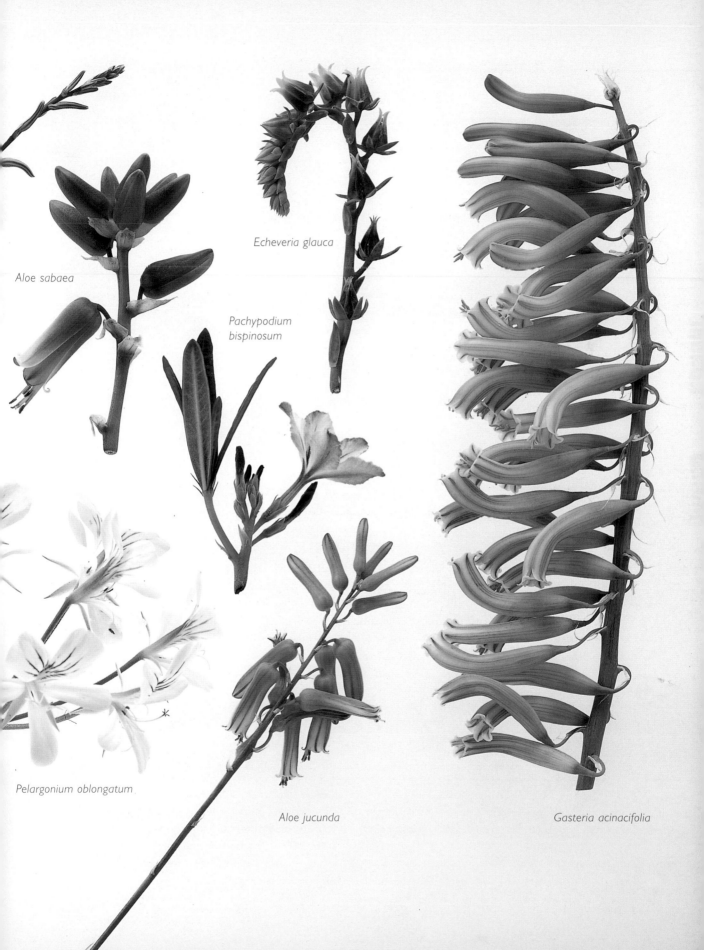

Aloe sabaea

Echeveria glauca

Pachypodium bispinosum

Pelargonium oblongatum

Aloe jucunda

Gasteria acinacifolia

This old grafted plant of *Echinocereus knippelianus* puts on an impressive annual display of flowers, but its appearance is quite unlike that of the plants found in habitat.

have three to five radial spines up to 2cm (¾in) in length. Where the tree has died and plants have become more exposed to the sun, the plant body shrivels and becomes more yellow in colour, while the spines grow longer and a central spine often develops. The same has been found in cultivation.

The flower colour, too, presents a very varied picture and includes white, bright red, orange, yellow, green and magenta blooms that are often bicoloured, with a white or red throat.

The genus is well documented, with work by Taylor (1995) and Blum, Lange, Rischer and Rutow (1998) providing useful reference points from which hobbyists and botanists can argue the merits of the current classification − such as the inclusion of *E. pensilis*, which was placed in the genus *Morangaya* by Gordon Rowley.

It would appear that the more that is known about a genus, the more we realize that there is a lot which still needs further investigation. DNA research indicates that plants previously considered varieties of a single species should be regarded as separate species, due to a difference in chromosome number that can only be determined in the laboratory. Observations of plants growing in cultivation and in habitat by hobbyists or botanists, such as those published in *Der Echinocereenfreund* by the specialist study group of the German Cactus and Succulent Society, are a great help in improving our understanding of the genus.

There are few problems in cultivation, with the pectinate-spined plants requiring rather less water but more sunlight than their green cousins. If the flowers have been pollinated to obtain seed, a careful eye should be kept on the ripening fruit, as in humid conditions they can be attacked by fungi that soon infect the whole plant.

Echinocereus brandegeei (Coulter) Schumann
This is a beautifully fierce-spined species from Baja California. The flattened central spines bear greater similarity to those of other Baja cacti, such as *Opuntia invicta* and *Stenocereus eruca*, the 'creeping devil', than to those of

many other *Echinocereus* species, perhaps with the exception of *E. barthelowanus*, which also comes from Baja California but is found only on the offshore Pacific Ocean island, Isla Magdelena.

While spine variation in species such as *E. engelmannii* has given rise to numerous names, this has not been the case with *E. brandegeei*. Here the colour of young spines can vary from a pinkish red to yellow and white. While the lower of the four spread central spines is often the most dominant, the length and shape of the remainder can vary greatly from broad, short and dagger-like to long and thin, reaching as much as 13cm (5in) in length.

Unfortunately, the plants are shy to flower in cultivation, but given the maximum all-year-round sunlight, it is possible to enjoy the bicoloured blooms, which are purplish lavender with a bright crimson throat and 7cm (3in) across.

Echinocereus knippelianus Liebner

This endangered species is unusual, in that in its small habitat on the border of the Mexican states of Coahuila and Nuevo Leon only the apex of the plant is exposed during the growing season, with the stem base and rootstock forming an underground water store. Following the growing season, the plants pull down into the ground and disappear, covered in dust and sand. The dark green stems usually remain solitary and the areoles bear few inconspicuous spines. The small pink flowers, which are up to 4cm (1½in) long, arise from areoles near ground level in *E. k.* var. *knippelianus* and from the apex of the plant in *E. k.* var. *kruegeri*, in which they are often a much lighter pink in colour, tending to white. This variety also produces offsets.

The habitat of this species lies in the Sierra Madre Oriental, where the plants grow at altitudes of 2,100–3,100m (6,800–10,100ft) in limestone soil that is rich in organic matter. At this altitude, the plants must be able to withstand severe cold weather. If this is reflected in the way we grow our plants in cultivation, then few problems are encountered, with the exception of red spider mites that appear to have a particular appetite for the succulent plant body's relatively soft epidermis.

Echinocereus longisetus (Engelmann) Ruempler

As in many other genera, it is the white-spined species that appear to attract the most attention from collectors, particularly when the white spines are accompanied by large flowers that contrast strongly in colour. Here, this niche is filled by *E. longisetus* and its variety *E. l.* var. *delaetii*, as well as by the dwarf *E. nivosus* and white-spined forms of the pectinate *E. reichenbachii*. In *E. longisetus*, flowers are pinkish purple to claret-red in colour with a white throat and 6cm (2½in) across. The petals have a darker midstripe.

ECHINOPSIS Zuccarini

Cactaceae

What is an *Echinopsis*? Once again, this is a genus that has undergone considerable revisions, by both 'splitters' and 'lumpers', since the German Joseph Zuccarini proposed it in 1837. Originally it covered low, globular or short, cylindrical plants from South America, but the modern view also includes *Lobivia, Chamaecereus, Helianthocereus, Soehrensia* and *Trichocereus*. The latter was a genus of tall, columnar plants such as *T. pasacana*, which can reach 6–10m (20–30ft) in height.

There is a strong opinion that these other genera should not have been included, as most (though not all) represent well-defined groupings of species and serve a useful purpose. The situation is very confusing for all but the botanists and the most dedicated cactus collectors, especially when one is confronted with a plant or seed list with an unfamiliar *Echinopsis* name that could apply to anything from a slow-growing tree to a golf ball that will flower within a year!

This is not the place for a critical in-depth review of the genus, but in brief overview it currently consists of the following six more-or-less defined groups of plants, plus some species that are intermediate between them – confirmation that nature resists 'pigeon-holing'.

Echinopsis

Plants with white or white and light pink flowers, with a long and slender flower tube, usually an adaptation to nocturnal pollination – indeed, many of the species have nocturnal flowers.

Lobivia

This former genus appears to be a very diverse assemblage of species with often brightly coloured flowers that can have short or long flower tubes, but in some cases also show characteristics associated with certain elements of *Rebutia*. There seem to be at least two major groups based on the form of the stem ribs: in one group the ribs are broken into spirally arranged tubercles, as in *Rebutia* etc, while in the other the ribs are continuous. Diversity is further illustrated by:

L. maximilliana, which has seed that differs dramatically from the other *Lobivia* species but is reported to show great similarity to that of *Trichocereus* species.

L. tegeleriana var. *incuiensis*, which has fruit that is uncharacteristically spiny, being similar to that of *Echinocereus* species.

Some or all species placed in *Pseudolobivia*, such as *L. ferox*, which unlike other *Lobivia* species are diurnal and white flowered.

Chamaecereus

Some argue that *Chamaecereus* should remain recognized as distinct from *Lobivia*, where it is currently placed. The thinner stem is very distinctive.

Trichocereus

This genus, in the narrowest sense, comprises white-flowered species with clearly columnar stems, whose usually funnel-shaped flower tubes are of greater diameter than in *Echinopsis*, *Lobivia* and *Chamaecereus*. The flower tube is long, but its scales are relatively short and generally broader, indicating a different type of development than in the above three genera. There is some uncertainty regarding the opening of the flowers: do all the species flower nocturnally, or are some diurnal and others nocturnal? In addition, there appears to be a profound genetic incompatibility in reciprocal crosses between *Echinopsis* and several species of *Trichocereus*.

Helianthocereus

This genus is usually placed in *Trichocereus*, but it has coloured diurnal flowers and it appears easier to cross species of *Helianthocereus* with *Echinopsis* hybrids than with *Trichocereus* species.

Soehrensia

This genus comprises globular and usually solitary species that were first placed in either *Trichocereus* or *Lobivia*. The characteristics that it shares with *Lobivia* include the brightly coloured and short-stemmed flowers. It is less obvious why some have included *Soehrensia* in *Trichocereus*.

As a stepping stone, there may be some merit in recognizing two broad genera:

Echinopsis, sens. lat. – comprising the three subgenera *Echinopsis*, *Lobivia* and *Chamaecereus*.

Trichocereus, sens. lat. – comprising the three subgenera *Trichocereus*, *Helianthocereus* and *Soehrensia*.

Echinopsis hybrids

While the botanists argue about the scope of the genus, there is plenty of time for the horticulturists among us to enjoy the spectacularly coloured flowers of a whole range of hybrids. These became extremely popular from the late 1950s, when Harry Hall produced a range of hybrids between *Lobivia* and *Echinopsis* that had large,

colourful, day-flowering blooms and became known as the Paramount hybrids. More recently (1997), many new hybrids have become available as the International Succulent Institute (ISI), in association with Huntington Botanic Gardens in Los Angeles, have included a large number of Bob Schick's hybrids on their annual list.

EDITHCOLEA N.E. Brown

Asclepiadaceae

This is a monotypic genus.

Edithcolea grandis N.E. Brown

When N.E. Brown described this plant in 1895, he considered it one of the most handsome of all stapeliads. He named the genus after Miss Edith Cole, who discovered it growing on rocky places in Somaliland in 1895, and even today, with all the taxonomic reviews that have affected so many plant names, it has retained its original name.

The plant has five-angled stems, about 30cm (12in) long, with spine-like teeth. The flowers are up to 12cm (5in) across and there is variation in their colour. The basic colour of the typical form is yellow, marked with brown towards the base and solid-colour purple-brown on the lobes, with olive-green tips. These beautiful patterns have prompted comparison to a Persian carpet.

This plant requires a lot of heat and moisture to grow successfully and seems to be very shy to flower under greenhouse conditions.

Edithcolea grandis has one of the most striking of all stapeliad flowers and fortunately no discernible offensive odour.

EPIPHYLLUM Haworth

Cactaceae

The plants in this genus are mostly epiphytes with a terete, woody main stem and branches that are flat and thin, almost leaf-like but sometimes three-winged. The areoles appear along the edges of the branches and are often spineless or only have some bristles. The large flowers provide the main attraction.

Haworth proposed the genus in 1812, but the name was first used for a plant listed by Hermann as early as 1689 as *Epiphyllum americanum*. Haworth's description is based on a plant first described as *Cereus phyllanthus* by Linnaeus in 1753. The name's origin is from the Greek and (incorrectly) means upon the leaf, indicating where the flowers appear.

Numerous names were added and have since disappeared. The CITES *Cactaceae Checklist* (1992) recognizes nine good species (*E. anguliger, E. cartagense, E. crenatum, E. grandilobum, E. laui, E. lepidocarpum, E. oxypetalum, E. phyllanthus* and *E. thomasianum*), with another ten species listed as 'provisionally accepted', all found throughout tropical and subtropical Central America from Mexico down to Uruguay, Paraguay and Argentina. Their habitat provides an indication that they are less cold tolerant than many other cacti.

Although these plants will thrive on neglect, if given a little care (see below) they will provide flowers that are breathtaking and among the most spectacular in the family Cactaceae.

Epiphyllum hybrids

In contrast to the collector of many other popular plants in cultivation, the cactus and succulent collector is usually keen to obtain true species of plants growing in the wild, rather than hybrids which have been grown to emphasize certain characteristics, most often flower size and colour.

Although there are a number of 'true' *Epiphyllum* hybrids, where both parents are species of *Epiphyllum*, the majority are the result of crosses with species from other genera, such as the epiphytic *Aporocactus, Disocactus, Heliocereus, Nopalxochia* and *Rhipsalis*. In addition, there are cultivars that have *Echinopsis* species as one of the parents, and many others where both parents are themselves registered hybrids.

In cultivation, we should recognize that the ancestors of these plants are often inhabitants of subtropical to tropical forests and that their epiphytic habitat, in or supported by trees, provides relatively shaded conditions.

The plants should be protected at all times from direct sunlight to avoid rapid and severe scorching of the stems, often incorrectly referred to as 'leaves'. Although many plants will survive temperatures of 5°C (40°F), many more will not and it is best to guard against temperatures dropping below 10°C (50°F), while some of the new American hybrids require a minimum of 15°C (60°F) in winter. Low temperatures will cause yellowing of the stems and eventually lead to rot. Such conditions also appear to reduce the intensity of the colour in yellow-flowered plants.

During the summer months the plants can be watered freely, provided that they are grown in a free-draining compost – stagnant water around the roots can cause rot. Regular feeding is recommended and here a regular houseplant fertilizer rather than a low-nitrogen cactus fertilizer should be used. Some growers swear by a layer of well-rotted cow manure at the bottom of the pot.

Propagation is by means of cuttings of mature, one-year-old growth and is best carried out from late spring to midsummer. Cuttings should be about 15cm (6in) in length and while some growers advise that the stem should be cut at its widest point, others prefer to cut at the narrowest point, at the bottom of a joint. The cut surface is allowed to dry for a few days and the stems are then potted into a damp potting mix containing 75 per cent grit. The stems can be left for several weeks like this, providing a convenient package to swap with other enthusiasts.

Do not water the cuttings for the first three to four weeks, until the first roots have formed. Watering can gradually be increased during the following month, and after about six months the plants can be transplanted into a more nourishing, humus-rich but still free-draining soil.

Unless pollination is carefully controlled with the aim of creating a new hybrid, propagation from seed is not recommended. The characteristics of the seedlings will be unpredictable and it will often take six to nine years before they produce flowers.

EPITHELANTHA F.A.C. Weber ex Britton & Rose

Cactaceae

The current view is that there is just one variable species in this genus, of which the other described species (*Epithelantha bokei, E. densispina, E. greggi, E. pachyrhiza, E. polycephala* and *E. rufispina*) are actually forms, or at best varieties.

Epithelantha micromeris has small white, globular stems that are very similar in size to golf balls.

Epithelantha micromeris (Engelmann) F.A.C. Weber
Originally described as *Mammillaria micromeris* by George Engelmann, these small globular, clumping, white-spined cacti do indeed at first glance resemble some of the *Mammillaria* species in the *Lasiacantha* group. They share their habitat in northern Mexico and western Texas with *M. lasiacantha* and its affiliated forms, but the small white or pale pink flowers are borne at the tip of the tubercles at the growing point of the plant, rather than from the axils as in *Mammillaria* species. The attractive bright red berries that often emerge in the year following flowering are both larger and more attractive than the flowers. Propagation from seed is easy.

The plants are slow growers and require a free-draining, calcareous soil and much warmth during the growing season. They should be kept dry during the winter rest period.

ERIOSYCE Philippi

Cactaceae

The scope of this genus has changed dramatically since the publication of the CITES *Cactaceae Checklist* (1992). Here we follow the views of Fred Kattermann in *Eriosyce (Cactaceae) The Genus Revised and Amplified* (1994), which has gradually gained acceptance among botanists and horticulturists. To illustrate the seemingly ever-changing names of plants, it is interesting to include a brief outline of the history of the genus.

Dr R.A. Philippi proposed the name *Eriosyce* in 1872 for plants which in many respects were similar to *Echinocactus*, used at the time as a 'catch-all' genus for globular plants. The new genus included plants where the apical flowers possess a floral tube produced beyond the ovary, with spines at the apex and with a dry fruit. *Echinocactus sandillon* became the type species for the new genus.

In 1922 Britton & Rose split *Eriosyce* into the new genera *Neoporteria*, for plants with funnel-shaped flowers and bristles on the flower tube, and *Malacocarpus* (*malaco* meaning soft, *carpus* meaning fruit), for plants with bell-shaped flowers and without spines at the top of the fruit, leaving *Eriosyce ceratistes* as the sole remaining member of Phillipi's genus. In 1929 Alwin Berger moved those species with hollow fruits from *Malacocarpus* to the genus *Pyrrhocactus* (species with reddish yellow, flame-coloured flowers) and *Notocactus* (yellow flowers).

Following his studies of the genus *Neoporteria* between 1934 and 1962, Curt Backeberg continued the splitting. He saw the Andes mountain range as a natural barrier and proposed the genus *Chilenia*, later split further into *Horridocactus* and *Neochilenia*, for plants found in Chile, west of the Andes, while those species from the eastern, Argentinian side were *Pyrrhocactus*. The western 'Pacific' genera also included species that were retained in *Eriosyce* and *Neoporteria*, as well as the genus *Islaya* from Peru.

The reunification was started in 1966 by John Donald and Gordon Rowley, who considered that *Horridocactus, Islaya, Neochilenia, Pyrrhocactus* and *Thelocephala* should all be placed under *Neoporteria*, but excluded *Eriosyce*, a name that preceded *Neoporteria*.

Kattermann's study completes the reunification and the older name is used. His concept of the genus includes 33 species of plants ranging in shape from globular to (rarely) columnar. The flowers are funnel-form, with a woolly or bristly pericarpel and flower tube, and are followed by a hollow dehiscent fruit that opens at the base.

The geographic distribution ranges from central Chile to southern Peru and eastwards to northwest Argentina, and covers a range of climates. All species require a gritty, well-drained compost and enjoy full sun. There is a short growing and flowering season in spring, during which the plants can be watered regularly, but after flowering heavy misting rather than use of the watering can is safer to avoid root loss and rot. Some of the species live in areas where rainfall occurs only every ten to 30 years with sea fogs providing the only source of moisture, and misting of plants in cultivation is recommended. Plants formerly included in *Pyrrhocactus* (Katterman retains the name as a subsection of *Eriosyce*) can be watered more freely and are easier to bring into flower.

Habitats range from mild-temperature sea-level zones up to alpine zones at an altitude of 3,000m (10,000ft), where the plants are often covered in snow. In cultivation, most will tolerate minimum temperatures of 5°C (40°F), provided that they are kept dry.

For the collector, these plants are worth growing for their wide range of very attractive body and flower colours – some species have bicoloured blooms – and spination. Propagation is mostly from seed, as few species produce offsets. Grown under the right conditions, they present no particular problems to the experienced grower, although some, particularly those in subsection *Chileosyce* (*E. esmeraldana, E. aerocarpa, E. krausii, E. tenebrica, E. laui* and *E. chilensis*) are more challenging.

Eriosyce senilis (Backeberg) Kattermann
In common with many in the genus, this variable Chilean species has a large, tuberous tap root that requires a deep pot with a gritty compost and careful watering. The dense, woolly to bristly spination can vary

Eriosyce senilis, formerly *Neoporteria nidus*. The flowers eventually manage to push through the dense spination.

in colour from snow-white to straw-yellow or dark brown to black. The flowers are 5–7cm (2–3in) long in varying shades of carmine-red, sometimes tending to pale pink or white towards the centre. The name *senilis*, meaning old, refers to the woolly white-spined form.

ESCOBARIA Britton & Rose
Cactaceae
The current opinion is that this genus, named after the Mexican naturalists Romulo and Numa Escobar who lived at the turn of the nineteenth/twentieth centuries, consists of some 16 species of small, globular cacti from northern Mexico, the western USA, southern Canada and Cuba. There is a close relationship with the genera *Coryphantha* and *Mammillaria*, and some botanists argue that *Escobaria* should be included in the former.

All these genera have tubercles, rather than ribs. In *Mammillaria* species there are two types of areole: one at the end of the tubercle that bears the spines, and one in the axil from which flowers and offsets emerge. In *Escobaria* species, these different areoles are also present and are connected by a groove (although in *E. roseana* and *E. agguirreana,* which were formerly members of the genus *Gymnocactus*, the spine- and flower-bearing areoles are united). *Coryphantha* species have a similar groove, but plants in this genus usually have pitted seeds, and often have a nectar-secreting gland on the stem which is absent in *Escobaria*. Most *Escobaria* species have fringed or ciliated outer perianth segments, while in *Coryphantha* these are found only in *C. macromeris*.

As a genus, these plants are probably among the most tolerant of the globular cacti to a wide range of environmental conditions, particularly when grown planted out in a well-drained hardy cactus bed, rather than in pots. They appear able to withstand many European winters in the open, taking frost and moisture as they come.

Escobaria vivipara (Nutt) F. Buxbaum
This species has the distinction of being the northernmost globular cactus, growing as far north as the province of Alberta in Canada, but also as far south as Central Mexico. It is no surprise that there is a great degree of variation over such a wide range and there are currently ten recognized varieties: *E. v.* vars. *vivipara, radiosa, neomexicana, arizonica, rosea, kaibabensis, bisbeeana, deserti, buoflama* and *alversonii*.

The small plants have stems that can reach 7cm (3in) in height and often cluster to form small clumps. The radial spines are translucent and shiny, and the central spines can be orange to brown in colour. Compared to *Mammillaria* species, the flowers can be considered as large and may reach 6cm (2½in) in length. They are bright pink to violet in colour and often have deep violet stigma lobes.

ESPOSTOOPSIS Buxbaum
Cactaceae

This monotypic genus was erected for a species that was previously moved around the genera *Cereus, Gerocephalus, Coleocephalocereus, Cephalocereus* and *Austrocephalocereus*.

Espostoopsis dybowskii (Gosselin) Buxbaum

This species comes from Brazil where the stems, which branch freely from the base, can reach heights of 2–4m (6–12ft). The stem, with up to 26 low ribs, is entirely covered with very dense greyish or yellowish white silky

Eulychnia breviflora f. *saint-pieana* lacks the very long spines of other forms but instead boasts appealing large, felted areoles.

wool, which hides the radial spines but allows the 3cm (1¼in) long central spines to poke through. The flowers are inconspicuous, hiding within the hair, which is longer in the flowering zone where a pseudocephalium is formed.

There are no particular problems in cultivation, where a standard succulent compost with some additional calcareous material should be allowed to dry out between waterings. During humid winters, the plants prefer temperatures of 5–10°C (40–50°F). In mild Mediterranean climates, they can be planted out in the open if some protection against frost can be provided.

EULYCHNIA R.A. Philippi
Cactaceae

This genus may be small in number (there are just five species, namely *Eulychnia acida, E. breviflora, E. castanea, E. iquiquensis* and *E. ritteri*), but it includes plants that are large in stature – the name is derived from the Greek words *eu*, meaning good, and *lychnia*, meaning candelabrum. They come from the coast and central valleys of the Chilean provinces of Acongua, Coquimbo, Atacama, Antofagasta and Tarapaca, where they grow with other desert plants on dry hillsides and can reach a height of 7m (22ft). The straight spines can reach a length of 20cm (8in). Local people use the plants for firewood and for hedging.

Eulychnia species make no special cultivation demands and are mainly grown in collections for their attractive spination, as the plants need to reach a considerable size before flowers can be expected. They like sunshine and enjoy misting to replace the coastal fogs that are a feature of their habitat.

Eulychnia breviflora R.A. Philippi

In habitat, the tall, slender stems of this plant, up to 4m (12ft) in height and 10cm (4in) in diameter, form large, bushy stands. The species is variable, now that plants previously regarded as separate species (*E. barquitensis, E. longispina, E. saint-pieana* and *E. spinibarbis*) are considered synonymous, or at best are recognized as forms. *E. b.* f. *longispina* and *E. b.* f. *spinibarbis* display the fiercest spination, with central spines that can reach 15cm (6in) in length, while *E. b.* f. *saint-pieana*, the most commonly found in cultivation, has long, snow-white woolly hair projecting from the large, round, grey-felted areoles. The large flowers, up to 8cm (3in) long, are white to pink in colour and have a very short, barely noticeable flower tube.

EUPHORBIA Linnaeus

Euphorbiaceae

This genus belongs to the fourth-largest of all families of flowering plants, which contains more than 3,000 other genera. The genus itself is also very large, containing some 300 species, a large number of which can be categorized as succulents. Their main attraction lies in their diversity of shape and size – they tend not to be grown for their flowers, which are small, but can have attractive, colourful bracts. Many species closely resemble cacti, with which the layman often confuses them.

Euphorbias are widely distributed throughout the world, being found in North and South America, Africa, the Canary Islands, Madagascar and India, and they grow in a wide range of climates. The plants do not like full sun so in cultivation some shade must be given, and they must never be allowed to dry out completely, even in winter. Some of the more difficult species can be grafted on to a more vigorous stock. For example, *Euphorbia piscidermis* is often found in cultivation grafted on to *E. ingens*.

Plants can be propagated from seed and it is also possible to root cuttings, but this is not as easy as in most cacti. This is due to the milky sap or latex which exudes when the plant is cut – spraying or dipping the cut surface in water will stop the bleeding. After the cutting has been taken, it is important to allow it to dry completely before potting it to set roots. Many species are dioecious with male and female flowers appearing on separate plants, so that plants of both sexes are needed in order to produce seed.

Euphorbia horrida Boiss.

The type locality of this plant is found in the Willowmore District of the Cape Province. The name *horrida* means spiny or bristly and indicates its cactus-like appearance. According to White, Dyer and Sloane in their monograph *The Succulent Euphorbiaceae of Southern Africa*, there are many varieties and natural hybrids.

E. horrida is a dioecious plant, reaching 1m (3ft) tall and 10–15cm (4–6in) thick. Older specimens branch from the base and form clumps. The stems have pronounced ribs and about 14 angles. The numerous spines are modified peduncles and are up to 3cm (1¼in) long, and the rudimentary leaves soon fall off. Although this plant is not a quick grower, it is not difficult to cultivate and makes a wonderful show specimen.

Euphorbia meloformis Ait.

The type locality of this plant is in the Uitenhage Dis-

Euphorbia geraldo is a new species from Madagascar introduced by W. Rauh and appears to be easy in cultivation.

trict of the Cape Province, South Africa. It was first introduced to the Royal Botanic Gardens at Kew by Thomas Masson as long ago as 1774, following a joint expedition with Carl Peter Thunberg, the 'father of South African botany', who described the plant as *E. pomiformis*, meaning apple-shaped, rather than melon-shaped as in the current name.

This is a dioecious species, globular in shape but sometimes becoming slightly elongated. It is spineless, but the remains of the peduncles persist, particularly in the male plant. These are not, however, spine-like, as in many euphorbias. The stem is usually divided into eight blunt ribs and is medium green in colour, often marked with lighter or darker green bands. Because this plant is somewhat variable in shape and markings, it is sometimes confused with *E. valida*.

This is an easy species to grow in cultivation. If it is kept warm in winter, it will soon form a large, clumping plant and make a handsome show specimen.

Euphorbia milii var. *splendens* (Boj. ex Hook.) Ursch & Leandri

Second in popularity only to *E. obesa*, this plant from Madagascar is probably the most cultivated of all succulent euphorbias. The slender stems are long and spreading and carry stout spines. The cyathia have bracts about 1cm (½in) in diameter and typically bright blood red, giving rise to the plant's common name of 'Christ's crown of thorns'. The species is very variable and Jacobsen's *Lexicon of Succulent Plants* lists 16 varieties or forms, often

Euphorbia lydenburgensis is another easy plant to grow, yet is not often seen in collections.

with bracts of different colours. The leaves are up to about 5cm (2in) long and 1cm (⅖in) wide, and will remain on the plant all through the winter if a minimum temperature of 10°C (50°F) is maintained and the soil is not allowed to dry out completely. In Madagascar, the plant is used for hedging and is bedded out in floral displays.

Euphorbia obesa Hook

The type locality of this plant is in the Graaf Reinet

Although it is not a member of the family Cactaceae, *Euphorbia obesa* is also known as the 'tartan cactus'.

District of the Cape Province, South Africa. This neat, dwarf, dioecious plant is probably the most popular of all succulent euphorbias with both beginners and experienced growers. It is globular or sometimes elongated, normally has eight ribs and remains solitary. The stem is grey-green and the whole plant is delicately marked with purplish bands. There are no spines, not even remains of peduncles, as these fall off when the flowers – which have a delicate, lime-tree flower perfume – have finished.

Cultivation is easy – with the caveat that the minimum temperature requirement of 10°C (50°F) must be followed or brown marks will appear on the stem, ultimately leading to rot.

There are many hybrid euphorbias, the most attractive being those from Madagascar, which have large, colourful bracts. Perhaps the best-known hybrid in cultivation is *E.* cv. 'William Denton', which arose from an accidental cross made by the late William Denton. The female plant was *E. obesa*, and although the male is not known with certainty, it was probably *E. mammillaris*. This plant grows to 50cm (20in) or more in height and 7–8cm (3in) across, branching freely, and has nine to 11 ribs that are notched into tubercles and spineless.

FEROCACTUS Britton & Rose
Cactaceae

This is a genus of large globular to short columnar cacti, similar to *Echinocactus* with which it shares the common name of 'barrel cactus', but from which it differs in its fruits and flowers. The name *Ferocactus* means ferocious cactus, from the often fierce armament of spines that protects the plant. Linnaeus based his description of *Cactus nobilis* on plants later known as *Ferocactus nobilis* and now included as a form of *F. recurvus*, which were collected some time before 1733 in Mexico by William Houston.

In habitat, in Mexico and the southern USA (California, Arizona, New Mexico and Texas), these plants can reach imposing proportions, up to 3m (10ft) in height and 1m (3ft) in diameter. Most species need to be a considerable size before they will produce their red, violet or yellow bell-shaped flowers, although some, like *F. macrodiscus,* will flower in cultivation as quite small plants in a 12cm (5in) pot.

Some species have a large distribution area while others, especially those from Baja California, are restricted to small locations. These include the attractive, heavily spined *F. chrysacanthus*, which is found only on Cedros Island and the adjacent coast of Baja California.

The greenish yellow flowers of *Ferocactus echidne* appear on relatively small plants.

A photograph in Britton & Rose's *The Cactaceae* shows how these plants may have saved many a desert traveller from a thirsty death. In a 1904 article, Dr F.V. Coville (after whom Britton & Rose named *F. covillei*) describes how the top of a large plant can be cut off, and by mashing the pulp, three quarts of drinkable liquid can be produced. The flesh can also be cut into slices that are then cooked in sugar and sold as candied sweets in Mexican markets.

All the species can be grown in a standard succulent compost with some added limestone gravel, which during the growing season should be allowed to dry out between waterings. The plants should be kept dry during winter dormancy and care should be taken that temperatures do not fall below 5°C (40°F), or higher if high humidity levels prevail, to avoid the epidermis becoming marked with corky patches.

Many species have nectar glands on young areoles. These can provide nutrition for sooty mould, which can cause unsightly patches on the epidermis but will not necessarily harm the plant or attract ants, which in turn may 'farm' mealy bugs.

Ferocactus echidne (De Candolle) Britton & Rose
Initially a solitary plant, in its native habitat in the Mexican state of Hidalgo this species will eventually produce offsets around its base, forming clumps of stems that can reach 20cm (8in) in height. Young spines are amber-yellow in colour and contrast nicely with the green to greyish green epidermis. The central spines can reach

Ferocactus pilosus var. *stainesii* – in 1961 this plant was named *Ferocactus stainesii* var. *pilosus* but the names are now reversed.

4cm (1½in) in length and often curve slightly downwards. Many species of *Ferocactus* need to grow to a significant size before flowers can be expected, but this species and a few others (listed below) will produce their flowers before outgrowing the space that most small collections can provide. The 3cm (1¼in) long petals are greenish yellow to yellow in *F. echidne*; whitish to pink or purple in *F. latispinus*; dark red to purple or carmine-red with a dark central stripe in *F. macrodiscus*; and yellow with a red centre in *F. setispinus* (formerly *Hamatocactus setispinus*). The latter also has an appealing perfume.

FICUS Linnaeus

Moraceae

This genus is endemic to Baja California in Mexico and is grown for its attractive foliage and caudex rather than its small flowers.

Ficus palmeri S. Wats.

From San Pedro Martin Island, these fig trees have a whitish, swollen base from which the branches – which can reach heights of 3–4m (9–12ft) – emerge. The leaves are heart-shaped and the bark varies from white to brown. The fruits appear in pairs, and although not as tasty as commercial figs, are eaten by the locals.

If this plant is bedded out in a frost-free greenhouse it grows easily. This also applies to the closely related *F. brandegeei* and *F. petiolaris*. Propagation is from seed and from cuttings, which are best taken during the growing season and can be rooted by placing the bottom in a jar of water or straight into a slightly moist soil. Once established, they continue to need plenty of water. Cuttings may take a number of years to form the caudex. Be careful with insecticides, some of which will defoliate and ultimately kill the plant.

FOUQUIERIA H.B. et K.

Fouquieriaceae

This is a small genus of 11 species from the desert regions of Mexico and the southwestern USA, and includes the monotypic genus *Idria*.

In the American southwest, these plants can be used in landscape gardens or grown in large pots, and may be watered as often as you remember. They are adventitious growers, and will leaf out whenever they receive water for a while. When grown in areas with winter rainfall, they will keep their leaves all winter but will drop them a couple of times during the summer when the soil dries out between waterings.

Fouquieria columnaris Kellog

Also known under the name *Idria columnaris,* the 'boojum tree' is well known from Lewis Carroll's *Alice in Wonderland* and forms dense populations in the valleys and rocky hillsides of Baja California. This plant's soft, spongy stem makes a tapering column that can reach a height of 16m (52ft). Growing together in forests, they present an eerie appearance, as their long beards of Spanish moss wave gently at you through the early-morning coastal fog. The creamy white flowers are produced at the top of the main stem during midsummer.

Fouquieria fasciculata (Humboldt ex Roem. et Schult.) Nash

This is the type species of the genus. It is a shrub that can reach a height of 2m (6ft) with its swollen, bottle-shaped basal trunk, which can measure up to 40cm (16in) across, as its most noticeable feature. The trunk is greenish in colour due to the chlorophyll in the cells below the epidermis with unusual, distinctive corky brown markings, to produce a plant with character. It has small leaves associated with spines and produces creamy coloured flowers from late winter to early spring. The leaves turn an attractive deep purple in autumn.

Fouquieria purpusii Brandegee

A species named by the German botanist Joseph Anton Purpus in 1907 in honour of his brother Carl Albert, who discovered the plant at Cerro de Coscomonte in the Sierra de Mixtrca in northern Oaxaca, this plant was not formally described until 1909 by K. Brandegee. It is very similar to *F. fasciculata* except that it grows bigger, reaching a height of 6m (20ft) with a diameter of 50cm (20in) across the base, and its leaves are smaller and linear.

Fouquieria splendens Engelmann

Probably better known by its common name 'ocotillo', this is the best-known species in the genus and is found throughout its distribution area. The plant is also known as 'coachman's whip', because of its slender, whip-like branches which can be up to 6m (20ft) in length. The brilliant red flowers (white in *F. s.* f. *albiflora*) make a lovely splash of colour, and both flowers and seed are part of the native Indians' diet. The stems are thorny and the small, oval leaves appear only briefly. The plant is the source of ocotillo wax, used in medicine.

FRAILEA Britton & Rose

Cactaceae

These unassuming, miniature globular to short cylindrical plants from South America were first classified as species of *Echinocactus,* starting with *E. pumila* as early as 1838, until Britton & Rose created the genus *Frailea* in *The Cactaceae* in 1922. The genus was named after the Spaniard Manuel Fraile, who for years looked after the cactus collection of the US Department of Agriculture at the time that Messrs Britton & Rose were preparing their book.

The plants often have cleistogamous flowers: the scaly flower buds are readily produced and in turn produce ripe fruit with large quantities of fertile seed without opening. The seed remains viable for only a short period and for best results should be sown as soon as the fruit is ripe. Many species also readily produce offsets that often develop roots while still attached to the mother plant.

The 23 species come from Brazil, Uruguay, Paraguay and Argentina, with a further two (*Frailea cataphracta* and *F. chiquitana*) reported from Bolivia. A further species, *F. columbiana,* was reported to come from Colombia, but a survey by botanists led by Dr Cardenas in 1967 failed to find the plants in the type location quoted (Dagua, on the Buenaventura to Cali railway at 1,500–1,800m/ 4,900–5,900ft), so that *F. chiquitana* is probably the northernmost species.

This is a poorly understood genus and it is rare for cactus and succulent journals to give space to articles about these little plants, yet they can make an interesting specialist collection for those with limited space. It is thought that the genus is closely related to *Parodia.* Unlike in most other genera, it is likely that there are many more species than names, with numerous distinct plants in circulation possessing only field collection reference numbers.

In cultivation the plants are best shaded from the hot midday sun, although one or two species seem to require a temperature of around 25°C (77°) at this time for their large yellow flowers to open fully – briefly. Full sun brings out the attractive bronze to red tones. Otherwise, they are undemanding plants, which can be grown in a range of soil mixtures and are resistant to cold if they are kept dry.

Frailea phaeodisca (Spegazzini) Ito

This small species is sometimes regarded as no more than a variety of another dwarf species, *F. pygmaea,* while the similar *F. asterioides* (syn. *F. castanea*) looks like a small sea urchin – the South American equivalent of *Astrophytum asterias* but without the white flecks. There are also some similarities between the seed types of the two genera and from time to time discussions flare up regarding possible affinities. The similarities are, however, quite superficial and are mainly found in their shape.

FREREA Dalziel

Asclepiadaceae

There is much discussion among botanists concerning the merits of this monotypic genus, with some arguing that it should be placed as a section within the genus *Caralluma*. There are also hybrids with *Huernia* (× *Frernia*), indicating another possible relationship.

Frerea indica Dalziel

This plant was first described in 1864 by N.A. Dalziel, the superintendent of the Bombay Botanical Gardens, in honour of Edward Frere, a prominent scientific researcher in India.

The type locality is close to the Shivneri Hill Fort near Puna in India. A feature that distinguishes the plant from other stapeliads is its expanded leaves, which may be up to 8cm (3in) in length. The plants grow low and prostrate, with stems some 2cm (¾in) in diameter. The flowers measure 1.5–2cm (½–¾in) across and are an almost black, dull purple in colour with bands of greenish yellow. This species should not be confused with *Caralluma indica*, which is a different species from the southern tip of the Indian subcontinent.

In cultivation, the species and its hybrids are easy to grow and can be propagated from cuttings. When dormant in winter, the leaves will drop but the plants must still be kept warm.

GASTERIA Duval

Aloeceae

The genus *Gasteria* is endemic to southern Africa and now has 16 recognized species. Since it was proposed in 1809, it has often been regarded as a 'problem' genus due to the extreme genetic variation and chameleon nature of the numerous species. Few of the original descriptions were supported by herbarium specimens.

The main centres of distribution are found in the dry savannah regions of the eastern Cape. It is easily distinguished from related genera by its belly-shaped flowers – the Greek word *gaster* from which the name is derived means belly.

Gasteria species are drought-resistant and shade-loving

The belly-shaped flowers of *Gasteria* (here *Gasteria nitida* f. is shown) led to the naming of the genus.

succulents. With their shallow roots and modest size they are well suited to pot cultivation.

Gasteria acinacifolia (Jacquin) Haworth

This species is confined to a narrow belt running along the southern Cape coast, from Knysna in the south to Port Alfred in the northeast. It is not known who first collected the plant, but according to Jacquin it was growing in Dutch gardens in 1809.

The two distinctive characteristics that make this so different from other *Gasteria* species are its 3.5–4.5cm (1½–1¾in) long capsule, which is truncate at the top, and its 6–8mm (¼–⅜in) long seeds. In these two characteristics, it is larger than any other *Gasteria* species. The leaves are rosulate, 22–60cm (9–24in) long and 4.5–10cm (1¾–4in) wide at the base, and dark green with dense white spots arranged in transverse bands; the epidermis is smooth. The flower colour is pink, the upper half being white with green striations. Like most *Gasteria* species, this plant is easy to grow, but it often becomes too large for pot culture.

Gasteria glomerata Van Jaarsveld

This is a dwarf species, discovered by Van Jaarsveld in the Cape Province near the Kouga Dam in 1991. It occurs on sheer quartzite sandstone rock faces in the Patensie district and proliferates freely from its base to form dense clusters.

The leaf surface has a bluish sheen and rough texture, and the flowers are an attractive red-pink in colour.

Easy to grow, if this plant is positioned in full sun the leaves will develop a very attractive sheen.

Gasteria rawlinsonii Obermeyer

This species is found in the mountainous Baviaanskloof region in the southeastern Cape, where it grows on the side of steep, shaded rock faces. The plant is most distinctive: its long, leafy pendent stems and leaves are armed with distinct white to green prickles, and different populations have either distichous or spirally arranged leaves. This is the only *Gasteria* species that cannot be propagated from broken leaf pieces, but propagation from offsets is very easy.

GEOHINTONIA Glass & Fitz.

Cactaceae

There is always a buzz of excitement in the cactus world on the occasions (few in recent times) when a new plant unlike any other known species is discovered and a new genus proposed. When this happens at the same time as the discovery of a new species in a previously highly sought-after monotypic genus, the buzz generates even more interest. This was the case in 1971 when Charles Glass and William Fitz Maurice described this plant and *Aztekium hintonii*, both named after their discoverer, George S. Hinton, found close to the type locality of *Aztekium ritteri* in Municipio Galeana in the Mexican State of Nuevo Leon, where they grow on steep gypsum hills and cliffs.

Geohintonia mexicana Glass & Fitz.

These solitary globular, sometimes shortly columnar plants grow to 11cm (4½in) in diameter with 18 to 20 ribs that bear the areoles. On new growth, these are covered with wool and spines up to 1.5cm (½in) long, but these soon disappear with age. The flowers emerge from the apex, are to 4cm (1½in) in diameter and deep pink to magenta in colour.

Gibbaeum album – in our opinion the prettiest species in the genus, but unfortunately a challenge to grow well.

As the genus and species are new, it is difficult to provide cultivation tips based on our own experience, but given its location, it is safe to assume that it should respond well to similar treatment to that provided for *Aztekium ritteri*. As it is becoming increasingly difficult to obtain plant material legally from Mexico, it is good to see that a reasonable number of grafted seedlings are now becoming available through European nurseries.

GIBBAEUM Haworth ex N.E. Brown

Mesembryanthemaceae

This is another genus of small, short-stemmed plants that produce pairs of round or egg-shaped, succulent-leaved bodies, from the Little Karoo area in South Africa. The name of the genus comes from the Latin word *gibba*, meaning hump or swelling, and refers to the shape of the

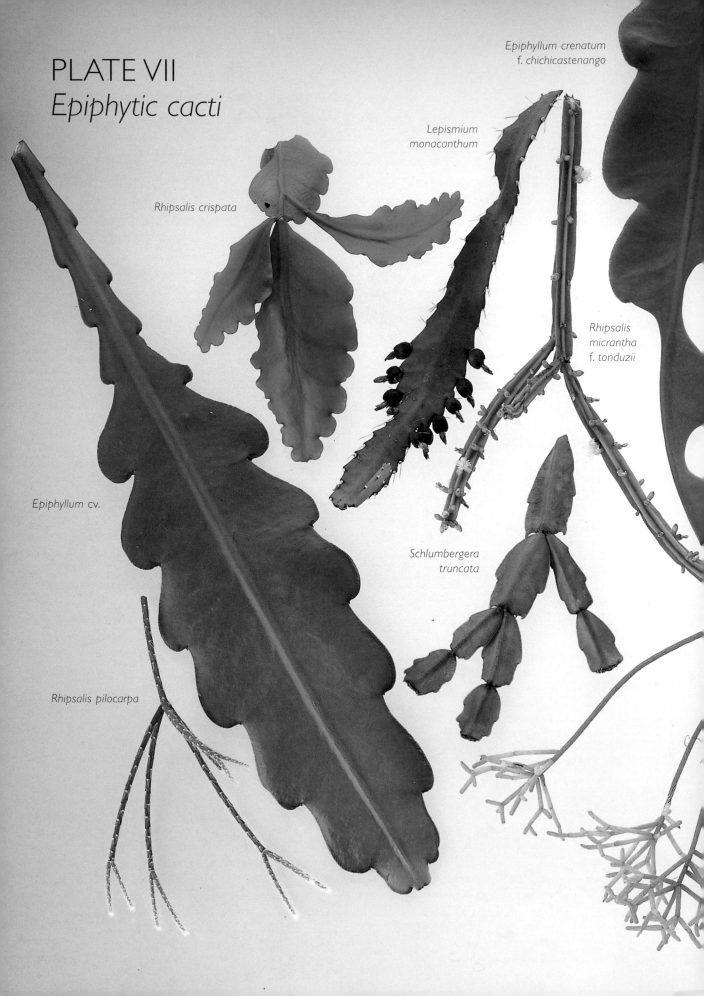

PLATE VII
Epiphytic cacti

Epiphyllum crenatum
f. chichicastenango

Lepismium
monacanthum

Rhipsalis crispata

Rhipsalis
micrantha
f. tonduzii

Epiphyllum cv.

Schlumbergera
truncata

Rhipsalis pilocarpa

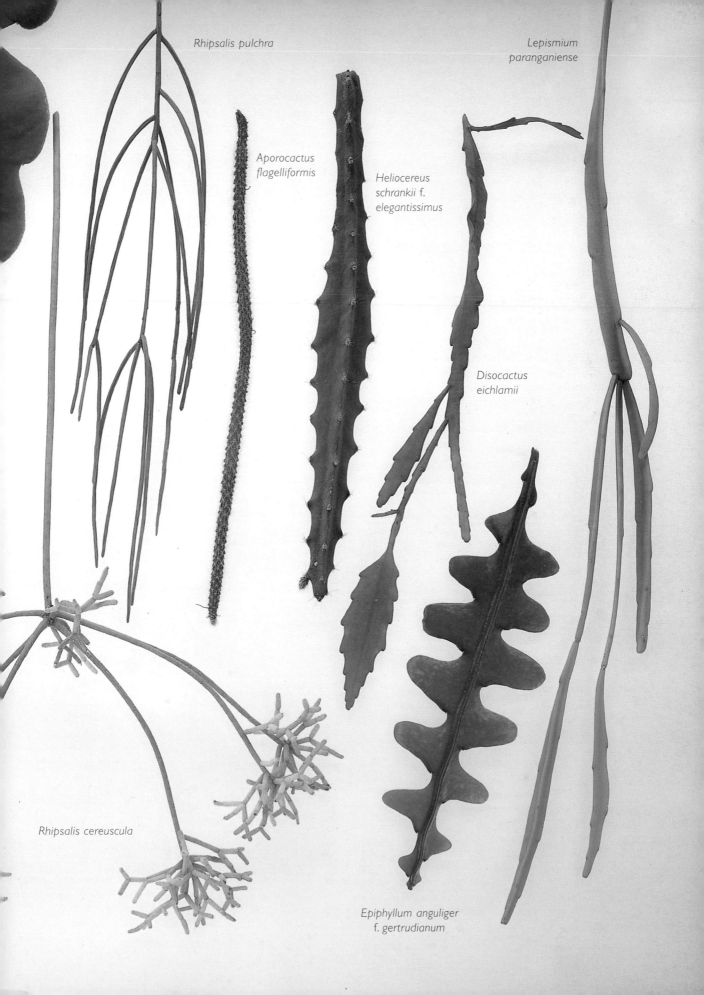

Rhipsalis pulchra

Lepismium paranganiense

Aporocactus flagelliformis

Heliocereus schrankii f. elegantissimus

Disocactus eichlamii

Rhipsalis cereuscula

Epiphyllum anguliger f. gertrudianum

leaf. The characteristic of the genus that separates it from other members of the family Mesembryanthemaceae with highly succulent bodies is the leaves, which are distinctly unequal in length, one of the pair usually being rounded at the tip while the other is more pointed. The leaves can be smooth, velvety or uneven in texture.

The plants can be tricky in cultivation as, like many members of the family, they have retained their native growing period, which in the northern hemisphere coincides with winter. They can be grown successfully in the greenhouse.

Gibbaeum album N.E. Brown

This plant is found in the Ladismith district of South Africa's Cape Province. The name *album* indicates the plant's white, fleshy leaves that give it an oblique-ovoid appearance. They are only about 3.5cm (1½in) long and 1.5cm (½in) wide. The flowers are white or purple in colour and appear at the start of the growing period, in late autumn or early winter. This plant is one of the most beautiful clump-forming species.

Gibbaeum heathii (N.E. Brown) L. Bolus

This species is also from the Ladismith district, but unlike *G. album* it is a spring- and summer-growing plant that should be kept dry in winter. It has almost spherical bodies, consisting of a pair of leaves that are about 3cm (1¼in) long and up to 2cm (¾in) wide and are united for half their length. The bodies are smooth and greyish green in colour. The flowers, 4cm (1½in) across, are creamy white tinged with pink and appear in spring. In habitat, the plants have a very long rootstock and often grow into large mat-forming clumps, but they are not particularly easy to flower in pot culture.

GYMNOCALYCIUM Pfeiffer

Cactaceae

This is a South American genus with plants distributed in southern Brazil, Paraguay, Bolivia, Uruguay and Argentina. Its distinguishing features are the naked flower buds (*gymno* meaning naked, *calycium* meaning calyx) and a ribbed plant body where the areoles are separated by prominent humps or 'chins'.

Unlike many of the genera of cacti, the genus *Gymnocalycium*, first proposed by Karl Pfeiffer in 1845 for a distinct group of plants previously described as *Echinocactus*, has remained fairly stable. As usual, a recent review has greatly rationalized the numerous names that were first applied to new discoveries, which when studied in more detail often turned out to be duplicates of others

discovered around the same time. The genus has been spared the splitting or unification with other genera that has occurred so widely in the family.

In cultivation these plants present few problems, provided that they are potted on regularly, say every two to three years. Some, like *Gymnocalycium saglionis*, will make a fair-sized solitary plant that will impress at shows for its size and strong spination, while others, like *G. bruchii*, will offset, forming clumps of relatively small heads. The recommended minimum winter temperature of 5°C (40°F) is adequate, provided that the plants are kept dry from late autumn until the danger of night frost has passed in spring. They can be watered freely during spring, but the soil should be allowed almost to dry out before the next watering. The frequency will depend largely on the pot size – soil in small pots dries out more quickly than that in large pots. In habitat, some species grow in the shade of small shrubs or trees, while others are fully exposed to the sun. In Europe, it is seldom necessary to provide shade, especially if the position where the plants are grown is well ventilated. Plants that offset can be propagated from cuttings, while all are readily raised from seed.

Gymnocalycium uruguayensis f. *artigas*. The smooth buds that give the genus its name open to produce a display of flowers.

Gymnocalycium vatteri. Unlike many other cacti, the flowers in this genus can last several days, half closing during the night.

Some mutations occur, where chlorophyll-less seedlings germinate. These can be grafted, so that the rootstock can provide the nutrients the plant is unable to produce itself. Although popular with the general public, the serious cactus collector tends to dislike such oddities.

Gymnocalycium uruguayensis (Arechavaleta) Britton & Rose

This is a variable species which, as the name implies, comes from Uruguay and now includes *G. artigas* and *G. guerkeanum.* The shiny green, flat-globular stems are 5–10cm (2–4in) in diameter and offset to produce clusters, which each produce flowers that can be greenish to pale yellow, white or pale pink in colour. Often the flowers are dioecious, with only the male or female parts of the bloom developed.

Gymnocalycium vatteri Buining

This is another variable species, that is perhaps related to *G. ochoterenae.* It comes from the Cordoba province in Argentina, where it grows at an altitude of 800–1,000m (2,600–3,300ft). A slow-growing plant, it remains solitary for many years before eventually producing some offsets. In habitat, plants grow to a height of 4cm (1½in) and reach a diameter of 9cm (3½in), but in cultivation the dull greyish to olive-green stems can often grow much larger. The plants are readily recognized by their spination, with one to three strong spines per areole, curved

towards the plant body on mature growth. The white flowers have a brownish grey throat and are up to 5cm (2in) long.

HATIORA Britton & Rose

Cactaceae

This small genus of Brazilian epiphytic cacti contains only five species (*Hatiora epiphylloides, H. gaertneri, H. herminiae, H. rosea* and *H. salicornoides*). It is closely related to the genus *Rhipsalis,* with which it is often united. The main difference lies in the flowers, which in *Rhipsalis* have widely spread petals, while those in *Hatiora* are erect. De Candolle originally used the name *Hariota* in 1834, to honour the sixteenth-century botanist and mathematician Thomas Hariot, but Adanson had already used this name for different plants in 1763, so that De Candolle's naming was invalid. The current name, created by Britton & Rose, is an anagram of the original.

Hatiora salicornoides (Haworth) Britton & Rose

This is the type species of the genus and forms a small epiphytic shrub, with erect rather than pendent ramifying stems, reaching a height of some 40cm (16in). The stems consist of short, first barrel-shaped, then bottle-shaped shoots with few spineless areoles along their side, justifying its common name of 'drunkard's dream'. The felted areole at the end of the shoot is much larger and it is from here that new shoots and the flowers emerge. There are two forms that previously were described as species: *H. s.* f. *bambusoides* and *H. s.* f. *cylindrica.*

HAWORTHIA Duval

Aloeceae

In 1809, the Frenchman Dr Duval proposed the genera *Haworthia,* named after the English botanist Haworth, and *Gasteria* for plants previously included in *Aloe.* All the 126 species listed by the National Botanical Institute of South Africa originate in that country. The plants are grown for their leaf shapes and attractive markings rather than for their flowers.

Haworthia koelmaniorum Obermeyer & Hardy

It is perhaps surprising to find this species growing as far west as Groblersdal in the Transvaal. In exposed places, the plants remain solitary, with rosettes reaching a diameter of 8–10cm (3–4in), while in deeply shaded locations they tend to offset, forming clumps of up to six rosettes. The leaves are deeply channelled, with both surfaces covered by irregular lines of raised tubercles. Grown in the shade, the leaves are turgid and dark green in colour.

Haworthia maughanii (shown here) and its cousin *H. truncata* are firm favourites with collectors.

During drought conditions, they turn a bronze-red shade.

Like most *Haworthia* species, this plant is not difficult to cultivate; it grows happily in full sun or shade, depending how you like your plants to look.

Haworthia maughanii von Poelnitz

Many collectors consider this small plant from the Little Karoo in the Oudtshoorn and Calitzdorp regions of South Africa to be one of the most attractive in the genus. The truncated leaves end in small 'windows' that in habitat enable the plant to diffuse the sunlight needed for photosynthesis, while the remainder of the plant body is pulled down into the soil. The semi- cylindrical leaves are in rosettes and are about 2.5cm (1in) long, the tips having a cut-off appearance. Unlike the related species *H. truncata*, it is very slow to offset.

Cultivation is not difficult, but this species takes a long time to produce a large plant.

HELIOCEREUS (Berger) Britton & Rose

Cactaceae

The name of this genus means 'cereus of the sun' and refers to the plant's day-flowering habit, rather than to

the preferred location – the plants grow in semi-shaded positions in Mexico and Guatemala. In spring, their large blooms are among the most beautiful of all cacti flowers and range from white to red. Another reason for the name is to differentiate between this genus and the night-flowering cacti of the genus *Selenicereus*, 'cereus of the moon'.

Unfortunately, the flowers only appear on mature specimens that will have grown into untidy, sprawling plants consisting of thin green stems several metres in length. In cultivation, they prefer a well-drained but nutritious soil with a high proportion of humus, and must not be grown in too large a pot. In contrast to our recommendation for most cacti, the soil should not be allowed to dry out completely, and these plants prefer a semi-shaded position rather than full sun. In winter, set the thermostat to a minimum temperature of 10°C (50°F). Plants are readily propagated from stem cuttings.

Heliocereus speciosus (Cavanilles) Britton & Rose

This species can often be traced back as one of the parents of many of the *Epiphyllum* hybrids found in cultivation, to increase the size and colour range of the flowers. The species has large, brilliant carmine-red flowers that are up to 15cm (6in) long and can first be expected on two- to three-year-old plants.

Heliocereus speciosus is used to produce many of the large-flowered *Epiphyllum* hybrids – the 'orchid cacti'.

HOODIA Sweet ex Decne

Asclepiadaceae

Plants in this genus are among the largest of the stapeliads. Under the new classification for *Hoodia* (Sweet ex Decne) there are now 16 species, the best known probably being *Hoodia gordonii*. In 1830 Robert Swan named the genus after Van Hood, a keen succulent grower. The majority of plants are found in the dry stretches of Namibia and South Africa, where they are especially prevalent in the northwestern Cape.

The plants are leafless stem succulents with thick, many-angled branches up to 1m (3ft) in height that are covered with warts, tubercles, spines or small teeth along the ridges. At the apex of the branches, striking large, papery, flat or bowl-shaped flowers arise from the grooves between the ridges. The elongated seeds are winged and are crowded in a papery sheath.

Hoodia gordonii (Mass) Sweet

This species is named after R.J. Gordon, who discovered the first plants on the northern bank of the Orange River during the eighteenth century. Later it appeared that it was widespread in Namibia and the northwestern Cape. It usually grows on rocky hills or slopes and in areas where the water drains quickly. The plant can reach a height of 60–70cm (24–28in) with branches about 5cm (2in) in diameter. The brownish flowers are cup-shaped and 7.5cm (3in) across.

In cultivation, this species likes plenty of water during the growing period, but in winter they should merely be misted occasionally to prevent them from drying out completely.

HUERNIA R. Brown

Asclepiadaceae

Robert Brown named this genus after Justus Huernius, a Dutch missionary who was one of the first Europeans to collect plants in South Africa. Some 60 species have been recorded throughout South and East Africa, Ethiopia and the Arabian peninsula, with a number of varieties. The plants in the genus have low-growing stems and short-stalked flowers, both of which are fleshy. The glabrous stems are grey-green or reddish in colour and are often armed with prominent tooth-like growths. The stems branch from the base to form clumps. The flowers are often spectacularly coloured and patterned, but unfortunately, like many others in this family, they have an unpleasant carrion-like smell to attract the flies that pollinate them.

Huernia hystrix readily produces its many flowers during the summer and autumn.

Huernia hystrix (Hook.) N.E. Brown

The clumps of this fine-flowered species have short, erect, five-angled stems that are 5–12cm (2–5in) tall and only up to 1cm (½in) in diameter. The edges of the stems have strong teeth. The flowers that usually appear from the base of the young stems are characterized by having ten points, five lobes and, alternating, five small teeth. The bell-shaped corolla is up to 4cm (1½in) in diameter. The five triangular, tapering lobes are pale green in colour on the outside and yellow on the inside, with red transverse lines, and are densely covered with fleshy, red-tipped, spine-like papillae that lead to the plant's common name of 'porcupine huernia'. The flowers of *H. h.* var. *appendiculata* are sulphur-yellow and have altogether more conspicuous markings.

This is an easy plant to grow and can be watered generously during the growing period.

HYLOCEREUS (Berger) Britton & Rose

Cactaceae

Hylocereus is a genus of slender-stemmed, epiphytic cacti that use their aerial roots to cling to the stems of huge jungle trees and 'climb' to their crowns – *hylos* is Greek for forest. They also grow hanging over rocks. The stems are three-edged or 'winged' with only very short, inconspicuous spines or none at all. The very large flowers (14–40cm/5½–16in long, depending on the species) appear during spring; they open at dusk but will have wilted by the next morning.

The plants' habitat is tropical regions in Mexico, Central America, the Antilles, northern South America and Peru. The most common species in cultivation is *Hylocereus undatus*, which has white flowers with the outer petals yellow.

During the growing season the plants require a fairly rich, acidic soil (achieved by adding peat moss), a warm position and thorough watering, but do allow the soil to dry out before watering thoroughly again. Feed with any good houseplant fertilizer containing trace elements, at one-quarter the recommended strength, in every second watering from spring through to autumn. In winter, the plants do not like to be too cold: 12°C (55°F) is the lowest temperature recommended. They enjoy bright, filtered sunlight and can be put outside in summer.

Propagation is easiest from cuttings, which should be about 15cm (6in) in length.

Hylocereus trigonus (Haworth) Safford

This species and *H. undatus* are vigorous plants often used as a rootstock for grafting, but as they are not tolerant of low temperatures they are less suitable for grafting plants kept in a cool greenhouse. The thin, three-edged stems measure only up to 3cm (1¼in) in diameter and will droop under the weight of the very large white flowers, but can reach a length of up to 10m (30ft). The plant grows in the forests of Puerto Rico, the Lesser Antilles and on the Virgin Islands.

KALANCHOE Adans.

Crassulaceae

This is a very widespread group of plants, occurring in Southern and tropical Africa, Madagascar, the Americas, India and Indochina, Malaysia, and on the islands of Cyprus and Socotra. In cultivation in the northern hemisphere, the plants are winter growing and spring flowering. The fleshy leaves often provide the main attraction for growing these small shrubs, as they can be beautifully coloured and in some species covered with wax or hair. *Kalanchoe beharensis* is probably the largest-growing species in the genus, reaching a height of 4m (12ft) in habitat. The large triangular, velvety leaves can

Kalanchoe tomentosa. Populations from different habitats can display variation in colour of the edging on the leaves.

be dried and are often used in flower arrangements. The inflorescence is a false umbel and is carried on a long stem, and the tubular, four-petalled flowers in white, pink, yellow or red are open at the tip. The flowering branches die after the seed has ripened but new shoots form around the base.

In Europe, many species can be grown outside in the garden during the summer, but unless you live in a frost-free area they must be dug up and overwintered in a cold greenhouse.

Kalanchoe tomentosa Baker

Also known as the 'panda plant', this species has green, oval leaves 7cm (3in) long that are edged with brown and covered in white hair. The long flowering stem carries whitish flowers but the plant is shy to flower in cultivation. It is a native of central Madagascar, and reaches a height of 50cm (20in). The stems have a tendency to form aerial roots, which makes it very easy to propagate plants from cuttings.

LAMPRANTHUS N.E. Brown

Mesembryanthemaceae

The name of this genus comes from the Greek words *lampros*, meaning bright or brilliant, and *anthos*, meaning flower. There are about 178 species from South Africa, where they are found throughout the Cape Province, Namaqualand through the coastal area to the Eastern Province, and Natal. One species, *L. tenuifolius*, comes from Australia.

The plants have upright, spreading or prostrate branches with many cylindrical or triangular leaves, that are blunt or tapering. They produce their showy white, pink, red, violet, orange or yellow flowers freely, but do require a bright position as the flowers only open fully in sunshine.

The plants are easy to grow and to propagate from either seed or cuttings. Most are fairly hardy and will tolerate temperatures down to near freezing.

Lampranthus coccineus (Haworth) N.E. Brown

This species grows near Cape Town and further west. It is a large shrub up to 60cm (24in) high with grey-green leaves of triangular cross-section, up to 2.5cm (1in) long. The flowers are about 4cm (1½in) across and a brilliant scarlet-carmine in colour (*coccineus* means scarlet). In the wild, the brilliant blooms are visible from a long distance.

Lampranthus haworthii (Don) N.E. Brown

The precise origin of this species, named after the English botanist Haworth, is not known, but it is found in the Cape Province. In cultivation, given a free root run, the freely branching shrub can grow up to 1m (3ft) high. It has semi-cylindrical leaves, up to 4cm (1½in) long and about 5mm (¼in) in diameter, which are light green, densely light grey-pruinose in colour. During late spring, the shiny, light purple flowers, which can be up to 7cm (3in) across, completely cover the bush, making a spectacular display.

LEPISMIUM Pfeiffer

Cactaceae

This genus of South American epiphytic cacti is found in Brazil, Paraguay, Argentina, Bolivia, Peru and Uruguay.

Since Pfeiffer proposed it in 1835, the concept of this genus and the closely related *Rhipsalis* has gone through a variety of changes. In their 1922 opus *The Cactaceae*, Britton & Rose recognized just one species, *L. cruciforme*, for which they listed 31 synonyms, many of which were originally attributed to the genera *Rhipsalis* and *Hatiora* (*Hariota*). The name *Lepismium* is derived from the Greek word for scale, referring to the small scales subtending the areole, and the plant was regarded as differing from *Rhipsalis* species by having sunken fruit. Over the years,

Lepismium houlletianum is an attractive plant for a hanging basket in a shaded corner. Not all cacti are sun-loving plants!

some species were included in *Lepismium* that did not have sunken fruits, while some that were described as *Rhipsalis* did.

In the latest revisions, carried out by Barthlott (1987) and Taylor (1995), the concept of these genera was modified so that *Lepismium* now includes those plants with laterally branching stems, while in the genus *Rhipsalis* the stem branches radiate out at the end of joints. In both genera, the stems may be flat, ribbed or cylindrical and both produce numerous tiny flowers that are followed by attractive berries.

Most plants flower in the winter period from autumn to spring, with just a few species in flower at any one time, although more appear to flower from midwinter onwards than before. In cultivation, occasional flowers are borne at other times of year. The plants should be grown in conditions very similar to those detailed for the genus *Epiphyllum*.

Lepismium bolivianum (Britton) Ewald

This species name is regarded as invalid, as Britton's original description was for *Hariota boliviana* rather than *Hatiora boliviana*. The plant has narrow, pendent, tape-like, spineless stems on which large purplish fruits are produced. This colour is very rare in the genus.

Lepismium cruciforme (Vellozo) Miquel

Pfeiffer named *L. commune* as the type species of the genus in 1835, but this name is actually synonymous with *L. cruciforme*, which was originally described as *Cactus cruciformis* in 1825.

The plant has green branches with white felted areoles and white flowers with light pink blotches. Once flowering is over, the attractive red fruits appear. There is an interesting variety – *L. cruciforme* var. *spiralis* – that was given its name because of the spiral growth of the dark green branches. This twisted appearance has also earned it the name of 'rope rhipsalis'. The branches have tufted, cottony areoles.

Lepismium houlletianum (Lemaire) Barthlott

This spectacular hanging-basket plant has long, gracefully cascading, notched, leaf-like stems and tiny yellowish, teardrop-like flowers with a red centre.

Lepismium micranthum (Vaupel) Barthlott

This plant consists of a lovely thick cascade of thin, three- or four-angled branches, some flattened, with white flowers.

Lepismium monacanthum (Grisebach) Barthlott

Slow growing and compact, this species produces minute orange blooms at every areole followed by small, round,

waxy fruit that decorate the plant for months. The spiny growth is both flat and triangular.

L. m. var. 'Espinoza' (ISI #95-9) is a relatively new variety that has spineless stems rimmed with orange flowers and purplish fruits, and is destined to become a very popular plant.

LEUCHTENBERGIA Hooker

Cactaceae

The single species in this genus is a very unusual-looking cactus from northern and central Mexico.

Leuchtenbergia principis Hooker

This species was described by Sir William Hooker in 1848 and named in honour of Eugene de Bauharnais, Duke of Leuchtenberg and Prince of Eichstadt (1781–1824), a stepson of Napoleon I. Hooker reported that the Mexicans in the states of San Luis Potosi, Guanajato and Zateca, and in the Sierra de la Paila in Coahuila, used it for medicinal purposes.

The plant's distinctive looks come from the unusually long, angular tubercles that can reach 12.5cm (5in) in length, at the end of which are thin, papery spines that may be 10cm (4in) long. Eventually the old tubercles die off and leave a scarred stem, not unlike that of a miniature palm tree. Plenty of water should be given during the growing season to produce the large yellow flowers, which emerge from the growing centre of the plant and remain open for up to six days. The large tap root can easily rot unless the plant is grown in an extremely well-drained compost.

Although this species looks like no other cactus, it appears to be related to the genera *Ferocactus* and *Thelocactus* and some interesting hybrids have been produced in cultivation, confirming this close relationship. In habitat, it can be found growing alongside *Agave lophantha*, to which, superficially, it bears a closer resemblance than to other cacti.

As the plant offsets only sparingly once it has reached a significant age, it is best propagated from seed, although it will take some six years for seedlings to reach flowering size.

LEWISIA Pursh

Portulaceae

The plants in this genus can only be considered as borderline succulents, taking their place alongside sedums and sempervivums as suitable border plants in the garden. They are cold hardy, but perform best

Selective breeding has created many hybrids of *Lewisia cotyledon* with a wide range of flower colours.

when grown on a slope and in a soil that provides really good drainage.

The genus is exclusively American and the state of California, with 19 species that exhibit a range of leaf forms and flower size and colour, is particularly rich. They hybridize very easily in cultivation, and many of the plants offered for sale in nurseries fall into this category, so that there is some confusion in naming. One of the most popular in cultivation is *L. cotyledon*, a native of Oregon and California.

Lewisias are glabrous, succulent, low-growing herbaceous plants with a fleshy rootstock that enables them to withstand long periods of summer drought. The flowers are usually large and showy, and often exhibit the brilliant pink and magenta colours associated with the family Portulaceae, although there are also several white-flowered species. The genus was first described by Frederick Pursh in 1814, based on a specimen collected by Captain Meriwether Lewis during the Lewis and Clark expedition. The last major revision of the genus was completed in 1966 by Brian Mathew of Kew.

Lewisias can also be grown in pots, when they need a rich compost and good drainage, and plenty of water during the growing period.

LITHOPS N.E. Brown

Mesembryanthemaceae

The name of this genus comes from the Greek *lithos*, meaning stone, and *opsis*, meaning appearance. *Lithops*, known as 'living stones', are the most popular of all plants in the family Mesembryanthemaceae due to their resemblance to pebbles. They are distributed over a wide area covering Namibia, the central districts of the Cape Province and the Transvaal.

The typical lithops consists of a pair of very thickened leaves, much the same as in *Conophytum* species, but whereas plants of the latter are quite variable, the leaves being separated into definite lobes or fused to reveal only a small slit, lithops are much more uniform in shape. The leaves are fused for most of their length, but are separated in the upper surface by a division extending across the whole width.

The leaf surface and its markings are important in the classification of the species. In some, the leaves may gape wider than in others. The upper surface is either flat or convex, and can be either smooth or rough, usually marked with lines, dots or blotched 'islands', with many species possessing more or less transparent 'windows' (see below). As well as over 130 species being described, there are now many attractive hybrids.

In habitat, the majority of the stem is withdrawn into the soil, with only the tops of the stems – the windows – exposed. This term is well chosen, as it is through these cells that sunlight is filtered to the cells below ground, where photosynthesis occurs.

The colour and markings of the windows bear close resemblance to that of the rocks and soil where each population is found, with those that match their surroundings best proving the most successful. This mimicry is a clever strategy to escape the attention of hungry animals. In cultivation, unusual-coloured forms, such as the very attractive *Lithops optica* var. *rubra*, are in great demand with collectors, while in habitat these colours break the mimicry defence so that such forms are not so successful.

The cultivation of lithops presents few problems and they are easily raised from seed. The main growing period is from early summer to early autumn, when they flower before starting the dormant phase of their growth cycle. When grown in pots in the greenhouse, they should be kept completely dry during the winter. Give the plants an occasional light watering in spring, but delay full watering until the old leaves shrivel and the new bodies appear. For species where the old leaves take a long time to shrivel, watering can commence once the new bodies emerge; some of the moisture in the old stems is used in the formation of the new bodies. It is not unusual for two pairs of leaves to emerge from a single pair, particularly if that head had flowers during the previous season. In this way, small clumps may form over many years.

In an interesting article in the *Cactus and Succulent Journal* of the American Society in 1980, James A. Robbins reports how many species planted out in the open in southern Arizona survived temperatures down to −17.2°C (1°F). This area at Sierra Vista experiences between 70 and 100 nights of frost each year.

Lithops dorotheae Nel

This species was first collected in 1935 by Mrs Aletta Helena Eksteen and named after her daughter, Dr Dorothea van Huyssteen. This very attractive and popular plant is much sought after by collectors, its distribution being in a small area near Pofadder. A very striking and distinctive species with very clearly defined windows, its colours are reddish brown, yellowish brown and some white, with margins and islands in various shades of opaque creamy, yellowish or pinkish beige, sometimes tinged green. It is clump forming, with bodies 2–3cm (¾–1¼in) high. The leaf ends have a large window containing small islands, with red dots and lines. The flowers are yellow.

Lithops fulleri N.E. Brown

This species was found by a Mr Fuller and occurs in Little Namaqualand. It is a clump-forming plant with bodies just over 1cm (½in) high and circular ends 2cm (¾in) across. These are greyish or reddish in colour, with grooves forming a honeycomb network over the surface. The outer edges carry notched marks, and short, rust-brown lines occurring in the serrations distinguish this species from all other similar ones. The colour of the flowers is white.

L. f. var. *chrysocephala* has a rather convex top surface, bluish grey and whitish in colour, with a pattern of grooves and lines plus scattered red dots. The inner edges of the leaf tips are transparent green and the flowers are again white.

Lithops hallii de Boer

This species was described by Dr H.W. de Boer in 1957 from specimens collected by Harry Hall in 1956 near Prieska in Cape Province. The plant bodies are up to 2cm (¾in) high, with almost flat ends about 2cm (¾in) wide and light brown in colour with dark markings. *L. h.* var. *ochracea* is distinguished from the type plant by

The markings on the windows of *Lithops dorothea* allow the plant to blend in with its surroundings.

The conspicuously coloured *Lithops optica* var. *rubra* is easily spotted in nature and flowers later than most in cultivation.

its opaque red-brown colour. Flowers are white in both.

Lithops optica (Marl.) N.E. Brown

This species comes from Great Namaqualand, where it forms clumps of 20–30 plant bodies each 2–3cm (¾–1½in) high and with a deep cleft between the leaves. The top surface is greyish green in colour and convex, with a window and a few or even no markings. The flowers are white.

L. o. rubra is probably the most popular and sought-after of all lithops. Thanks very largely to H.W. de Boer, this mutation is well established in cultivation, where it grows well from seed although only a small percentage come true. In habitat it is a very rare plant, because its bright colour cancels out the mimicry that protects its less colourful relations. Flower colour is white.

LOPHOPHORA J. Coulter

Cactaceae

More has probably been written about this genus than about any other species of cactus. Known locally as 'peyotl', the sap of these plants (like that of many other cacti) contains hallucinogenic alkaloids – including mescalin – which are similar in their effect on the brain to the drug LSD. Once ingested, they produce visions of brilliant colours and flashing alterations of spatial forms. Aztecs and Toltecs used these cacti during their religious ceremonies and believed they could thus communicate directly with their gods. These rituals, regarded as magic, are still practised in some religious ceremonies of the Native Americans.

Possession of these plants is prohibited in many countries, including the USA, where it grows in southern Texas and New Mexico. In California, possession of the plants alive, dried or even as seed is illegal. Those convicted face a fine or gaol term (in 1998, $10,000 or one year). The plants are variable, which has given rise to half a dozen different species that are separated mainly on flower colour.

Lophophora williamsii (Lemaire ex Salm-Dyck) J. Coulter

Although six species have been described over the years, only two (this and *L. diffusa*) are recognized today, with *L. echinata, L. fricii* and *L. jourdaniana* all reduced to synonymy with *L. williamsii*, while *L. lutea* is regarded as no more than a form of *L. diffusa*. *L. williamsii* has white or pink flowers.

The forms seen in cultivation as *L. fricii* and *L. jourdaniana* have very decorative dark red flowers in the middle of a white cushion of silky hairs at the apex, instead of the sometimes poorly discernible white, pink or yellow flowers of other forms.

MAIHUENIA (Philippi ex F.A.C. Weber) Schumann

Cactaceae

As explained in Chapter 3, there are many types of desert, some of which do not necessarily fit into the stereotypical desert image. Similarly, not all cacti are true desert plants. In fact, most species are found in areas where the rainfall is significantly higher than the 25cm (10in) annual precipitation that in part defines a desert. It should therefore come as no surprise that there are members of the family Cactaceae that also defy the stereotype of a spiny plant, and the two species that make up the genus *Maihuenia* certainly fit into that category. In habitat, the average annual rainfall is 130–220cm (51–87in), which is comparable to the annual rainfall in western Britain.

The genus was created in 1883 and the name is derived from the native name 'maihuen', the Mapuche word for woman, for the type species *Maihuenia poeppigii*. The other species is *M. patagonica*, with *M. albolanata, M. brachydelphys, M. cumulata, M. latispina* and *M. valentinii* all reduced simply to synonyms of *M. patagonica*, while *M. philippii* is now regarded as *M. poeppigii*. Both species were first described as species of *Opuntia* and were later moved to *Pereskia*.

The plants have 6cm (2½in) long cylindrical segments, similar in appearance to those of some opuntias but with no glochids, and the stems bear small, sedum-like permanent leaves. The yellow or white flowers are about 3cm (1¼in) long and have no flower tube. *Maihuenia* species are currently classified as belonging to the subfamily Pereskioideae alongside the genus *Pereskia*, with which they share characteristics of seed, pollen and spines. However, DNA studies by Rob Wallace indicate that the two genera are not closely related, so that *Maihuenia* may deserve a subfamily of its own. The plants are natives of the arid steppes of Patagonia in the southern Andean region of Argentina and Chile, as indicated by the species name *patagonica*.

In cultivation, given the rainfall that these plants experience in habitat, they are best treated like alpines rather than cacti and can be grown outside in Europe if planted in a well-drained position. They will endure continued frost for several weeks, surviving temperatures down to −10°C (15°F).

Maihuenia patagonica (Philippi) Britton & Rose
This species is known by the locals as 'espina blanca', after its white spines that are weak and described by Britton & Rose as only 1–1.5cm (½in) long. This needs to be revised if the other species are now to be included, as *M. valentinii* is reported to have spines up to 6cm (2½in) in length. The stems form hemispherical mounds and have numerous short side branches emerging from nearly every areole. The plant has white flowers

Maihuenia poeppigii (Otto) F.A.C. Weber
This species has recently been reported from the Parque Nacional Torres del Paine, situated at latitude 50° 58′ S, and can therefore claim to be the southernmost species of cactus, beating the previous 'record' held by *Pterocactus australis* by some 65km (40 miles). These locations are a similar distance from the equator as is the city of Southampton on the English south coast.

This plant differs from *M. patagonica* by forming large mats rather than mounds, with segmented stems that branch near their tips, longer leaves and shorter spines. The flowers are sulphur-yellow or paler. It has both superficial and deep-reaching root systems, so that plants can obtain the optimum water in both small and large rainfall events. The thick, branched tap roots of this plant are very mucilaginous and act as water storage to help the plants survive periods of drought.

MAMMILLARIA Haworth

Cactaceae

There are still nearly 500 accepted or provisionally accepted species in this genus, despite some very thorough research in recent years. *Mammillaria* species are among the most popular cacti – many are easy to grow and, as they remain relatively small, rarely outgrow their welcome. Most can be relied upon to produce an abundance of flowers that are followed later by often brightly coloured berries.

Most *Mammillaria* species are freely offsetting and form large clumps of globular stems, each being 5–10cm (2–4in) in diameter. There are, however, many exceptions, with some species – such as *Mammillaria matudae*, where the 3¼cm (1¼in) diameter stem can reach 20–30cm (8–12in) in length – forming a snake-like plant that has given rise to the variety name *serpentiformis*. Other species remain as solitary stems that over many years can grow to 50cm (20in) tall and 30cm (12in) across.

New species continue to be discovered in Mexico, but are seldom seen in cultivation as the Mexican government has forbidden the export of plants and seed.

Mammillaria guelzowiana Werdermann
Mammillarias tend to impress because of their willingness to produce great numbers of flowers year after year, rather than because of the size of the blooms. They are often arranged in turrets around the top of the stem. This species is the exception to the rule and produces the largest flowers in the genus – up to 6cm (2½in) across and an intense purplish red in colour, with green stigmas and a striking greenish bronze colouring of the outside of the flower tube. The flower petals are covered with very fine hairs on the outside and are seemingly irritated by sudden gusts of cool air, which cause the flower to close with remarkable speed. It is a member of the series *Ancistracanthae*, known for its larger-than-average flowers and for presenting some challenge in cultivation.

Without its flowers, the plant looks much like the

Lophophora williamsii: one variable species in a monotypic genus, or several species distinguished by flower colour?

If the unusual long-stemmed flowers of *Mammillaria theresea* are fertilized, the fruit remains hidden in the plant body.

Mammillaria woodsii is often regarded as a less hairy, extreme form of *M. hahniana*. Both these species hail originally from Guanajuato in Mexico.

popular *M. bocasana*, with long, white, hairy radial spines. It is, however, a little more tricky to keep alive, requiring extra grit in the soil and a minimum winter temperature of 10°C (50°F), with a dry set of roots and low air humidity. The species is named after Herrn Guelzow, who imported the first of these plants from the state of Durango in Mexico to Europe. The hooked central spine is usually reddish in colour, although *M. g.* var. *splendens* is a form with yellow central spines.

Mammillaria theresae Cutak

This species is named after Theresa Bock who, together with her husband John, discovered the plants on the eastern slopes of the Coneto Mountains in Durango, Mexico, in 1966. It is one of the most distinctive dwarf members in the series *Longiflorae* and comes from the Sierra Madre Occidental, where it is found only at its type locality.

The olive-green, sometimes purplish-tinged bodies rarely exceed 4cm (1½in) in length and 2.5cm (1in) in diameter. The slender tubercles are about 6mm (¼in) long and at their tip is an areole with some 30 white, plumose radial spines. The flowers are up to 3cm (1¼in) across and can reach a length of 4.5cm (1¾in). They are violet-purple in colour with deep yellow anthers and pale yellow stamens.

Plants can be propagated from seed, which can be difficult to harvest as the fruit remains hidden within the plant body. Wait until just before the first watering of the year in spring for plants that flowered the previous summer. As the stem is still quite soft, it is possible to inspect the axils to find the aperture to a chamber that contains the fruit. Open the entrance to this chamber gently with a pair of tweezers and extract the fruit.

In common with the newly discovered *M. lutheyi*, this species has a stout tap root and care must be taken not to overwater, to prevent rot damaging the roots.

MATUCANA Britton & Rose

Cactaceae

This genus is named after the small Peruvian town of that name, some 80km (50 miles) east of Lima, where the type species, *M. haynei*, was first collected. The 19 species are found only in a strip 50–150km (30–90 miles) wide and 1,000km (625 miles) long in the western Peruvian Andes, where they mainly grow at altitudes of around 2,000–4,000m (6,500–13,000ft).

It is possible that by the time that this book appears, this genus, introduced in 1922 by Britton & Rose, will have been re-submerged in the genus *Oreocereus*. It has been the regular subject of taxanomic 'lumping' and 'splitting', possibly because the original description by Britton & Rose was insufficiently precise, leaving out details of the fruit and seed. Here we will continue to consider *Matucana* on its own merits, using the definition and classification given in Rob Bregman's monograph *The Genus Matucana* (1996), which includes those species previously classified under *Eomatucana* and *Submatucana*.

The plants are globose to short cylindrical, sometimes ceroid, with long, more or less zygomorphic flowers that are borne from the new areoles. The flower shape is an adaptation to pollination by hummingbirds, although the yellow-flowered *M. aureiflora* is thought to be pollinated by bees. The fruit is very characteristic: globose to oval, usually about 1cm (½in) in diameter, and green with a red or brown base. The fruits are ribbed and split along three vertical slits, which stretch to over halfway up the fruit. The seed is a dull yellowish brown to black in colour, short bag-shaped and relatively broad. The closest relatives of this genus are *Oreocereus* (in particular those species previously classified under *Arequipa*, *Morawetzia* and *Oroya*) and possibly *Denmoza*. It differs from both these genera in flower, fruit and seed details, in particular the dehiscence of the fruit.

The plants are easy in cultivation and have few special requirements. Some species, from the Maranon basin, are cold sensitive and although a minimum temperature of 5°C (40°F) is tolerated, it is perhaps safer to set the thermostat a little higher to avoid brown spots forming on the epidermis. *Matucana myriacantha* and *M. oreodoxa* are noticeably sensitive to excess moisture, when the roots are prone to rot. The other cold-sensitive species are *M. paucicostata*, *M. tuberculata*, *M. krahnii*, *M. formosa* and *M. madisoniorum*.

Matucana madisoniorum (P.C. Hutchison) Rowley

First described as a species of *Borzicactus,* then of *Submatucana,* Gordon Rowley moved this plant to *Matucana* in 1971, before it was briefly classified in *Loxanthocereus* and *Eomatucana*. The dull grey-green body grows to a height of 15cm (6in) and a width of 10cm (4in), and is usually almost spineless. New areoles do bear up to five short spines, but these become easily detached. The slender flower is up to 10cm (4in) long and usually orange-red in colour, although a much sought-after white-flowering albino form is now also available. The plant occurs only in a small area, where it has suffered from commercial over-collection.

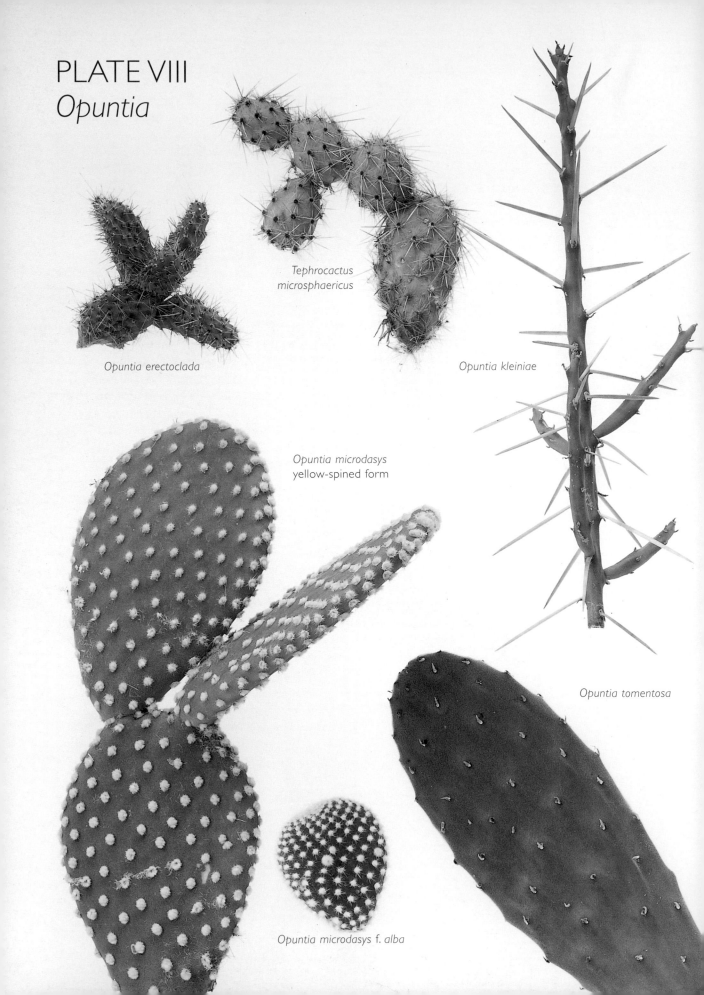

PLATE VIII
Opuntia

Opuntia erectoclada

Tephrocactus microsphaericus

Opuntia kleiniae

Opuntia microdasys yellow-spined form

Opuntia tomentosa

Opuntia microdasys f. alba

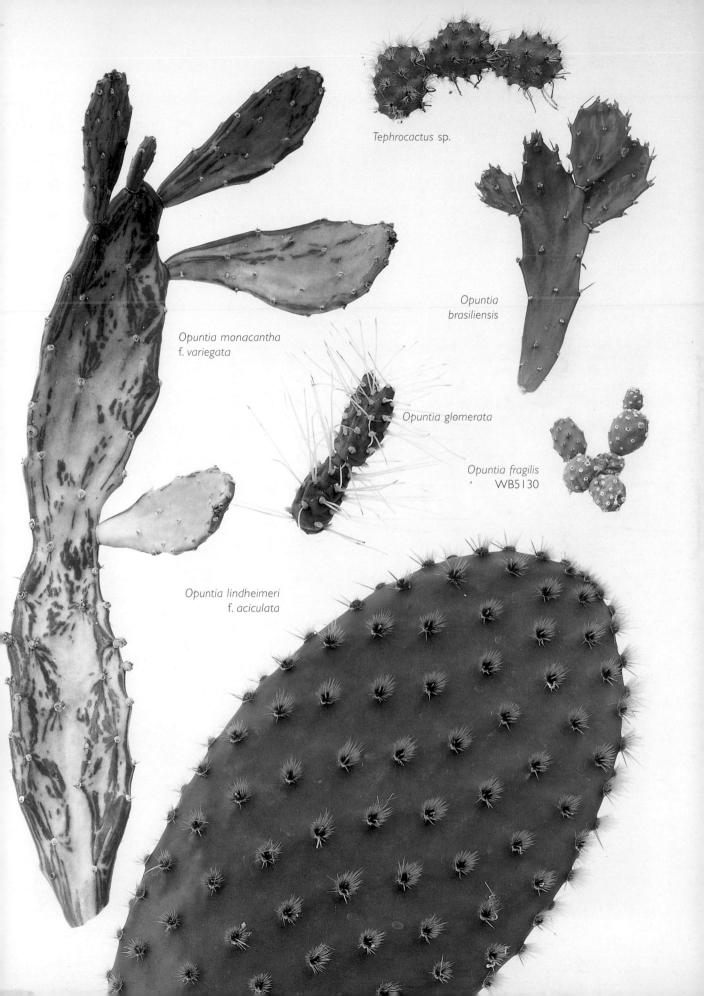

Tephrocactus sp.

*Opuntia
brasiliensis*

*Opuntia monacantha
f. variegata*

Opuntia glomerata

Opuntia fragilis
WB5130

*Opuntia lindheimeri
f. aciculata*

MELOCACTUS Link & Otto

Cactaceae

Many species from the West Indies now classified in this genus were among the first cacti to reach Europe and were then known under the name *Echinomelocactus.* Tournefort shortened the name to *Melocactus* while Linnaeus, in 1753, used the name *Cactus*, until Link & Otto restored the name *Melocactus* in 1827.

Mature plants are globular, conical or subcolumnar and remain solitary unless the growing tip zone is damaged, in which case several offsets may occur at various points

Melocactus neryi. Sometimes mistaken for a scion grafted on a larger rootstock, the cephalium is the flower-bearing organ.

on the plant body. If the main plant body has a cephalium, these unnatural offsets may also soon set cephalia. The epidermis ranges from dark shiny green (*Melocactus violaceus*) through pale green (*M. matanzanus*) to striking frosty blue (*M. azureus* and *M. glaucescens*). They may be miniature, measuring just 9–12cm (3½–5in) in diameter (*M. matanzanus* and *M. violaceus*), up to very large barrels, almost 1m (3ft) tall including cephalium (*M. intortus* and *M. pachyacanthus*).

Most *Melocactus* species have prominent ribs and are armed with strong, colourful spines. When they reach maturity, they produce an apical cephalium that usually consists of numerous red, brown or orange bristles and white wool, which gives rise to the common name of

'Turkish cap'. Cephalium-producing plants vary in age according to their eventual mature size. The smaller-growing species, such as *M. matanzanus* from Cuba and *M. violaceus*, can produce cephalia in two to four years from seed. The larger-growing species often take several years more.

Coincidental with cephalium production is the advent of flowering. The flowers are small, only 1–2cm (½–¾in) long, diurnal, usually pink or red in colour and borne in great abundance throughout the late spring, summer and early autumn. The flowers have no discernible fragrance and are mostly self-fertile – the most notable being *M. glaucescens*, which produces very few fruit, even after vigorous use of a paintbrush in an attempt to pollinate the flowers artificially. The blooms usually open in the late afternoon.

The fruit is a small, juicy, conical berry that is usually pink in colour, occasionally white, as in *M. azureus* and *M. pachyacanthus*, and rarely red, as in *M. glaucescens* and *M. ernestii*. As the plants are self-fertile, the fruit is also borne in great abundance – often well into the winter months – and is constantly being expelled by cephalic pressure, so that the cephalium is soon littered with fruit in various stages of drying unless it is harvested.

As each fruit may contain around 30 seeds which readily germinate, these plants provide a perfect opportunity to experiment with propagation. Seedlings need the same general treatment as most other seedling cacti, except that temperatures below 10°C (50°F) are not well tolerated. The seedlings grow rapidly and soon become plump, symmetrical globes.

The plants are very variable in spination, body colour and size, and this has given rise to a confusingly large number of specific names in the genus. In addition, there are a large number of plants in circulation that are merely known by the field collection numbers of Horst and Uebelmann, HU. The following selection of plants will fit comfortably on the average windowsill: *M. concinnus, M. glaucescens, M. matanzanus, M. neryi* and *M. violaceus.*

MICRANTHOCEREUS Backeberg

Cactaceae

These are upright, columnar plants from Brazil, reminiscent of the thicker-stemmed *Cleistocactus* species from Bolivia. They are usually sparingly branched from the base, although occasionally they branch higher. The epidermis is usually a frosty blue of varying intensity.

The stems of these plants have numerous shallow ribs, densely armed with fine, sharp spines. In most species, the areoles on the side of the stems facing the strongest sunlight enlarge and become very woolly, coalescing into a kind of open, lateral pseudocephalium.

From this flowering zone emerge a great abundance of blooms, usually in winter and carrying over into spring. The flowers are diurnal, very small and tubular in shape. They are brightly coloured in shades of red, orange, pink and purple, and have no discernible fragrance. Manual pollen dispersal with a paintbrush is usually required to produce the fruit, which are small and commonly reddish brown in colour.

Plants are readily propagated from seed, although cuttings are also easily rooted. Tip cuttings taken and rooted in late summer will usually produce cephalia and flowers during the following winter or spring.

All species can be grown successfully as small specimens, in most up to about 30cm (12in) in height in 10cm (4in) containers.

Micranthocereus densiflorus Buining & Brederoo

This is by far the most floriferous species in the genus, bearing a great abundance of bright, reddish orange flowers for many weeks during winter and early spring. The spines are stiff and sharp, and the flowering zone has the aspect of a loose and open lateral cephalium. The plant branches quite freely from the base, and soon makes a nice clustered specimen.

Micranthocereus streckeri Van Heek & Van Criekinge

This is a particularly handsome plant, with somewhat thicker stems than the other species that are covered with soft, golden yellow spines. At maturity, the apical regions of the stems produce a mass of rich brown bristles and pale yellow wool that soon forms into a distinct lateral cephalium. The large, deep purple flowers are borne in great profusion and, along with the cephalium, make a striking contrast with the golden stems. Unlike the other species of this genus, the flowers of *M. streckeri* appear to be self-pollinating, producing an abundance of plump, juicy, purple berries that are almost identical in colour to the flowers. As in *Melocactus* species, the fruit is ejected from the cephalium.

MONADENIUM Pax

Euphorbiaceae

F. Pax created the genus *Monadenium* in 1895, based on a plant that was discovered in 1885 in east Africa by G.A. Fisher, which he named *M. coccineum*. By 1913, 24 species

Its larger flowers make the genus *Monadenium* (*M. reflexum* is shown) one of the most desirable of the Euphorbiaceae family.

were recorded, and this has now risen to over 60.

Monadenium species are found almost only in tropical east Africa, with three species as far as west Africa; the greatest number and variety of species are concentrated in the region of Tanzania. Although members of the family Euphorbiaceae, they differ from *Euphorbia* species in possessing a zygomorphic cyathium, which is the specialized inflorescence found in many genera in the family. The genus itself is quite diverse. Many of the species form an underground caudex from which annual stems and leaves appear, while others have fleshy cylindrical or angular stems with or without thorns.

In cultivation, the plants prefer a warm, sunny position in summer, while in winter they should be kept dry and at a minimum temperature of 10°C (50°F), with a little water given if the plants show severe shrivelling.

Monadenium reflexum Chiov.
A species from Sidamo in Ethiopia and from Kenya, this plant has a fibrous root and very fleshy stems covered with long tubercles pointing downwards or, as the name indicates, reflexed. It is one of the dwarf succulent members of the genus, with stems that may be up to 30cm (12in) tall and 6cm (2in) in diameter. The small, fleshy terminal leaves soon drop off. The cyathia are small and greenish in colour.

MUIRIA N.E. Brown

Mesembryanthemaceae
This is a monotypic genus.
Muiria hortenseae N.E. Brown
This curious plant is named after Dr John Muir, who discovered it, and his daughter Hortense. It has the distinction of being probably the most succulent of all leaf succulents. The growth consists of a pair of more or less compressed, cone-shaped leaves, about 5cm (2in) tall and 1.5cm (½in) or more thick. The fusion of the leaves is almost complete, there being only a small slit – not at the top but towards the side of the plant body – which is pale green and covered closely with fine hairs. Brown skins around the base are the remains of former plant bodies. The flowers appear in early winter and are pinkish white in colour. Its habitat is at Springfontein in the Riversdale district of the Cape Province.

This is not an easy plant to grow in cultivation and extra care must be taken with watering during its short growing period, which occurs from mid- to late summer in habitat but from early autumn to early winter in cultivation in the northern hemisphere.

NOTOCACTUS (Schumann) Fric

Cactaceae
Following the revision of this genus, the consensus since the publication of the CITES *Cactaceae Checklist* (1992) is that all *Notocactus* species are now regarded as members of the genus *Parodia*. But what happens to the 51 species that did not transfer and remained on the *Checklist* as 'provisionally accepted' *Notocactus* names?

The *Checklist* is a list of some 6,500 Cactaceae binomials that was compiled from 12,000 names from various sources. Those that were not included in the published version were dismissed as archaic synonyms that are only likely to be encountered by the most dedicated specialist researcher. The term 'provisionally accepted' is applied to those taxa that 'made the top 6,500', but where further study is required either to promote them to 'accepted' status or to reduce them to synonymy. The *Checklist* should not be regarded as a dogmatic statement of what is right and what is wrong, merely as a snapshot of the then current opinion of a group of people from a predominantly botanical background, which acts as a useful and convenient reference point for further study.

In cultivation, there is the usual mix of easy and difficult species. Many can grow an extensive root system, and if this should die off it is difficult to re-establish the plant. This might happen if the soil becomes too alkaline – the plants prefer a neutral to slightly acidic soil – or if they are given too long a winter rest: two months is long enough. *Notocactus* species readily set seed that germinates easily. As most species flower at the same time, this can lead to unintended hybrids and may explain why there were so many names in existence. Those species that offset freely can be propagated from cuttings.

Rather than looking at an individual species, we will look at a group that falls into the grey area of plants that in 1992 were provisionally retained in *Notocactus* and are still regularly seen in collections and nurseries in the UK under these names. The plants in question were placed in Notocactus Group 1: *Mammulosi*, based on (then) *Notocactus mammulosus*, a very variable species. Seedlings offered for sale are usually globular plants that in a few years will become short cylindrical stems, some producing many offsets.

The distinguishing feature of the *Mammulosi* group is the flowers, which are short tubed and bell shaped, with a receptacle that widens just above the nectary into a flat basin. The stamens arise in a single group from close to the red to dark purple lobed stigma, but bend away from it. The dominant flower colour is yellow, with some pale pink forms. As the fruit ripens, it elongates and the fruit wall becomes thin. As it dries, the wall tears at the bottom of the fruit and the 50–100 seeds fall on to the soil.

This species was, however, moved into the genus *Parodia*, together with some of the other members of the group: *P. allosiphon, P. buiningii, P. mammulosa, P. muellermelchersii, P. rutilans* and *P. werdermanniana.* Other species – *Notocactus floricomus, N. mueller-moelleri, N. roseoluteus* and *N. submammulosus* – were reduced to synonymy with *Parodia mammulosa*, while *N. orthacanthus* and *N. schlosseri* have remained in *Notocactus* pending further study.

Notocactus orthacanthus (Ik. & O.) Hert.

First described in 1827, from the vague details provided the identity of this plant remains in doubt. More recently, collected plants from Uruguay seen offered under this name appear to be related to *Parodia rutilans.* Unless more detailed information can be found about the material originally described, it may be better to disregard this old name and re-label the newer plants in our collections as a form of *Parodia rutilans.*

Notocactus schlosseri van Vliet Succulenta 53: 10, 1974

Named after the person who collected it in Uruguay, Hugo Schlosser, this plant was for many years known only by its collection number: Schlosser 51. It is related to *Parodia mammulosa* and with its very dense, reddish spination is an attractive plant, even without the shining lemon-yellow flowers.

OBREGONIA Fric

Cactaceae

This monotypic genus is found only in the Valley of Jaumave in the Mexican state of Tamaulipas.

Obregonia denegrii Fric

Briefly included in the genus *Ariocarpus*, as *A. denegrii*, and later, together with some species of *Turbinicarpus*, in *Strombocactus*, this plant is now back in favour under its original name. This commemorates two Mexican politicians, Alvaro Obregon and Senor Denegri, respectively President and Minister of Agriculture at the time that the plants were discovered in 1923 by Alfredo Fric.

This is a popular species with the more experienced cactus collector, as it is quite unlike the 'usual' cactus in appearance. The plant has evolved spirally arranged tubercles that in habitat form a flattened rosette up to 20cm (8in) in diameter, while in cultivation the plants tend to be more globular. The broad but pointed tubercles are a rather dark greenish brown in colour, have a smooth surface and at first sight give the plant the appearance of a very short, rosette-leaved succulent or a very short, tubercled *Ariocarpus trigonus*, with which it shares its habitat. The tubercles are keeled on the lower side, with a few short, flexible spines appearing at their tips. The white flowers, about 2.5cm (1in) across, appear throughout summer from the woolly centre of the plant. If they are fertilized with pollen from another specimen, whitish brown fruits are produced that dry out and split to give large numbers of very tiny seeds.

In habitat, the plants grow abundantly in rocky limestone, packed solidly around the stems of shrubs on east-facing slopes at the bottom of the valley, pulled down into the soil. Below the surface is a large, tuberous root. With age, large plants may produce a few offsets, but this is rare in cultivation. Although abundant, they are found only in this small, limited area, where collection by the locals (the plant is used to treat rheumatism) and by commercial collectors appears to pose the greatest threat to its survival. Perhaps the Mexican government can be persuaded to declare the valley a nature reserve, so that this rare species' chances of survival are improved.

Until recently, many of the plants offered for sale in Europe and North America had been collected from the wild. They are slow growing and the small seedlings, which can be prone to rot and should initially be grown in a shaded position, take some five years to reach a diameter of 2.5cm (1in). At this size, they can be expected to produce their first flowers and to be of some commercial value.

Grafting the seedlings will speed the growth somewhat and often results in sparingly offsetting specimens. The offsets can be taken as cuttings and rooted. If plants are grown in free-draining standard succulent compost with the addition of some limestone, they can be watered freely during the height of their growing season. At other times, water should only be given when the soil has been allowed to dry out completely. From late autumn the plants should be kept completely dry. Young plants are said to be prone to scorching in extreme sunlight, but this tends not to be a problem at higher latitudes in Europe and North America.

OPUNTIA (Tournefort) Miller
Cactaceae

A large genus ranging throughout the North and South American continents, *Opuntia* competes with *Mammillaria* for the honour of having the largest number of recognized species – both boast nearly 400 in the CITES *Cactaceae Checklist* (1992). To arrive at this position, many species formerly included in separate genera have been 'lumped' into *Opuntia*, a trend that seems soon to be reversed as the need to distinguish between extremes has brought some of the older names back in favour. Due to their high variability and ability to hybridize and propagate very successfully vegetatively from joints that become easily detached, the genus is often regarded as a taxonomic minefield.

In habitat and cultivation, too, *Opuntia* has few friends. Those that have bumped accidentally into the sharp, barbed spines have christened them UFOs – Ugly Flipping Opuntias – or stronger! In cramped collections they soon outgrow their welcome, unless kept pot-bound, creating 'bonsai' plants that rarely flower. Yet in habitat, I was impressed by large groups of plants such as *Opuntia basilaris* in full bloom that persuaded me to add a few to my collection. There are a few choice miniatures and not all are rampant; some present a real challenge when cultivated in cool, humid climates. Many species are now gaining popularity as hardy cacti, suitable for growing in a well-drained cactus garden.

The genus includes the record holder for the title of northernmost cactus species in the form of *O. fragilis*,

which has been reported growing near Fort St John in British Columbia, Canada, at a latitude of 58° 15' N, similar to Stornoway in the Outer Hebrides.

Opuntia albiflora Schumann

More accurately *O. salmianae* var. *albiflora*, this plant is unusual among opuntias for the mass of white flowers that it produces. Schumann reported it as having been collected in Paraguay. It is weakly spined and the dark green to purplish cylindrical joints, which can reach 7.5cm (3in) in length, are only 1.5cm (½in) in diameter.

In a pot, the plant will make an attractive branched bush that can grow to a height of 50cm (20in), although when cultivated without root restriction it can reach a height of 2m (6ft). The flowers can be up to 4cm (1½in) across.

Plants are readily propagated by breaking off and rooting at the joints. As with most opuntias, the fruits also readily root to form new plants.

Opuntia basilaris Engelmann & Bigelow

As indicated by its common name of 'beavertail cactus', the flat pads of this opuntia are broad at the top and narrow at the bottom, resembling the tail of a beaver. The joints are an attractive blue-green in colour, turning purplish in cold weather due to a build-up of betacyanin pigment. When growing in sandy terrain, the pads, half-buried in the sand, form chains that radiate outwards from the plant's first pad, giving the impression of a freight train travelling through the desert.

The round areoles are spineless (with the exception of *O. b.* var. *treleasei*, which has one to five short spines) but are covered in brown glochids that, although only some 3mm (⅛in) in length, can be just as painful on contact. The flowers can reach 7.5cm (3in) across and are described as cerise in colour, although plants with yellow flowers are also reported.

Like many of the North American species, this opuntia grows during hot weather when, given water, plants can grow quickly. Both *O. basilaris* and *O. b. pulchella* are, however, very sensitive to being wet for prolonged periods. After several good soaks in early summer, when they start growing, the soil should be allowed to dry out between waterings. By autumn, most North American species lose all interest in water and stop using it even if it is present. They flower late compared to most cacti,

The tiny glochids of Opuntia microdasys ('bunny ears') have been used as one of the ingredients in itching powder because of their irritant quality.

in late spring to early summer, and grow during the warmest months.

Opuntia tunicata (Lehmann) Link & Otto

This is a member of the group often referred to as chollas, with cylindrical joints that in this species can reach 15cm (6in) in length. It is found in the highlands of Mexico, although it has also been reported from Ecuador, Peru, northern Chile and the Glass Mountains in southern Texas, possibly making it the most widely distributed species of *Opuntia*. The six to ten spines can be white, yellow or reddish in colour and grow to a length of 5cm (2in) in habitat, although in cultivation a stunted dwarf form with rather unimpressive spines emerges. This form is also found growing in the wild. A silvery white sheath covers each barbed central spine and this dominates the plant's overall appearance in the wild.

Del Weniger, not known as a lover of opuntias, commented in his *Cacti of the South-West*:

> … most people find them the least interesting of the cacti, and many people associate them too strongly with unpleasantness to be able to appreciate them at all.

But even he was so impressed by this particular species that he wrote:

> When growing robustly, *Opuntia tunicata* is an amazingly beautiful plant. A good specimen is a small bush so compact in its branching and so covered with its shining silver sheathed spines that it glistens, even from across a canyon, like an ice-covered bush in the sunlight of a northern winter, or like a globe of the finest Spanish silver filigree.

But watch those spines!

OREOCEREUS (Berger) Riccobono

Cactaceae

This genus has been established since 1909 and, when Britton & Rose wrote *The Cactaceae* in 1922, was considered to be a monotypic genus containing only *Oreocereus celsianus*. By 1992 the genus was considered to include *Arequipa*, *Morawetzia* and *Arequipiopsis*, resulting in five species (*O. celsianus*, *O. doelzianus*, *O. hempelianus*, *O. pseudofossulatus* and *O. trollii*) with a further six species that require further study. More recently, the genus *Matucana* is also being considered for inclusion, but here has been kept separate.

These are columnar cacti that form large clusters of strongly ribbed and spined, 2m (6ft) long stems where the spination is often hidden among dense, long white hair. The name *Oreocereus* derives from the Greek and

Orostachys iwarenge from Japan can be grown outside during the summer months to improve its colour.

means mountain cereus, as they grow in the South American Andes Mountains in Argentina, Bolivia, Chile and Peru at altitudes above 4,000m (13,000ft). The long-tubed, zygomorphic flowers are pink to purple in colour and can reach up to 11cm (4½in) in length.

Recognizing their habitat, the plants like a very sunny position with as great a difference between night and daytime temperatures as is practical. As a result, they are not particularly suited to windowsill cultivation, where such differences are difficult to achieve. In winter, night temperatures may be allowed to drop below 0°C (32°F), provided that a daytime temperature of 10°–15°C (60°–70°F) can be achieved. Good ventilation is another requirement, as stagnant heat and low aerial humidity do not suit.

Oreocereus doelzianus (formerly *Morawetzia doelziana*) branches densely from the base and has a terminal cephalium from which the blue-carmine flowers appear.

Oreocereus celsianus (Lemaire) Riccobono

This and *O. trolli* are probably the best-known members of the genus in cultivation, where the young seedlings are popular for their hairy appearance. The long white to brown hair hides the long spines, which on mature specimens can reach up to 12cm (5in) in length.

O. c. var. *celsianus* has yellowish to reddish brown spines and dirty pink flowers; in *O. c.* var. *fossulatus* the spines are a translucent honey-yellow and the flowers are red; and *O. c.* var. *ritteri* has long, brilliant yellow spines hidden among snow-white hair, through which the carmine to carmine-violet flowers appear.

OROSTACHYS Fisch.

Crassulaceae

These are small, summer-flowering, rosette-forming plants which occur from the Ural Mountains across to China, Japan and Korea. They are very closely related to the genus *Sedum*, looking like extremely succulent sempervivums. All the species are monocarpic and are on the borderline of being cold hardy.

Orostachys iwarenge (Makino) Hara

This species is native to Japan, where it grows on roofs near the sea. It is a pale green plant with large, flat leaves and is a biennial that grows easily from seed. There are some beautiful cultivars with highly colourful and attractive leaves, but unfortunately they are not easy to obtain.

ORTEGOCACTUS Alex.

Cactaceae

This frequently neglected monotypic genus was first described in 1961, and was briefly included in Britton & Rose's genus *Neobessya* until this was itself included in the genus *Escobaria*.

Ortegocactus macdougallii Alex.

This small, offsetting, globular, pale green plant forms stems about 4cm (1½in) in diameter. The spines are black or whitish with a black tip and the flowers, which are almost as large as the plant body, are pure yellow.

The plants should be grown in a free-draining, high-mineral cactus compost, as the roots do not like stagnant moisture. Unlike the other former *Neobessya* species, this plant from the State of Oaxaca in Mexico does not tolerate low temperatures during winter, which cause ugly orangey brown marking of the epidermis. In cool, humid northern European climates, a minimum temperature of 12°–15°C (55°–60°F) will prevent this.

OTHONNA Linnaeus

Compositae

This genus from South Africa and Namibia consists of small perennials and shrubs, many of which are of interest to the collector of succulent plants, although not all species in the genus are succulents. A synopsis of the genus given by Gordon Rowley in Hermann Jacobsen's *Lexicon of Succulent Plants* recognizes four main groups:

1 Soft, prostrate to decumbent herbs with more or less terete evergreen leaves.
2 Shrubby or long caudiciform plants with slender, non-succulent branches.
3 Geophytes, with more than half the caudex being below the ground.
4 Short caudiciforms with more than half the caudex above the ground.

In the northern hemisphere, the last three types are dormant during the summer and grow during the winter months, not having reset their biological clock to reflect cultivation in their new home.

Othonna cacalioides Linnaeus

A member of the short caudiciform group and one that is likely to appear on the wanted list of many succulent plant collectors, this is one of the smallest of all succulents in the family Compositae, and one of the slowest and most difficult to grow in cultivation.

It is a miniature, deciduous, highly stem-succulent perennial consisting of a flattened potato-like caudex that can reach up to 9cm (3½in) in diameter and is covered in very tough, dark brown skin. Leaves and yellow flowers arise from the woolly tufts on top of the caudex. The plant comes originally from Van Rhyns Pass in the Clanwilliam District of the Cape Province and from Namibia.

Othonna herrei Pill.

This is one of the most sought-after species, also proving to be one of the most difficult to grow successfully. From Stinkfontein in Little Namaqualand, it is another species from the short caudiciform group and has a thickened stem that usually grows up to 8cm (3in) tall and 1cm (½in) in diameter, and is knobbly in appearance. It only branches with considerable age. The oval leaves are about 6cm (2½in) long and 3cm (1¼in) wide, pale blue-green in colour, and appear in the autumn and fall during spring. The plant should be kept dry during the summer resting period. The flowers are yellow.

Othonna retrorsa De Candolle

A geophytic species, this domed cushion plant forms a many-headed, woolly caudex, is densely covered in the remains of dead leaves and has a woolly growing point. The leaf rosettes, up to 10cm (4in) high and 30cm (12in) across, appear at the end of short, thick, forking branches. The flowers are yellow. The delightful plant grows in South Africa, in the Cape Province and Little Namaqualand, but is not easy in cultivation.

Pachycereus marginatus. Many of the plants in habitat are reported to suffer from a virus that disfigures the stem.

PACHYCEREUS (Berger) Britton & Rose

Cactaceae

Whereas the saguaro (*Carnegia gigantea*) dominates the landscape of southern Arizona, these giant tree-shaped or bushy columnar cacti are the main feature of many a Mexican vista. Like their Arizona brethren, they make impressive landscaping plants for gardens in areas that are free from frost. The Greek word *pachys* means thick and in the name refers to the girth of the stem, which can reach 1m (3ft) across.

Pachycereus militaris (Audot) D. Hunt

Ironically, the brightly coloured cephalium – the densely spined area of mature stems from which the flowers emerge, and which therefore plays an important role in this plant's reproduction and ultimately the species' survival – nearly caused its extinction. During the 1970s, when the plant was known under the name *Backebergia militaris*, habitat plants were decapitated and the cephalia-bearing tops exported to Europe, where they had become popular in cultivation. The golden, densely spined cephalium resembles the military busby in all but colour and gave rise to the name of the species. From the cephalium emerge the greenish white flowers, which are about 7cm (3in) long and 4cm (1½in) across.

Fortunately, the threat of extinction through over-collecting has now passed, thanks to the tighter controls enforced by the Mexican government. Hobbyists are unlikely to grow this plant to flowering size, as in habitat

The ribs of *Pachycereus pringlei* allow the girth of the stem to increase dramatically when water is available.

Pachyphytum oviforum, the 'sugar almond plant', is ideal for beginners, but do not touch the leaves as this will mark them.

it can reach a height of 6m (20ft) – unless it is planted out in a warm, dry climate where the temperature rarely drops below 5°C (40°F).

Pachycereus pringlei (S. Watson) Britton & Rose

In habitat – Baja California and along the coast from Sonora to Nayarit – this cactus tree can reach a height of 12m (40ft) or more. The plant is known locally as the 'senita'.

Pachycereus schottii (Engelmann) D. Hunt

Still often referred to under its old name *Lophocereus schottii*, this plant is probably better known for its strange, spineless monstrose form than for the regular-spined form. The monstrose plant is like a man-made statue and invariably visitors to my collection feel the need to touch the smooth epidermis. Engelmann named the species after his friend, the cactus collector A. Schott.

The stems can reach a height of 3–5m (10–15ft) and branch from the base of the plant. Once the stem has reached maturity, the upper areoles develop long, hair-like bristles and later the reddish white nocturnal flowers emerge from these areoles.

Plants can be propagated from seed or from stem cuttings, although these appear reluctant to root once the cephalium has started to develop.

PACHYPHYTUM Link, Klotzsch & Otto

Crassulaceae

This small Mexican genus superficially resembles some of the thick-leaved *Echeveria* species. They differ from the latter in the flower, which in *Pachyphytum* species has a pair of scales on the lower, inner surfaces of each petal.

Pachyphytum oviferum J.A. Purpus

J.A. Purpus, superintendent of the Darmstadt botanical gardens, described this species in 1910 based on plants collected in the state of San Luis Potosi in Mexico.

Pachypodium bispinosum from South Africa is easy in cultivation and produces many white to pink flowers during the summer.

The plant forms a small shrub, about 20cm (8in) high, with fat, succulent leaves crowded together to form rosettes about 10cm (4in) across. The leaves are bluish to lavender and heavily covered with a white coating, and have been described as resembling sugared almonds. It is important not to touch the leaves as they mark very easily – once the white coating has been removed, it will not return. The flowers appear during spring and are greenish white in colour.

This is an easy plant to cultivate and likes plenty of water during the growing season. A bright position is needed to obtain the best colour from the leaves. A large, well-grown plant makes a wonderful show specimen, even if some of the leaves drop off in transport. These can be placed in the soil, where they will soon root and form new plantlets.

PACHYPODIUM Lindl.

Apocynaceae

This genus contains about 17 species, of which five (*Pachypodium namaquanum, P. bispinosum, P. succulentum, P. saundersii* and *P. lealii*) are native to South Africa, from the Cape region through Little Namaqualand up to southern Namibia, while the remainder are found widespread throughout Madagascar, with the exception of the rainforest region on the eastern coast. Here the Greek word *pachys*, meaning thick, refers to the base (*podium*) of the barrel- or bottle-shaped succulent stems. There are shrubby and arborescent species, with the latter (*P. lealii, P. rutenbergianum, P. lamerei* and *P. geayi*) growing on to become trees up to 10m (30ft) in height.

The African species are much easier to grow than the Madagascan ones. Due to their size, the plants rarely achieve their magnificent stature in cultivation in a heated greenhouse, although those fortunate enough to live in a moderate, frost-free climate may like to include them in their landscaped garden. All the South African species will tolerate temperatures down to 5°C (40°F).

Pachypodium brevicaule Bak.

The habitat of this plant is the Itremo region of Madagascar and on Mount Ibity near Ansirabe, where it grows on quartzite rocks at an altitude of 1,600–2,000m (5,200–6,500ft). It has a flat caudex up to 1m (3ft) across, from which short, thick branches arise that are covered with a silvery grey skin, similar in colour to the quartzite rocks. Large plants, often many hundreds of years old, are said to resemble a heap of potatoes. The 1.5cm (½in) long lemon yellow flowers are slightly asymmetrical in shape and are borne on the ends of the branches. This is a very slow-growing species: three-year-old seedlings are not much bigger than a pea and are much in demand by collectors. It requires warmth and dryness during dormancy and sparse watering during the growing season.

Pachypodium decaryi H. Poiss.

This species from the extreme northern tip of Madagascar has the largest flowers of all, reaching 5–8cm (2–3in) in length, although it can be very shy to flower in cultivation. When they do appear, the flowers are greenish white in colour and the pure white lobes have a yellow blotch at their base. The swollen, grey-skinned caudex can reach a height of 3m (10ft) and measure up to 40cm (20in) in diameter at the base. This is not a plant commonly seen in collections and is now also becoming extremely rare in habitat.

Pachypodium namaquanum (Wyley ex Harv.) Welw.

This highly desirable species is always sought after by collectors. It is the only one in the genus with a simple cylindrical stem, which grows to a height of about 2.5m (8ft) and will then measure 30cm (12in) across at the base, tapering to 10cm (4in) at the top. It is one of the most heavily spined species, with stems covered in tubercles each armed with two to three leather-brown, downcurving spines that can reach a length of 7cm (3in). The tips of the stems always tilt towards the sun (in habitat, to the north) at an angle of 30 degrees. Its habitat is on dry quartzite rocks in Namaqualand and Namibia, where its silhouette has earned it the nickname of 'half-mens'. The cup-shaped flowers are born in rings at the top of the plant. They are up to 5cm (2in) long and 1cm (½in) across, yellowish green on the outside and a velvety purple to reddish brown, with yellow stripes, on the inside.

Pachypodium rutenbergianum Vatke

This is a tree species that covers a wide area, ranging from the southwest corner to northwest tip of Madagascar. It has a stout, bottle-shaped trunk that can grow to 8m (25ft) in height and measures 60cm (2ft) at the base. The branches are heavily armed with paired brown spines up to 15cm (6in) long. The showy white flowers are large (up to 3.5cm/1¼in long) and asymmetrical. This is perhaps one of the most difficult species in the genus to cultivate, as in winter there is a tendency for the tips to die back.

PARODIA Spegazzini

Cactaceae

This genus is named after the Argentinian botanist Dr Lorenzo Raimundo Parodi (1895–1966) and enjoyed a 'fashionable' phase between 1965 and 1975, when many new but doubtful species were introduced. Sometimes plants from the same population but with different-coloured flowers might be described as separate species, although flower colour is regarded as having little or no taxonomic value. Recently, the number of species recognized in this genus has increased further, due to the inclusion of the genus *Notocactus* for plants with mainly red stigmas to the flowers, and the associated genera of *Malacocarpus, Eriocephala, Brasilicactus, Eriocactus, Wigginsia* and *Brasiliparodia*. At the same time, the review rationalized the existing names so that the CITES *Cactaceae Checklist* (1992) recognizes only 29 species with a further 77 regarded as provisionally approved, while another 51 provisionally approved names remain uncomfortably as *Notocactus* for the time being. The genus is closely related to the miniatures in the genera *Blossfeldia* and *Frailea* but not, as originally thought, to *Uebelmannia*. More research on the genus is indicated.

Found throughout South America, east of the Andes, these are attractive plants, even when not in flower, due to their often dense, brightly coloured spination. They are small to moderate in size, globular or elongated and mostly solitary, but offsetting from the base in some species. The stems usually have tubercled ribs and are often very spiny (with some hooked spines); they produce dense wool, particularly on young growth. Compared to most cacti, the rather large red to yellow flowers last much longer, often for several days.

In cultivation, we should recognize that these plants come from less extreme conditions than those endured by some of their colleagues. They prefer a nutritious soil with a little added humus and a constant but low level of moisture during the growing period, with good ventilation as protection against excessive heat. In winter, the plants should not be kept completely dry as this can cause unsightly corking around the base, and they therefore prefer the temperature to be kept above 10°C (50°F). A bright windowsill is as much appreciated as a heated greenhouse.

Parodia chrysacanthion (K. Schumann) Backeberg
This densely golden yellow-spined plant from the Argentinian provinces of Jujuy and Salta, with its crown covered in thick, yellowish wool, makes an attractive plant all year round. The yellow flowers that appear in fours and fives from the top of the plant are only 2cm (¾in) across and have difficulty pushing through the spines. There are some 30–40 hair-like straight spines, up to 2.5cm (1in) in length, per areole.

Parodia magnifica (Ritter)
First described as an *Eriocactus* species, then (and probably still best known) as *Notocactus magnificus,* a large clump of this bluish green plant, with its white radial spines and golden yellow central spines, certainly lives up to its name. It comes from the Rio Grande do Sul area of Brazil, and during winter prefers a minimum temperature of 10°–15°C (50°–60°F) to reflect the more temperate climate of its natural habitat.

Parodia schwebsiana (Werdermann) Backeberg
By contrast, this species from Cochabamba and Chuquisaca in Bolivia has blood-red or salmon-coloured flowers that stand out beautifully against the dense white wool that covers the top of the plant. There is a dominant, hooked lower central spine and all the spines can be white, yellow or brown in colour.

PEDILANTHUS Necker

Euphorbiaceae

This American representative of the family Euphorbiaceae is to be found in Central America, the Caribbean islands, Florida and Mexico. About 14 species are described, some of which can only be considered borderline succulents. They form large clumps and their size can vary considerably, from small shrubs less than 50cm (20in) high to large trees over 7m (22ft) tall. The stems are partly woody, with the typical milky sap. The leaves are quite large, lanceolate or oval and usually deciduous. The cyathium is different from that of the genus *Euphorbia* in that it is oblique with a one-sided spurred appendage, giving a bill- or beak-like appearance.

Pedilanthus tithymaloides Poit.
This highly variable species is one of those most often

Pedilanthus tithymaloides. The unusual shape of this small flower is typical of the genus.

seen in collections, and many subspecies have been described. It is very widespread, ranging in habitat from Mexico to Colombia. Over the years, the plant has been given a number of different names by various botanists. It can grow up to 1m (3ft) tall with thick, partly woody, partly succulent stems. The leaves are partially deciduous and may reach a length of 16cm (6in) and a width of 10cm (4in), but some forms are much smaller. The flowers, at the ends of the shoots, are reddish, and because of the bill- or beak-like appearance of the cyathium, the species is often referred to as the 'robin plant'.

This plant is easy to grow provided the recommended minimum winter temperature of 10°C (50°F) is maintained, with plenty of water during the growing season.

PEDIOCACTUS Britton & Rose

Cactaceae

The name *Pediocactus,* from the Greek meaning cactus of the plains, reflects the general habitat of the one species, *Pediocactus simpsonii,* that Britton & Rose included when they proposed the genus in 1913 for a plant that had previously been included in *Mammillaria* and *Echinocactus*. The most recent review of the genus by Fritz Hochstätter, *The Genera Pediocactus – Navajoa – Toumeya Revised* (1994), recognizes six species – *P. bradyii, P. knowltonii, P. nigrispinus, P. paradinei, P. sileri* and *P. simpsonii* – and retains the associated monotypic genera for *Navajoa peeblesiana* and *Toumeya papyracantha*, that others respectively include in *Pediocactus* and *Sclerocactus*.

Although these plants are found over a large area from 500km (300 miles) south of the Canadian border in Washington State, through Idaho, Oregon, Montana, Wyoming, Colorado, Utah and Nevada, to Arizona and New Mexico, they are all considered rare as they are usually found only in small populations, often occupying no more than a few square metres. Such distribution has given rise to a certain amount of variation between different populations and a number of subspecies and varieties are recognized.

In habitat, most *Pediocactus* species endure tremendous temperature variations between hot summers and icy winters and are able to draw themselves below ground for protection, to re-emerge in spring and autumn. Within a single species, there are populations with yellow, brownish, greenish/brownish or red-brownish coloration of the epidermis, depending on the colour of the soil in which they grow. This mimicry allows the plants to blend into their surroundings and it is best to look for them in habitat during their flowering period, as at other times they are often impossible to find.

In cultivation, the plants present some challenge – apparently taking a strong dislike to the much more moderate conditions with which we pamper them, they are not suitable for the usual living-room windowsill. The difficulties begin with attempts to raise plants from seed. In habitat, the seed experiences a scarification process where a combination of heat and cold, together with the abrasive properties of the soil, wears down the hard seed coat so that germination takes place. In cultivation, there are various means of imitating this process, such as treatment with acid, sandpaper or a sharp knife. The fruit is ripe within about four to six weeks, but the seeds remain viable for several years.

Plants on their own roots are difficult to grow in the greenhouse and are usually grafted on *Harrisia jusbertii* or *Echinopsis spachiana*, while a more cold-hardy stock, such as hardy *Echinocereus* species or perhaps *Opuntia rutila, O. fragilis* and varieties, should be used for plants that are grown in the open. The typical drawing into the soil will obviously not be observed on grafted plants. The plants prefer to retain the two short spring and autumn growth periods and are prone to rot if watered outside these times.

Pediocactus bradyi L. Benson

Known as the Marble Canyon cactus, this small (5cm/2in diameter), light green, globular cactus spends most of the summer and winter months hidden among loose limestone fragments on low, flattened banks along the Colorado River in Marble Canyon, at an altitude of around 1,000m (3,250ft). After heavy thunderstorms in late winter and early spring, the usually solitary plant bodies swell and appear some 4cm (1½in) above ground level. Towards the middle of spring – some four to six weeks earlier than with most *Pediocactus* – the cream to straw-yellow flowers, up to 3cm (1¼in) across, followed by fruits that are first green, then reddish brown in colour, present the best opportunity to find the plants.

Fritz Hochstätter has recently re-classified two closely related species, *P. despainii* and *P. winkleri*, as subspecies of *P. bradyi*.

P. b. subsp. *despainii* was discovered at San Rafael Swell in Utah, at higher altitudes of 1,600–1,800m (5,200–5,900ft). The stems are larger than those of *P. bradyi* and are usually solitary, although multiheaded plants are now also reported, sometimes caused by grazing cattle that damage the apical growing centre of the plant. The pale apricot to deep pink flowers that appear in mid- to late spring are also larger, but the fruit capsule is shorter. There are fewer, thinner and shorter radial spines. Like the other subspecies, this is a rare plant that is under threat from all-terrain vehicles, cattle and beetle larvae that bore into the plant body and ultimately kill it.

P. b. subsp. *winkleri* is endemic to lower elevations of the Colorado Plateau in Wayne County, south-central Utah, and only four populations are known, all at altitudes of 1,400–1,650m (4,600–5,400ft). These populations total about 20,000 plants that grow on widely separated parcels of habitat 1–20 hectares (2.4–48 acres) in size, and are threatened by collection and by habitat disturbance due to mining, recreation and livestock. The US Fish and Wildlife Service has determined that this is a threatened species, and it is now under the protection of the amended Endangered Species Act of 1973. The plants differ from *P. bradyi* in having woolly areoles and in the flowers, which appear later, from mid- to late spring, vary-ing from salmon, through pale to deep pink, to cream or even greenish in colour. The seed is also somewhat larger.

PLATE IX
Leaf succulents

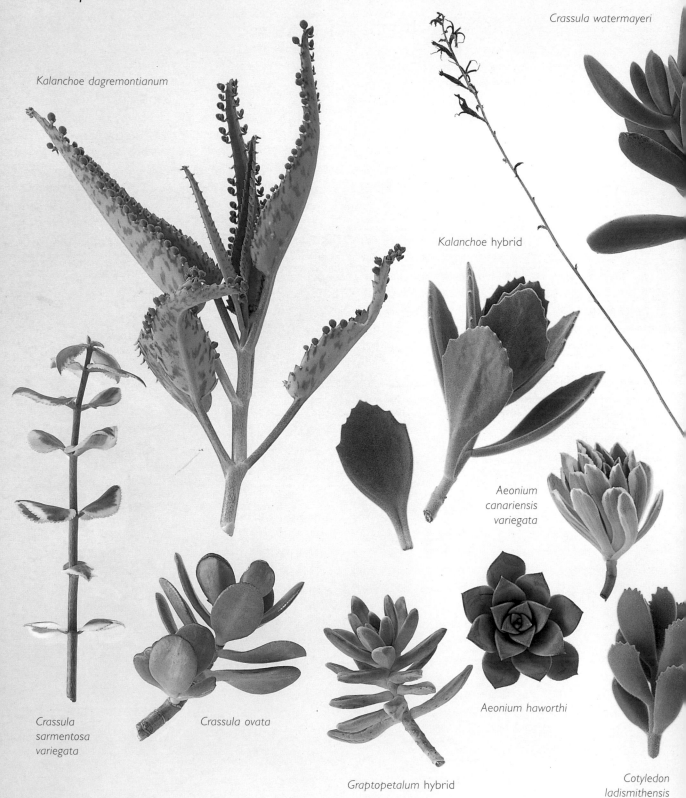

Kalanchoe dagremontianum

Crassula watermayeri

Kalanchoe hybrid

Crassula
sarmentosa
variegata

Crassula ovata

Aeonium
canariensis
variegata

Graptopetalum hybrid

Aeonium haworthi

Cotyledon
ladismithensis

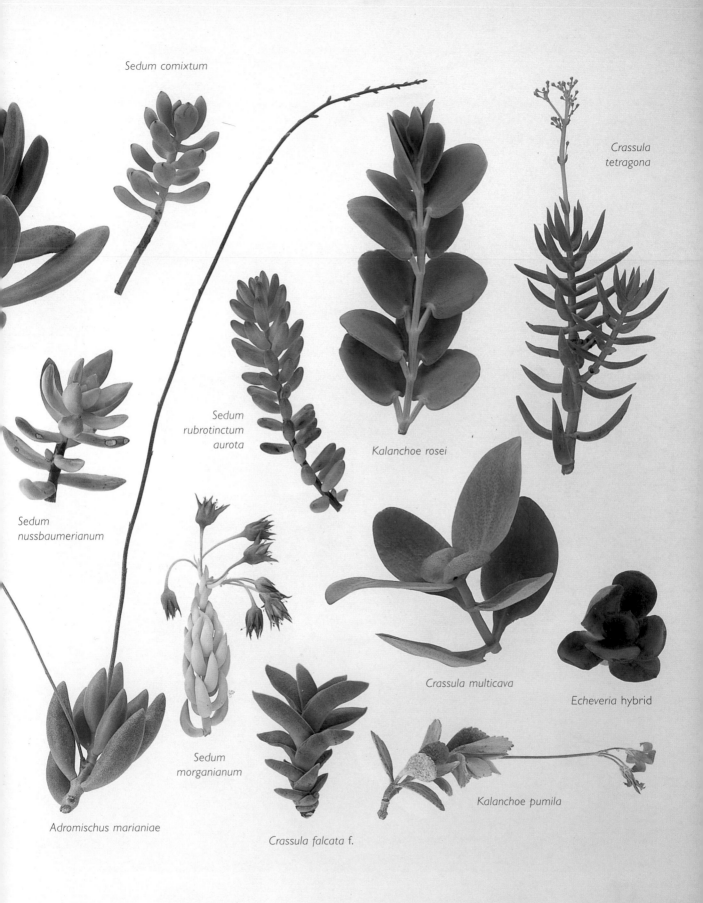

Sedum comixtum

Crassula tetragona

Sedum rubrotinctum aurota

Kalanchoe rosei

Sedum nussbaumerianum

Crassula multicava

Echeveria hybrid

Sedum morganianum

Adromischus marianiae

Crassula falcata f.

Kalanchoe pumila

PELARGONIUM L'Her.

Geraniaceae

The genus *Pelargonium* contains some 280 species, of which the majority (some 225) can be considered as true succulents, yet in general horticulture the species found on windowsills and as garden plants are the non-succulent ones. These have showy flowers in various shades of red and white and are widely grown in gardens and pots in North America and Europe.

The term geranium is frequently used as the common name for certain species of *Pelargonium*. However, true geraniums and pelargoniums are easily distinguished vegetatively: pelargoniums are thick-stemmed, succulent and usually strongly scented, while plants of the genus *Geranium* are low, spreading and unscented. The name

The beautiful flowers of the compact *Pelargonium oblongatum* are a must for all lovers of succulent pelargoniums.

Pelargonium refers to the stork, due to the shape of the fruit which resembles a stork's bill.

Most succulent pelargoniums are easy to grow, but like so many South African plants they usually grow in autumn and winter in the northern hemisphere and should be rested during summer. When in growth, they should be watered generously. They are susceptible to white fly, and once these take hold they can be very difficult to eradicate. The following succulent species are among the most desirable found in cultivation.

Pelargonium alternans Wendl.

This small, branched shrub is easily grown and originates in the South West Cape area of Africa. The plant has 2–3cm (1–1¼in) thick stems and grows to a height of 70cm (28in). The small flowers are white.

Pelargonium boranense Frilis & M.G. Gilbert

This is a striking plant that is characterized by its well-developed, perennial succulent stem and very large,

bright orange-red flowers, which are possibly the largest of any of the species. It was discovered in 1972 by a joint expedition of the Institute of the Systematic, University of Copenhagen, and the National Herbarium, Addis. The plant is found in grassland in Sidamo Province, Borana Awraja, in Ethiopia.

In cultivation, this is one of the more challenging plants in the genus. The habitat experiences two rainy seasons, and in cultivation the plants can be watered generously at these times – from mid- to late autumn and from early to mid-spring – but are best kept dry for the rest of the year. The minimum temperature required is 10°C (50°F).

Pelargonium carnosum (Linnaeus) Ait.

This species was first introduced to cultivation in England as early as 1794. The thick, spreading stems form a small shrub that can reach a height of 30cm (12in). Its popularity is partly due to its ease in cultivation, where it will reward you with an abundance of small white flowers which are unusual in that the petals are often shorter than the sepals. In habitat, in Namibia, Namaqualand and the southwest of Cape Province, it grows in sandy soil among semi-desert vegetation.

Pelargonium cotyledonis (Linnaeus) L'Her

This rare species, endemic to the island of St Helena in the Atlantic Ocean, is threatened due to overgrazing by goats that were introduced by men. The remaining plants are confined to the steep cliffs, out of reach of the goats. Fortunately, the plant is not difficult in cultivation and is readily propagated from seed. It forms an attractive branched shrub with succulent stems and simple, closely spaced, heart-shaped, leathery leaves that have prominent veins and are densely woolly on their lower surface. The flowers are pure white.

Pelargonium oblongatum E. Mey. ex Harv.

The species name recognizes one of the main characteristics of this plant: the oblong tuber that can reach a length of 15cm (6in). This has a peeling bark and is usually crowned with the remains of old stipules and petioles. The leaves are large, and their shape varies from cordate ovate to orbicular or even obovate. The leaves are rather fleshy, glandular and covered with coarse hairs. The plants have retained their annual growing cycle, so that in the northern hemisphere they are summer dormant. They commence into growth in early autumn and shed their leaves in early spring as the weather becomes warm, then produce the tall inflorescence of spectacular large, pale yellow flowers that are the main attraction of this species. Distribution is restricted to the Richterveld and to the northern part of Namaqualand.

PELECYPHORA Ehrenberg
Cactaceae

The name of this genus of only two species is derived from the Greek words *pelekys*, meaning axe, and *phoros*, meaning bearing, and reflects the appearance of the long, narrow, axe-like tubercles with short, pectinate spines. Like other species that are used by the locals in religious ceremonies, the plant sap contains hallucinogenic alkaloids that in this case are reported to have medicinal properties. The Mexicans in San Luis Potosi use the name 'peyote' for both species in the genus; the name is used further north for *Lophophora williamsii*.

The thick, beet-like tap root is rather prone to rot if the mineral soil is not allowed to dry out thoroughly between waterings. Natives of the Mexican states of San Luis Potosi and Nuevo Leon, the plants like a warm, bright space in the greenhouse, but some protection from the strongest midday sun will prevent scorching of the greyish green stems. A minimum winter temperature of 10°C (50°F) is recommended.

Both species are rare in habitat and are highly valued by collectors, with the systematic commercial collection of plants from the wild presenting the main threat to their survival. The small original locations where the plants were first discovered have now been stripped of these plants and the other species of collectable cacti that grow there, which include *Ariocarpus retusus, Echinocactus platyacanthus* and a number of species of *Thelocactus* and *Turbinicarpus*. Fortunately, some new sites have recently been discovered that are not yet widely known.

Pelecyphora aselliformis Ehrenberg

This is a very attractive little cactus, with bodies that can reach 10cm (4in) in height and 5cm (2in) across. Also known as the 'woodlouse cactus', the elongated areoles that sit on top of the 5mm (¼in) tall tubercles are covered with around 60 short, pectinate spines – leading to the comparison in appearance with this insect. Magenta flowers emerge from the axils of the tubercles in late spring and early summer and are 2cm (¾in) in diameter. The plant was first described in 1843.

Pelecyphora strobiliformis (Werdermann) Fric & Schelle

The conical shape of the stem of this plant has given rise to the common name of 'pinecone cactus'. Its pointed, woolly apex rises about 4cm (1½in) above ground level and the areole, found at the end of the triangular, slightly keeled tubercles, contains seven to 14 short, thin, flexible spines that fall off with age. The magenta flowers are 3cm (1¼in) across.

PENIOCEREUS (Berger) Britton & Rose

Cactaceae

With their name derived from the Latin word *penio*, meaning tail, the 15 species in this genus all have long, thin stems up to 3m (10ft) in length but only 2.5cm (1in) across, and a thick tap root. Their attraction is the long nocturnal flowers that appear simultaneously within populations on mesas (high-altitude flatlands) and in valleys throughout northern Mexico and the southern USA, as though orchestrated by some invisible power.

Peniocereus greggii (Engelmann) Britton & Rose

In habitat, the dark green, almost black stems of this species are virtually spineless and the plants are difficult to find, looking much like dead sticks among the desert sagebush shrubbery, until the slender white flowers open at dusk. These can be up to 20cm (8in) across and are extremely fragrant, earning the plant the common name of 'queen of the night'. Around Tucson, Arizona, it is reported to flower between 12 and 16 June, with many of the flowers opening on the same night. By covering the flowers once they have opened, thereby preventing them from being exposed to sunlight, their magic can be captured in photographs without the use of a flash.

Below the ground, the plants have a giant tap root, up to 60cm (24in) thick with a weight of more than 60kg (130lb), indicating some of the difficulties of growing this plant successfully in a container. The tap root is prone to rot if overwatered and the plants do not tolerate frost.

PERESKIA P. Miller

Cactaceae

If your reason for growing cacti is their unusual shape or fierce spines, then plants of this genus, which have woody stems and leaves as in other 'conventional' plants, are unlikely to attract your interest. But if you like the unusual, then a cactus with leaves certainly deserves a place in your collection.

Named after Nicholas Claude Fabry de Peiresc (1580–1637), first by C. Plumier in 1703 and then by Philip Miller in 1754, the genus is sometimes still found with the alternative spellings *Peirescia, Peireskia* and *Perescia*. These are tolerant plants that can be grown in a range of nutritious soils and are found from Florida in the USA, through Mexico and the West Indies, into South America to northern Argentina. They are only slightly succulent shrubs or trees with leaves that are dropped during their rest period, yet they must be watered only moderately but regularly, as they do not like protracted periods of drought. This is generally considered to be the most primitive genus within the family Cactaceae.

Pereskia aculeata P. Miller

This leafed cactus is ideal to train along a conservatory wall where, given a few sunny days during mid- to late autumn, it will be covered with strongly perfumed pale pink flowers with orange to red centres. After flowering the plant can be pruned back hard, in a similar way to a grape vine.

Pereskia grandifolia Haworth

Although this species can grow into quite a tall tree, it will flower once it has reached a height of around 60cm (24in), producing its beautiful deep reddish purple flowers throughout late summer and early autumn.

PERESKIOPSIS Britton & Rose

Cactaceae

The ending *–iopsis* in the generic name, meaning like, indicates the similarity of plants in this genus to those in *Pereskia*, with their bushy stems bearing flat leaves. In contrast to *Pereskia* species, the areoles on the stem have glochids and the seeds a hard, white testa, placing the genus in the subfamily Opuntioideae. Native to Mexico, Honduras and Guatemala, the stems of these vigorous plants are less woody than in *Pereskia* species, making all eight plants in the genus (*Pereskiopsis aquosa, P. blakeana, P. diguetii, P. gatesii, P. kellermanii, P. porteri, P. rotundifolia* and *P. scandens*) very suitable for the grafting of young cactus seedlings. They are unlikely to be grown for their ornamental value.

PILOSOCEREUS Byles & Rowley

Cactaceae

The name of this genus is derived from the Latin word *pilosus*, meaning hairy, and refers to the hairy pseudocephalium: areoles that have been adapted to bear the 4–10cm (1½–4in) long nocturnal flowers. The term pseudocephalium is used when this hairy flowering zone extends only to a few ribs on one side, rather than to the whole circumference of the stem. Although this genus was not established until 1957, it was proposed to replace the similarly named genus *Pilocereus*, which had been described invalidly by Lemaire in 1839. Lemaire had used *Cephalocereus senilis* as the type species of the genus.

Following the latest (1995) thorough review of the genus in *Pilosocereus (Cactaceae): The Genus in Brazil* by Daniela Zappi, 35 species are included. There is an interesting distribution pattern, with members of the genus growing naturally from Central Mexico, through Central America and the Caribbean islands and on the southern tip of Florida in the USA, and into South America in northern Peru, Ecuador, Columbia, Venezuela and along the Atlantic coast into Brazil and Paraguay. There are two centres of greatest diversity, one in Central Mexico and another in the Brazilian state of Minas Gerais.

The plants are tree-like or bushy, columnar cacti with, as already mentioned, nocturnal flowers that appear from specialized areoles or in a pseudocephalium. Although frequently seen offered for sale, their purchasers are often disappointed when the stems mark badly or the plants die after exposure to low temperatures during the winter months. A minimum temperature of 10°–15°C (50°–60°F) is recommended to avoid such disappointments.

Pilosocereus leucocephalus (Poselger) Byles & Rowley

This is a particularly popular plant in cultivation for its dark to azure-green ribbed stems, with dense grey-white wool from the areoles completely covering the edges of the ribs. In habitat, in the Mexican State of Tamaulipas, plants can reach up to 6m (20ft) in height, with slender stems up to 8cm (3in) in diameter.

The 8cm (3in) long, funnel-shaped, purplish red nocturnal flowers appear only on mature plants (a pink-flowered form is also available), but the attractive stems are worth growing for their beautiful colour and hairy appearance alone, if the extra heat required for this genus can be provided during the winter months.

PLUMERIA Linnaeus

Apocynaceae

This small genus of plants, also known as frangipani, will in its tropical American habitat grow to the size of a tree, with succulent stems and foliage. In habitat, plants are often collected and grown in gardens as ornamentals for their large perfumed, showy flowers that can vary from white to purple in colour. They are easy to propagate from either seed or cuttings and present no problems in cultivation, where plants can be bedded out to produce an even greater number of flowers. They are mainly grown for their ornamental qualities rather than as real collector's plants, and are used extensively as decorative garden plants in warmer frost-free areas.

Plumeria acuminata Ait.

This is by far the most common species seen in cultivation. It has large, oblong leaves and flowers during the late spring and summer months, when it can be watered quite freely. The flower buds are white and open to reveal yellow or red petals. As the plants come from tropical Mexico, a minimum winter temperature of 15°C (70°F) is recommended. Unfortunately this plant is very prone to red spider mite.

PSEUDOLITHOS P.R.O. Bally

Asclepiadaceae

This genus of only five species (*Pseudolithos caput-viperae, P. cubiformis, P. dodsonii, P. horwoodii* and *P. migiurtinus*) from Somalia is most unusual in appearance. The plants consist of a short, leafless, unbranched succulent stem, not unlike a grapefruit-sized, spineless, globular cactus. The grey to grey-green stem is covered with wart-like tubercles and the masses of small, insignificant flowers appear in umbels.

All species are a challenge in European cultivation and are often grafted on to tubers of *Ceropegia woodii* to improve their chances of survival. Even so, the minimum temperature should not drop below 10°C (50°F).

Pseudolithos migiurtinus (Chiovenda) P.R.O. Bally

This species comes from an area near the mouth of the river Nogal in Somalia. It was first described in 1956 and moved to the current genus in 1975. This dwarf, hemispherical succulent rarely grows larger than 6cm (2½in) in height and is covered with many-angled, small, blunt

Plants in the genus *Pseudolithos* are renowned for being difficult to grow, but *P. migiurtinus* is probably the easiest.

tubercles, while four rows of larger transverse, elliptical tubercles run vertically down the stem. Although the plant usually remains solitary, it may produce small branches if it becomes damaged. The flowers occur in clusters and are brownish green in colour.

Cultivation of this species is not easy. The plants require an absolute minimum temperature of 10°C (50°F) and plenty of moisture during the growing period. They burn easily, so need a shaded position in a heated greenhouse. Although this is certainly not a plant for beginners, more experienced growers will enjoy the challenge of raising a mature specimen that will attract attention at shows. The plants can be propagated from seed which, if fresh, will germinate quickly.

PTERODISCUS Hook

Pedaliaceae

These dwarf plants have a stem less than 30cm (12in) tall, with a swollen base or underground tuber. There are at present about 12 recognized species that occur in tropical Africa, with a further three from the Transvaal. They need the heat of a warm greenhouse and grow during the European summer months. Plants are easily raised from seed and cuttings.

Pterodiscus aurantiacus Welw.

This species is characterized by bluish leaves that are comparatively wide with shallowly lobed margins, and by flowers that vary from pale yellow through to pink. The bottle-shaped caudex can grow up to 30cm (12in) tall and has several thick stems at the apex. The plant comes from Angola, Namibia and Great Namaqualand.

This species is fairly easy to grow in cultivation, but care must be taken with watering. It has winged seed, which germinate readily.

REBUTIA Schumann

Cactaceae

First described in 1895, this genus was named in honour of the Frenchman, Rebut and enjoyed a phase of immense interest during the 1960s and 1970s, mainly through the work resulting from a series of expeditions to the plant's Andean habitat and the extensive reclassification work that resulted from the new species that were found. The main expeditions were well documented in many cactus and succulent societies' journals at the time by (among others) Alfred Lau, Friedrich Ritter, Werner Rausch and Alfred Buining. The plants collected by each of these explorers were numbered and details of their

location noted before they were sent home. Here the material was studied further and identified, with new descriptions produced where it was felt appropriate. Later, comparisons of these individual efforts revealed a number of instances where different names had been created for the same or very similar plants. This, and the trend at the time to focus on differences between plants rather than their similarities, gave rise to over 500 new taxa.

The trend was reversed during the early 1990s with many of the species, including those formerly placed in *Sulcorebutia* and *Weingartia*, now combined in a streamlined genus that in the CITES *Cactaceae Checklist* (1992) lists 38 species, of which nine are provisionally accepted.

The plants present few problems in cultivation and cheer the greenhouse for weeks on end with their abundance of yellow, red, orange and magenta flowers, which in some forms and hybrids are bicoloured. As may be expected from their high Andean habitats, they are fairly hardy and can be kept in a warm greenhouse; some will survive short periods of light frost, provided they have been kept completely dry from late autumn. Those species that develop a large tap root (often those formerly in *Sulcorebutia*) need careful watering and a slightly deeper pot, to prevent the roots from rotting. The plants are prone to attacks of red spider mite and the hidden spaces between the numerous offsets are the ideal breeding ground for mealy bug, but regular treatment with different sytemic insecticides will usually prevent any such problems.

Rebutia canigueralii Cardenas

This species provides a good illustration of the confusion that can arise when a review reduces many old and familiar names to synonymy. Named after its discoverer, Father Canigueral, the original description is for plants found in the Cara Cara Mountains around Sucre, in the Department of Chuquisaca in Bolivia, at an altitude of 2,200–3,000m (7,200–9,750ft).

In the CITES *Cactaceae Checklist* (1992) the following names, previously placed in the genera *Sulcorebutia* and *Weingartia*, have been included in the wider concept of a much more variable species: *alba, alboides, brevispina, callecallensis, caracarensis, crispata, fischeriana, frankiana, inflexiseta, losenickyana, pasopayana, perplexiflora, pulchra, rauschii, ritteri, rubro-aura, saxatilis, tarabucina, tarabucoensis, vazqueziana* and *verticillacantha* var. *albispina*, var. *aureiflora* and f. *brevispina*. Many of these species had originally been described in the leading cactus and succulent

Rebutia canigueralii – after recent 'lumping', how do we ask the nurseryman for this form with gorgeous bicoloured flowers?

societies' journals, but details of the reasoning behind this massive change have been poorly communicated to the hobbyist collector.

While we are not in a position to argue the botanical merits or otherwise of this particular change, it is a shame that many plants which differ quite widely in appearance are now all known by the same name. The original description is for a plant with gorgeous bicoloured flowers: orange-red petals with a bright yellow throat. Most of the referred species have far less attractive, uniformly magenta flowers. Many of the old names are now used to describe the different forms of the new species, while others are merely referred to by the field reference number under which they were originally collected.

This last point introduces a complication, in that strictly speaking these numbers should only be used for material that has been vegetatively propagated from the plants originally collected. Over the years, many of the field numbers have become attached to plants raised from seed that closely resemble the original plants. As these plants take some years to fill a 10cm (4in) pot, it is quite interesting to build up a collection of the wide range of forms for their equally wide range of body colours, length and colour of spines, and flower colours. *The Collector's Guide for Sulcorebutia and Weingartia* (1985), written by John Pilbeam with excellent photos by Bill Weightman, provides a good reference point for such a collection. It also indicates those names that were mere duplicates of earlier names.

Rebutia heliosa Rausch

This species and its two varieties – *R. h.* var. *cajasensis* and *R. h.* var. *condorensis* – now also include the former species

At the peak of flowering, *Rebutia heliosa* var. *condorensis* is hidden beneath a cover of flowers.

R. narvaecensis and *R. perplexa* and have been crossed with other species, notably *R. albiflora*, to produce some interesting and attractive flower colour variations. The long-tubed orange flowers have a white throat deep inside the flower and appear from the lower part of the plant.

The unusual spination of *R. heliosa* makes it an all-year-round attraction in the greenhouse. All forms readily offset or can be propagated from seed, although in a mixed collection of the genus, where these floriferous plants all tend to flower at the same time, some unexpected results may occur. The long tap root should be planted in a very free-draining compost and care should be taken not to overwater the plants. It is wise to root some offsets and keep them in reserve, as this species appears not to be long lived and after several years seems to exhaust itself with its annual bounty of flowers.

RHIPSALIS Gaertner
Cactaceae

This is another old genus that was first proposed in 1788. The confusion between this and the closely related genus *Lepismium* is outlined under that heading. Gaertner chose the name, meaning wickerwork in Greek, because of the slender, pliable branches that become tangled and give the appearance of wickerwork. Today the genus includes 40 species, of which at least 15 require more detailed study.

Interestingly, the occurrence of some species in tropical Africa, Madagascar and Sri Lanka (formerly Ceylon) forms the only possible exception to the American natural distribution of cacti.

Rhipsalis species can become marvellous hanging-basket plants with their long, slender, cylindrical stems

Epiphytes displayed on a bark-covered frame: *Rhipsalis teres* (left) and 'Spanish moss', *Tillandsia usneioides* (right).

or flattened leaf-like joints, and producing showers of fingernail-sized blooms. The tiny flowers are borne profusely at almost every areole and most blooms resemble each other throughout the genus. Most plants flower in the winter period from autumn to spring, with just a few species in flower at any one time, although more appear to flower from midwinter onwards than before. In cultivation, occasional flowers are borne at other times of year. Any collection of epiphytic plants would be incomplete without a few hanging *Rhipsalis* species to complement and offset the other lovely plants.

This genus has similar cultivation requirements to that of the other 'less spiny' epiphytic cacti *Discocactus, Hatiora, Lepismium* and *Schlumbergera*, so that it is possible to build up a specialist collection of these plants without the worry of widely different requirements. A minimum winter temperature of 5°–10°C (40°–50°F) is recommended, while during summer the temperatures should not exceed 30°C (85°F) as this can lead to plants shedding some of their branches. They are happy in a shaded position and should be protected from direct sunlight, especially during the hot summer months. The soil should not be allowed to dry out completely, so regular watering should be carried on throughout the year. The plants like quite a humid atmosphere, but only if sufficient ventilation can be provided to prevent the air from becoming stagnant.

Propagation is easy from stem cuttings that will usually root within a couple of weeks. It is also possible to raise plants from seed, but it will take some years before the seedlings reach flowering size. It is therefore rare to see these plants on seed lists.

Rhipsalis baccifera (J. Miller) W.T. Stearn

This is possibly the most widely distributed species of cactus, found along the American Atlantic coast from Florida south throughout Mexico and Central America, and in South America into Brazil and westwards into Peru. There are a number of subspecies: *R. b.* subsp. *fasciculata*, from Brazil, and *R. b.* subsp. *horrida* and *R. b.* subsp. *fortdauphinensis*, both from Madagascar.

The plant consists of a cluster of pencil-thin (up to 0.5cm/¼in thick), cylindrical, pendent stems and it flowers during late winter, with many white blooms followed by berry-like fruits that decorate the plant for many months.

Other species include:

Rhipsalis burchellii A very nice delicate, pendent plant from Brazil, with white flowers that hang downwards

from the ends of thread-like stems. This species dislikes drying of the soil more than most.

Rhipsalis cereuscula, sometimes referred to as the 'rice cactus', has a multitude of tiny, cylindrical stems that are borne at the ends of long, slender branches.

Rhipsalis cereuscula* f. *simmleri has fine, dark green, lacy branches and is minuscule. The main branches spread out into hundreds of finer branches that bear creamy white blooms, making this an excellent hanging basket plant.

Rhipsalis crispata has many differently shaped, light green segments and becomes a rather stiffly branched plant. Some of the segments are cylindrical with wavy margins and others are long and narrow with a prominent stem. The flowers are yellowish in colour.

Rhipsalis dissimilis with long, very green, smooth, cylindrical branches, has (relatively) very large white flowers with a hint of rose.

Rhipsalis mesembryanthoides is also known as the 'mistletoe cactus', with cylindrical stems bearing many tiny spiralling, short joints, taking on a bush-like appearance. The flowers are white.

Rhipsalis micrantha has thin, three- or four-angled or sometimes flattened stems and white flowers. The former species, now *R. m.* f. *rauhiorum*, is rather slow growing and bears some resemblance to *Schlumbergera* species. The pendent branches are made up of light green, scalloped segments.

Rhipsalis pilocarpa has hairy, pendent stems and white flowers that can reach 3.5cm (1½in) in diameter if the plant is grown in an even, high temperature, but significantly less if the temperature fluctuates between 4°C (39°F) and 18°C (64°F).

RHYTIDOCAULON Bally

Asclepiadaceae

This small genus of eight species (*Rhytidocaulon fulleri, R. macrolobum, R. paradoxum, R. piliferum, R. richardianum, R. sheilae, R. subscandens* and *R. torta*) occurs in Ethiopia, Somalia and Yemen.

Rhytidocaulon macrolobum Lavranos

In the dry, rocky countryside of south barh (dry shrubland) and Wadi Dabab in Yemen, this erect, leafless plant grows to a height of 25cm (10in). The sparingly branched, cylindrical stem is waxy-grey and rough, and is covered with warts but without fleshy wings or prickles. The flowers appear scattered over the new growth of the stem, and are dark purple in colour with vibrant white hairs. This is probably the least difficult species to grow,

Seeds and plants of *Rhytidocaulon macrolobum* are still difficult to obtain from nurseries.

but in saying that, care must be taken not to overwater the plants. During the resting period, an occasional misting will prevent dieback of the tips.

SANSEVIERIA Thunbg.

Dracaenaceae

This genus, until recently a member of the family Agavaceae, has over 50 species and new discoveries are being reported all the time. The plants grow in the wild throughout South Africa, West Africa, Kenya, Madagascar, India and Yemen. They have short, thick rhizomes from which spring fleshy, decorative, often variegated leaves arranged in rosettes. The flowers are borne in racemes and are usually small and white.

In our experience, potted plants grow much better indoors than in the greenhouse, and throughout Europe windowsills full of the popular 'mother-in-law's tongue' (forms of *Sansevieria trifasciata*) can be found. In some species, particularly the large-leaved *S. grandis*, the thick rhizome can grow at such a rate that it frequently pushes the plant out of the pot. Propagation is by removing and potting up the shoots that seem to appear around the mother plant wherever the rhizome reaches the surface of the soil. Leaf cuttings can also be taken. The flat-leaved species seem to be particularly prone to attacks of the relatively new (to the UK) pest called western flower thrip, which attacks the heart of the plant where the young leaves emerge.

Sansevieria hyacinthoides (Linnaeus) Druce

This species comes from the eastern and northern Transvaal, where it is generally found growing beneath trees. It is an acauline plant with a creeping rhizome. The flat, lanceolate leaves are 20–40cm (8–16in) long with a diameter of about 3–8cm (1¼–3in) and are very fleshy. The flowers are arranged in racemes that can reach a length of 5cm (2in) and, as its name implies, resemble an off-white to cream-coloured hyacinth in appearance. Unlike the hyacinth, however, they have only a slight fragrance. Highly decorative orange berries appear after the flowers have finished.

This plant has many uses. The leaf fibres can be employed as thread, while in the eastern Cape the plant is used as medicine by the locals, who cut the leaves and use the dripping sap as a remedy for earache and toothache.

Sansevieria trifasciata Prain

This is the most common species seen in collections but its precise origin in nature is unknown. The plants can be found in tropical west Africa. The broad leaves are nicely marked and there are a number of variegated cultivars including 'Hahnii', with leaves up to 15cm (6in) long and yellowish ('Golden Hahnii') or silvery white ('Silver Hahnii') markings. The plants look like small aloes.

SARCOCOULON De Candolle

Geraniaceae

Plants from this genus are known as the 'bushman's candle' because of their highly inflammable waxy coating. They shed their leaves during their resting period and can remain in this dormant state for several years, until conditions are right for growth and reproduction.

In cultivation, plants should never be left completely dry and can be given an occasional misting throughout the year. When grown in cultivation in the northern hemisphere, leaves and flowers appear mostly in spring or early summer. Stem cuttings can prove difficult to root, so the plant is usually propagated from seed.

R.O. Moffett, a leading authority on this genus, recognizes 14 species. Plants can be found from Angola and Namibia, to the Cape and Little Namaqualand, where they are widely distributed over the more arid areas.

Sarcocaulon l'heritieri (De Candolle) Sweet

This species was first described from plants found near Grahamstown; it grows in Namibia. The plants adapt well to cultivation, where they become fleshy, spiny shrubs, up to 75cm (30in) high and 60cm (24in) across. The flowers, pale lemon in colour, are 2cm (¾in) in diameter.

Sarcocaulon peniculinum Moffett

This species' habitat is restricted to an area between Rosh Pinah and Dreigratdrif in Namibia. It is a fleshy,

The delicate leaves of *Sarcocaulon peniculinum* make this an attractive plant even when it is not producing its delightful pale to rose-pink flowers.

dwarf, prostate shrublet, only 8cm (3in) in height and diameter, with stems that branch at or just below ground level. The roots are not swollen, and there are seldom more than two branches. The flowers are rose to pale pink in colour and do not have the throat markings found in other species.

SCHLUMBERGERA Lemaire

Cactaceae

Probably one of the best-known and most popular houseplants in the world, these compact, free-flowering plants are seen in full bud during the weeks leading up to Christmas in the northern hemisphere, everywhere that plants are sold. Although the genus contains six species, most of the plants sold are hybrids that have been created to produce larger blooms and a wide range of flower colours, from pure snow-white through soft shell-pink to orange-yellow and bright ruby-red. Some of the new hybrids even have bicoloured flowers.

These many-branched, epiphytic shrubs, their 'branches' consisting of 2–3cm (¾–1¼in) long, flat, leaf-like stems with a pronounced central vein, are marvellous patio and houseplants. They can be grown in almost any type of container, bloom at a time of year when flowers are rarely seen, and bear more blooms and become more handsome as the years pass. Offered for sale as 'Christmas cacti', most will flower for several weeks some time around Christmas.

Schlumbergera species prefer a shady location with filtered rather than full sunlight. A standard houseplant fertilizer can be given at one-quarter the recommended strength, but do allow the soil to dry out somewhat between waterings. Another tip is not to over-pot this plant and to provide several weeks of short days (long nights) to induce flowering. About six to eight weeks before Christmas, make sure that the plant does not get any light after daylight has gone outside. Even a streetlight close to the windowsill where the plant is kept can prevent flowering; cover the plant until daylight arrives in the morning. Turning the plant once the buds have formed can lead to their dropping off before opening.

Schlumbergera opuntioides (Loefgren & Dusen) D. Hunt
This is a remarkable plant with growth that could easily be mistaken for that of a small opuntia. Raspberry-purple flowers are just like those of most other Christmas cacti in size and shape.

Schlumbergera orssichiana Barthlott & MacMilan
This is a recent discovery from the Brazilian mountains and is still rarely seen in cultivation. Producing extra-wide growth, it bears pendent white flowers with pinkish red edges; these are 6–9cm (2½–3½in) across and sometimes surprise you by appearing out of season.

SCLEROCACTUS Britton & Rose

Cactaceae

The concept for this genus has grown to include species formerly under *Ancistrocactus, Glandulicactus, Navajoa, Toumeya* and *Utahia*. Plants in this genus offer a real challenge to those who want to grow them in cultivation outside their natural habitat, the Great Basin Desert that covers parts of California, Arizona, Nevada, Utah, New Mexico and Colorado in the USA. Here they are found in small, inaccessible, isolated colonies, growing in some of the most inhospitable environmental conditions.

The name is derived from the Greek *skleros*, meaning dry, hard, parched, which describes these conditions admirably. This is a landscape of weathered and eroded limestone and granite rocks where water drains away quickly. At these high-altitude locations, up to 2,500m (8,000ft), temperatures can drop to below −18°C (0°F) during winter, when the plants are often completely covered by snow for several months, yet relative humidity is very low. Not only do they have to survive these conditions, but human activity in the area – mining, road construction and military installations – has wiped out complete colonies, while others have been decimated by natural pests.

You would think that plants which can survive these conditions would flourish when looked after and nourished in the greenhouse or on the windowsill. Not so. The challenge starts with raising the plants from seed. Unlike most cactus seed, that of *Sclerocactus* species has to be scarified to encourage germination. The young seedlings are very prone to rot and are often grafted when only a few weeks old. This introduces a further problem: *Sclerocactus* can tolerate, in fact need, low temperatures so that their stomata can open to allow exchange of carbon dioxide and oxygen with the atmosphere, but the stock on which they are often grafted is not as cold resistant and it is usually the death of the stock plant that spells the end of the *Sclerocactus* species that has been grafted on to it.

In habitat, most species form heavy-spined, solitary globular to short cylindrical stems, up to 30cm (12in) tall, earning them the name of 'small barrel cactus'. They rarely offset: what appear to be offsets are usually young seedlings growing around the mother plant.

Sclerocactus mariposensis (Hester) Taylor

Like many cactus names, this one has 'been around'. Originally described in 1945 as *Echinomastus mariposensis*, the plant has also spent time briefly under the names

Echinocactus mariposensis (1969), *Neolloydia mariposensis* (1970) and *Thelocactus mariposensis* (1978), before classification as a *Sclerocactus* species in 1987, where it and other former species of *Echinomastus* sit uncomfortably.

Fritz Hochstätter, in his review of the genus published since the CITES *Cactaceae Checklist* (1992), excludes the former *Echinomastus* species from *Sclerocactus*, for although they share many features, their habitats are outside the Great Basin Desert. The name *mariposensis* indicates the place where the plant was first discovered: Mariposa in Brewster County, Texas. The plants are winter hardy and frost-resistant but dislike high humidity when it is cold.

A rare sight in most hobbyist collections: a mature specimen of *Sclerocactus mariposensis* in flower.

Plate X
Ceroid cacti 2

Espostoopsis dybowskii

Cleistocactus strausii

Micranthocereus streckeri

Espostoa melanostele f. churinensis

Weberbauerocereus johnsonii

Pilosocereus glaucochrous

*Espostoa (Thrixanthocereus)
senilis*

*Coleocephalocereus
(Buiningia) aureus*

Angola, Botswana, Somalia and Ethiopia. There are five species: *Sesamothamnus benguellensis*, *S. busseanus*, *S. guerichii*, *S. lugardii* and *S. rivae*. Most have large, white or whitish pink flowers, although in *S. guerichii* the blooms are golden yellow.

Sesamothamnus lugardii N.E. Brown

Usually found in the dry, hot parts of the northern and eastern Transvaal, but also reported from Zimbabwe, the name of this species honours E.J. Lugard. The thick, fleshy, tapered trunks can reach a height of 4m (12ft), with a number of short, spiny branches at the top – the spines are modified leaves. The large flowers are cream coloured and have a nice fragrance.

The plants are best grown in a warm greenhouse, where they can be propagated from seed but are slow to grow on.

STENOCACTUS (Schumann) Backeberg & Knuth

Cactaceae

Taylor and Hunt resurrected this genus in 1980 as the name precedes that of *Echinofossulocactus* Lawrence (1841). Both names refer to the 30–100 narrow, wavy ribs (*steno* meaning narrow, *fossulo* meaning ditch or little furrow) that are characteristic of most plants in the genus and not found in any other.

The plants are extraordinarily variable in spination, flower colour and number of ribs. This has given rise to a host of poorly defined names. The CITES *Cactaceae Checklist* (1992) still recognizes eight species, but Taylor suggests there are only four: *Stenocactus coptonogonus*, with the fewest number of ribs (ten to 14), indicating an affinity with *Ferocactus*; *S. crispatus*, with which most of the old names fall into synonymy; *S. phyllacanthus* and *S. vaupelianus*.

All the species are native to Mexico, where they are found in the central states of Hidalgo and Zacatecas and through to northern Coahuila. They are unlikely to grow to more than 20cm (8in) in height with a diameter of up to 10cm (4in), usually remaining solitary but sometimes clustering to form groups up to 30cm (12in) across. The flowers can be yellow, cream or purple, but the most sought-after forms have attractive white-and-purple striped flowers. None of the species is particularly difficult in cultivation.

Stenocactus crispatus f. *violaciflora* is an unusual-looking cactus with a large number of narrow ribs and attractive striped flowers.

Stenocactus crispatus (De Candolle) Berger

Plants found under this name are highly variable, particularly in the size of the central spine, which is usually flattened and dagger-like, up to 3.5cm (1½in) long, straight and curved upwards. The flowers are up to 3.5cm (1½in) long, with white outer petals that have a broad, median violet-brown stripe and a violet edge, while the other petals are violet with a carmine-red median band.

STENOCEREUS (Berger) Riccobono

Cactaceae

The 23 species of this genus of tree-forming or bushy, columnar cacti are found from Arizona through Mexico and the Caribbean islands down to northern South America. The genus has taken in species formerly included in *Machaerocereus*, *Isolatocereus*, *Lemaireocereus*, *Ritterocereus*, *Hertrichocereus* and *Marshallocereus*, while *Stenocereus marginatus* and *S. weberi* have been transferred to *Pachycereus*.

Steno- means narrow and indicates that, considering their length, the stems are remarkably thin, with *S. dumortieri* and *S. griseus* probably competing for the thickest woody trunk, at a diameter of 40cm (16in). These species can reach a height of 15m (50ft) in their Central Mexican and South American habitats.

Many of the species are valued for their edible fruits, while *S. gummosus* is used in Baja California as a fish poison by local fisherman, who bruise the stems and throw these into running streams.

The further south these plants are found, the less tolerant of cold they become. In cultivation, a minimum winter temperature of 10°C (50°F) will prevent the often beautifully coloured epidermis from developing unsightly cold marks.

Stenocereus eruca (Brandegee) Britton & Rose

This is an unusual member of the genus, because its 3m (10ft) long stems grow prostrate with only their tips slightly raised, giving it the common name of 'chirinola', the 'creeping devil cactus'. The specific name *eruca* is Latin for caterpillar. Britton & Rose placed the plant in their new genus *Machaerocereus* that derived its name from the Greek *macaera*, meaning dagger, because of the dagger-like 3.5cm (1½in) long central spine. This is reminiscent of the robust lower central spine found in *Echinocereus brandegeei* and the spination of *Opuntia invicta*, with which *Stenocereus eruca* shares its Baja California habitat.

In habitat, the plants propagate vegetatively. As the

Only the stem tips of *Stenocereus eruca*, the 'creeping devil', are raised off the ground as it appears to climb over rocks.

older parts of the stem die, the roots that develop on the underside of the sprawling stem continue to sustain the plant. The raised heads 'crawl' over logs and stones as well as other branches of the same original parent plant. For those unable to travel to Baja California, there is an impressive display of this plant in the Huntington Botanical Gardens in Los Angeles. The 12cm (5in) long white nocturnal flowers are rarely seen in cultivation.

STROMBOCACTUS Britton & Rose

Cactaceae

The generic name is derived from the Greek meaning coiled in spirals, referring to the way that the tubercles spiral around the flattened, globular body. There is only one species in the genus.

Strombocactus disciformis (De Candolle) Britton & Rose
Originally described as *Mammillaria disciformis* by De Candolle in 1828, the nineteenth-century names that have been reduced to synonymy (*Echinocactus disciformis, Echinofossulocactus turbiniformis, Cactus disciformis* and *Anhalonium turbiniforme*) provide an indication of the genera to which this plant is related. It is native to central and northeastern Mexico.

More recently, and only for a short while, the genus was enlarged to include *Obregonia denegrii, Pelecyphora/Normanbokea pseudopectinatus* and *Pelecyphora/Normanbokea valdezianus,* as well as species of *Turbinicarpus*, before returning to its monotypic status.

The plants are solitary and slow growing, rarely reaching more than 10cm (4in) in diameter, and produce 2cm (1½in) long white flowers from the centre. The short spines and white wool that are found on young areoles later disappear.

Strombocactus disciformis. By grafting this usually solitary plant, offsets are produced that can be removed and rooted.

TACITUS Moran

Crassulaceae

Often incorrectly attributed to Moran & Meyran, Moran proposed this monotypic genus for a plant discovered in 1972 by Alfred Lau in Chihuahua, Mexico. It is closely related to *Graptopetalum* but differs in various important floral characteristics.

Tacitus bellus Moran & Meyran

Above this plant's echeveria-like rosette rises a short inflorescence bearing a few very large flowers of striking appearance: 3cm (1¼in) across and brilliant magenta-red in colour. Each five-part flower is star-like in shape and beautifully crowned by ten large, stiff stamens. The five carpels are also red. The corolla is peculiar in having a short tube which is closed at the top by a lip-like over-hang embracing the filaments, which suggests why Moran gave the genus its name – implying closed lips.

The striking flowers of *Tacitus bellus* created a great demand for this plant when it was first introduced in 1972.

A plant of easy culture, it is nevertheless worthy of a place in any succulent collection, where the only problem likely to be encountered is that mealy bugs love to hide underneath the lower leaves.

TAVARESIA Welwitsch ex N.E. Brown

Asclepiadaceae

This genus was established in 1854 by Friedrich Welwitsch in order to accommodate *Tavaresia angolensis*, which had been discovered the previous year in Angola. In 1870, Decaisne placed this plant in a new genus, *Decabelone*, and this generic name remained in use until 1904, when N.E. Brown re-established the old name *Tavaresia* in *The Flora of Tropical Africa*, and this is retained under today's classification. Both names are still encountered in collections. The plants present some challenge in cultivation and can be grafted on to tubers of *Ceropegia woodii*.

Tavaresia grandiflora (K. Schumann) Bgr.

This plant is widespread in Namibia and the northern Cape. The 14-angled stems reach a height of 20cm (8in) and the pale yellow flowers, specked with purple, are 10cm (4in) long and 4cm (1½in) across. If this plant is kept at or above the recommended minimum winter temperature it will soon form a fair-sized clump, and can make a wonderful show plant.

Thelocactus hexaedrophorus var. *fossulatus*. With its large, showy flowers and ease of cultivation it is surprising that this genus does not enjoy greater popularity. It is highly suitable for beginners.

THELOCACTUS (Schumann) Britton & Rose

Cactaceae

This is a genus of medium-sized cacti that are globular to short columnar or somewhat flattened in shape, with few low ribs or more often with large tubercles that give rise to the genus' name: *thelo* is the Greek word for nipple. The plants rarely exceed 40cm (16in) in height and 15cm (6in) in diameter for the short columnar species. The flowering tubercles are more or less grooved on their upper surface and the large, campanulate flowers are born on young areoles at the centre of the plant, opening during the daytime. The fruit splits at the base to reveal the black, finely tuberculate seeds which have a large basal hilum.

The plants are distributed in Mexico and along the Mexican border in the southern American state of Texas, where they grow on slopes in predominantly limestone

At first glance, a small plant of *Tavaresia grandiflora* could almost be mistaken for a cactus. Do not overwater this plant.

soil and are exposed to near-freezing temperatures during the winter.

These are good plants for beginners, quite tolerant of different soil mixtures provided that the compost is free draining and is allowed to dry out between waterings. They love sunshine and will then readily display their beautiful flowers, which in some species are bicoloured. Some of the species have nectaries on their areoles which produce a sugary sap that can lead to the formation of a black sooty mould, which may not harm the plant but will detract from its natural beauty. Misting the plants will wash away the sugary excretion, and if a fungicide is occasionally added this will prevent the mould from appearing.

Thelocactus bicolor (Galeotti ex Pfeiffer) Britton & Rose
This is probably the most common *Thelocactus* species found in collections, possibly because of the large flowers which essentially, despite the name, are tricoloured, with a red or deep magenta throat, lighter-coloured petal tips and a white band between these two zones. The different proportions of these three bands and the variable spination of the plant have given rise to numerous synonyms and variety names. In some plants the white band has almost completely taken over, producing white flowers, while in others the deep colour of the centre of the

flower dominates, almost to the exclusion of the other zones. The flowers can measure up to 8cm (3in) across.

The plants occur along the Mexican border in Texas and in the northern Mexican states of Chihuahua, Coahuila, Nuevo Leon, Tamaulipas, Durango, Zacatecas and San Luis Potosi.

T. b. var. *bolaensis*, from the Sierra Bolla in Coahuila, forms tall, cone-shaped stems that are densely covered with light-coloured spines that almost totally hide the green body of the plant.

TRICHOCAULON N.E. Brown
Asclepiadaceae
The proposed new name for this genus is *Larryleachia*, but as yet this is not fully accepted in all circles. But what's in a name? The genus is found in the Cape Province in South Africa and throughout Namibia. The highly succulent stems are often densely tuberculate, with the tubercles arranged in ribs or spiralling up the stem, and often carry hairs or bristles at their tip.

Trichocaulon cactiformis (Zeyher) N.E. Brown
Carl Zeyher, who named the species *Stapelia cactiformis* although it does not resemble a cactus in any way, first discovered this plant in 1840. N.E. Brown placed it in the genus *Trichocaulon*. The plant is found in the vicinity of

Trichocaulon cactiformis. Two seedlings from the same batch sown in 1995 have reached flowering size over a period of three years and are now planted in 7cm (2¾in) pots and show both solitary and offsetting forms.

the Orange River in Little Namaqualand. Its small chocolate-coloured flowers measure only 0.5cm (¼in) across. In cultivation, it grows easily from seed but, like all asclepiads, black rot and mealy bugs are its worst enemies.

TURBINICARPUS (Backeberg) Buxbaum & Backeberg

Cactaceae

At the time that the CITES *Cactaceae Checklist* (1992) was published, this genus of small, globular plants was included in *Neolloydia*, but as there were doubts about the true affinities of *N. conoidea*, the type species of the genus, *Turbinicarpus* was retained for the purpose of the *Checklist*. There is still some controversy about the inclusion of some former *Gymnocactus* species (*G. beguinii*, *G. gielsdorfianus*, *G. goldii*, *G. horripilus*, *G. knuthianus*, *G. mandragora*, *G. subterraneus*, *G. viereckii* and *G. ysabelae*), but the inclusion of the former *Normanbokea* species *N. pseudopectinatus* and *N. valdezianus* is more generally accepted. While some of the species in the genus have been known for many years, there are also some exciting recent discoveries that have stimulated interest in these small plants.

To grow them requires a very well-drained compost (50:50 soil and grit) and careful watering, especially at the start of the growing period, as they can sometimes absorb too much water and split. Propagation is usually from seed that spills out of the fruit when this has dried and split. Germination is quick, but growth seems very slow. Many species retain their juvenile spination – often small clusters of short, whitish radiating spines, without central spines – for some time and look quite different from mature plants. To increase the numbers of plants available in cultivation, they can be grafted and will off-set profusely, especially if the mother plant is decapitated. Each offset can be rooted to increase the number of plants in cultivation.

All *Turbinicarpus* species are CITES Appendix I plants. It is hard to single out one or two of my favourites, so get a couple of small trays and grow them all! The following two species are new discoveries since the publication of the CITES *Cactaceae Checklist*.

Turbinicarpus alonsoi Glass & Arias

There was a buzz of excitement at the annual May Cactus Fair in 1996. Some of those attending had just received their copy of the now sadly defunct *Cactus File* magazine with a beautiful photograph on the cover of what appeared to be an *Ariocarpus* species with a deep

Turbinicarpus schmiedickeanus var. *klinkerianus*. Seed falls from the top of the plant and readily germinates around its base.

magenta flower, but with spines on the younger areoles. On page 8 we were introduced to Alonso Garcia Luna, who at the age of 14 had been on an expedition to northeastern Guanajuato with Charlie Glass. For most of us, this was the first time that we had seen photographs of *Turbinicarpus alonsoi*, two years after its discovery by young Alonso. It would be another year before we saw the first plants in cultivation; some were weathered habitat plants collected illegally, others were fresh young grafted seedlings raised from seed that had also left Mexico illegally. Fortunately, some of these plants were acquired for extortionate sums of money by keen hobbyists. They were able to raise significant quantities of seed that, through grafting of the young seedlings, has resulted in many more plants now becoming available in Europe, at more reasonable prices and without endangering the plants in habitat.

Unlike many species in the genus, this plant has long, flattened tubercles, looking rather like a cross between *Obregonia denegrii* and an *Ariocarpus* species.

Turbinicarpus jauernigii G. Frank

Dr Gerhart Frank first described this species in the Dutch Society's journal *Succulenta*, based on a plant found by Johan Jauernig in 1991 north of Las Palomas, in San Luis Potosi, Mexico, as follows:

25(–50)mm diameter, 10(–20)mm high. Juvenile plants have 7–10 white radial spines, 3–5mm long, old plants only have a single central spine with a dark tip, flowers 25mm long and 15mm wide, light yellow-brown, with a darker mid-stripe.

The plants are similar in appearance to *T. schwarzii*, with a greyish purple body.

UEBELMANNIA Buining

Cactaceae

There was quite a furore when the first plants of this genus, found in 1965 by Horst and Baumhardt north of Diamantina, Minas Gerais, in Brazil, were imported into Europe by the Swiss nurseryman Werner Uebelmann during 1966. A photograph of a plant, simply labelled HU 106 and nicknamed 'the treasure from Brazil', appeared on the cover of the September issue of the *National Cactus and Succulent Journal* in England in 1967, followed by its first description as *Uebelmannia pectinifera* in the December issue. In the meantime, the new genus *Uebelmannia* had been proposed in the November issue of the Dutch society's journal *Succulenta* for a group of plants that were similar to, yet different from, the genera *Parodia, Notocactus, Blossfeldia, Frailea* and *Eriocactus*, mainly based on fruit, seed, embryo, seedling and flower characteristics.

Recently some botanists have expressed doubts about this relationship. Nigel Taylor, while working on his definition of the tribe Cereae, suggested the possibility that *Uebelmannia* might be a member of that group, although his evidence and conclusions tended to reject the idea. Recent DNA studies, however, confirm this.

To understand the cultivation requirements of these plants we need to look at their habitat. This is located on a high plateau at an altitude of around 1,000m (3,250ft) some 240km (150 miles) inland from the Atlantic east coast of Brazil, where the plants grow in an acidic mixture composed of quartzite sand and leaf mould. Average temperatures are 17°C (63°F) during the winter months and rise to 22°C (72°F) during summer, with very hot days but cool nights and a heavy rainfall of around 25cm (10in) per month – quite unlike conditions in the North American deserts! In cultivation, a minimum temperature of 10°–15°C (50°–60°F) is recommended.

In habitat, the epidermis is often encrusted with lichens. On cultivated plants, it is worthy of a closer look with a magnifying glass to reveal a layer of clear mucilage-filled cells that have been compared to those of the 'windowed' *Haworthia* and Mesembryanthemaceae species. In some species, the epidermis and older spines have a whitish wax coating, creating a dark grey-white appearance.

These are first globular, later short cylindrical plants that rarely offset until they reach a great age. The stems can grow up to 30cm (12in) in height. Spination on habitat plants is impressive (2–3cm/¾–1¼in in length) for the size of the plants, but rarely reaches these lengths in cultivation.

It is perhaps surprising that after the first descriptions of the three species – *U. gummifera* (including its subspecies *buiningii* and variety *rubra), U. buiningii*, and *U. pectinifera* (with its varieties *pseudopectinifera* and *multicostata*, and subspecies *horrida* and *flavispina*) – between 1967 and 1984, no new species have been discovered.

Uebelmannia pectinifera Buining

This beautiful plant is bound to attract attention in any collection. The dark bodies turn a reddish brown at the apex, while the acute ribs are covered with very closely spaced areoles that are white-woolly on new growth with porrect spines pointing away from the plants. Most of the plants found in cultivation are grafted on a low stock that is often concealed in the pot below a layer of grit, to give the impression that the plants are growing on their own roots.

UNCARINA (Baill.) Stapf

Pedaliaceae

Jacobsen dismisses the nine known species in this genus, all of which are endemic to the island of Madagascar, as 'of no significance in cultivation'. In habitat, they form much-branched trees and shrubs that can grow to a height of more than 4m (12ft). The flowers can be yellow, white or red, although yellow appears to be the most common. The fruit is quite remarkable: the pods are flat at one end, pointed at the other and are armed with numerous barbed hooks. The local people use them as mouse traps, as any small rodent soon gets caught in the barbs.

Uncarina decaryi Humbert

Although officially this is an invalidly published name, this is the most common species in the genus, both in the wild and in cultivation. It is found in the dry regions in the southernmost part of Madagascar, near Fort Dauphin (now called Tolanaro). It has a greyish bark with thick branches growing to a height of 3m (10ft). The hairy-waxy coating found on the leaves helps to protect the

plant from the extreme heat. When the leaves are crushed, they emit an unpleasant smell. The flowers are up to 4cm (1½in) across and bright yellow on the outside, magenta to maroon inside. This species can be watered freely during the growing season.

Uncarina stellulifera Humbert

This succulent shrub grows in the dry southwest corner of Madagascar, where it is found on the Mahafaly limestone plateau. It has disappeared from many regions due to a considerable cutting of thickets to provide grazing for the zebu (a Madagascan cow). It grows to about 3m (10ft) tall with leaves that are ovate-triangular in shape. The flowers appear in clusters, coloured pinkish white with reddish carmine veins on the outside. Once again, this species is easy to grow in cultivation, with plenty of watering during the growing season.

WEBERBAUEROCEREUS Backeberg

Cactaceae

Curt Backeberg named this genus after German botanist August Weberbauer (1871–1948) who studied the flora of the Peruvian Andes, where all four 'accepted' species (*Weberbauerocereus cuzcoensis, W. longicomus, W. weberbaueri* and *W. winterianus*) originate. There are four more species (*W. churinensis, W. johnsonii, W. rauhii* and *W. torataensis*) that in the CITES *Cactaceae Checklist* (1992) are provisionally accepted, pending further study.

These are bushy, columnar cacti where the main stem may grow to 2m (6ft) in height and 15cm (6in) across. From this main stem, long and thinner branches grow, ultimately producing a plant of tree-like proportions. The flowers are 6–12cm (2½–5in) long, and are radial symmetrical in some species but zygomorphic in others.

In cultivation, these plants can safely be grown in a greenhouse where temperatures are kept above 5°C (40°F). In frost-free areas, these decorative columnar cacti can be grown outside in the garden, where their dense, attractive-coloured spination will eventually form an impressive stand.

Weberbauerocereus winterianus Ritter

The attraction of this plant is the dense, golden yellow spination on young stems, but unfortunately this fades and becomes less dense on mature stems. The spines are usually only 1.5cm (½in) long, but on flower-bearing areoles there are longer, more bristle-like golden spines that can reach a length of 7cm (3in). These announce the impending arrival of slightly longer flowers that have very pale pink inner petals, with the outer petals a darker pink. *W. w.* var. *australis* is a more robust plant.

WEBEROCEREUS Britton & Rose

Cactaceae

This is a genus of epiphytic cacti producing long, slender stems with many aerial roots, that climb up and then hang from trees. The stems are often only 1cm (½in) in diameter and have only weak spination. The funnel- to bell-shaped flowers open at night and can be up to 6cm (2½in) long and across. Seedlings and new growth are similar to that of *Rhipsalis* species, but *Weberocereus* species produce much larger flowers and fruits that are quite different. Their native habitat is in Central America (Costa Rica, Ecuador, Guatemala, southern Mexico, Nicaragua and Panama).

The genus is named after the Frenchman Dr Albert Weber (1830–1903) and now embraces nine accepted species, including three (*Weberocereus glaber* from Guatemala, and *W. imitans* and *W. tonduzii* both from Costa Rica) that were formerly included in the genus *Werckleocereus*.

Weberocereus biolleyi (Weber) Britton & Rose

Weber was sent a specimen of this plant by P. Biolley and first described it in 1902 as *Rhipsalis biolleyi*, but at that time he had not seen its flowers. In 1903 he wrote to Schumann suggesting that he now considered the plant to be a *Cereus* species. Later, plants sent to Britton & Rose in Washington DC produced flowers which led to the plant's reclassification as a member of their new genus *Weberocereus*. This species is found only in a limited area in the provinces of Alajuela, Guanacaste and Limon in northern and northeastern Costa Rica.

In cultivation, this unusual cactus forms a rambling, much-branched vine of pencil-thick stems, often with aerial roots, that can be grown against a trellis or in a hanging basket, and flowers well. The pinkish, fragrant flowers are up to 6cm (2½in) in length and appear only at night.

Uncarina roeoesliana can be planted out in a bed and if given a free root run will soon produce a marvellous plant.

SUMMARY CHART

The chart gives general guidance for all the genera described in the A–Z section of this book. Plants marked ★ retain their southern hemisphere growing and flowering times when grown in the northern hemisphere, so that such a plant shown in the chart as flowering, for example, in midwinter (in the northern hemisphere) will flower in midsummer in its native habitat.

KEY
C CUTTINGS
S SEED
🌿 GROWING plants may be watered, easing the plant into growth during the first month and reducing the frequency in the last month
❀ FLOWERING
blank DORMANT do not water

	GENUS	PROPAGATION	MIN TEMP °CELSIUS	Midwinter	Late winter	Early spring	Mid-spring	Late spring	Early summer	Midsummer	Late summer	Early autumn	Mid-autumn	Late autumn	Early winter
1	Acanthocalycium	S	5				🌿	🌿❀	🌿❀	🌿❀	🌿❀	🌿			
2	Adenia	C & S	15				🌿	🌿	🌿❀	🌿❀	🌿❀	🌿❀			
3	Adenium	C & S	10–15				🌿	🌿	🌿❀	🌿❀	🌿❀	🌿❀			
4	Aeonium★	C & S	5	🌿	🌿	🌿❀	🌿❀	🌿❀				🌿	🌿	🌿	🌿
5	Agave	C & S	5				🌿	🌿	🌿❀	🌿❀	🌿❀	🌿❀			
7	Alluaudia	C	10				🌿	🌿	🌿	🌿	🌿	🌿			
	Note: rarely flowered in cultivation in Europe														
6	Aloe★	C & S	10–15					🌿	🌿	🌿❀	🌿❀	🌿❀	🌿❀	🌿❀	🌿❀
	Note: plants from Madagascar require a minimum temperature of 10°C														
8	Aporocactus	C	5		🌿	🌿	🌿❀	🌿❀	🌿						
9	Argyroderma	C & S	5							🌿	🌿	🌿	🌿❀	🌿❀	
10	Ariocarpus	S & grafting	5				🌿	🌿	🌿		🌿	🌿❀	❀		
11	Arrojadoa	C & S	10			🌿	🌿	🌿	🌿❀	🌿❀	🌿❀	🌿❀	🌿		
12	Astrophytum	S	10				🌿	🌿	🌿❀	🌿❀	🌿❀	🌿❀	🌿		
13	Austrocactus	C & S	0			🌿	🌿	🌿❀	🌿❀			🌿			
14	Aztekium	S & grafting	5–10					🌿	🌿	🌿❀	🌿❀	🌿			
15	Bijlia★	C & S	5	🌿❀	🌿❀	🌿❀	🌿❀						🌿❀	🌿❀	🌿❀
16	Blossfeldia	C, S & grafting	10				🌿	🌿❀	🌿❀	🌿❀					
17	Brachystelma	C & S	5				🌿	🌿	🌿❀	🌿❀	🌿❀	🌿❀			
18	Bursera	C & S	5				🌿	🌿	🌿❀	🌿❀	🌿❀	🌿❀			
19	Carnegiea	S	5				🌿	🌿❀	🌿❀	🌿❀	🌿				
20	Carpobrotus	C & S	5					🌿	🌿❀	🌿❀	🌿❀	🌿❀	🌿❀		
21	Cephalocereus	S	10				🌿❀	🌿❀	🌿❀	🌿❀	🌿❀	🌿❀	🌿❀		🌿❀
22	Cephalopentrandra	C & S	10				🌿❀	🌿❀	🌿❀	🌿❀	🌿❀	🌿❀			
23	Ceropegia	C & S	10				🌿❀	🌿❀	🌿❀	🌿❀	🌿❀	🌿❀			
24	Cleistocactus	C & S	5				🌿❀	🌿❀	🌿❀	🌿❀	🌿❀	🌿❀	🌿❀		

Legend for season columns: ○ = leaf (growth) symbol; ✿ = flower symbol (shown with leaf).

	GENUS	PROPAGATION	MIN TEMP °CELSIUS	Midwinter	Late winter	Early spring	Mid-spring	Late spring	Early summer	Midsummer	Late summer	Early autumn	Mid-autumn	Late autumn	Early winter
25	Conophytum★	C & S	5	○	○					○	○	✿	✿	✿	○
26	Copiapoa	C & S	5–10		✿	✿	✿	○			○	✿	✿	✿	
27	Coryphantha	C & S	5							✿	✿	✿			
28	Crassula	C & grafting	5	✿	✿	✿	✿						✿	✿	
29	Didymaotus	S	5							○	○	✿	✿	✿	○
30	Dioscorea★ (elephantipes)	S	5	✿							○	○	○	○	✿
31	Discocactus	S	10–15				○	○	✿	✿	✿	✿	✿		
32	Dorstenia	C & S	10						✿	✿	✿	✿	✿		
33	Dracaena	S	10					○	○	○	○	○	○		
	Note: unlikely to flower in cultivation until tree-sized														
34	Dudleya★	C & S	5	✿	✿	✿						✿	✿	✿	✿
35	Echeveria	C & S	5						✿	✿	○	✿	✿	✿	
36	Echinocactus	S	10								✿	✿	✿		
37	Echinocereus	C & S	0					✿	✿	✿	✿				
38	Echinopsis	C & S	5						✿	✿	✿	✿	✿		
39	Edithcolea	C & S	10					○	○	○	○	○	○		
	Note: do not dry out during dormancy. Rarely flowered in cultivation in Europe														
40	Epiphyllum	C & S	5–10	○	○	✿	✿	✿	✿	✿	✿	✿		○	○
41	Epithelantha	S	5							✿	✿	✿			
42	Eriosyce	S	5				✿	✿	✿						
43	Escobaria	C & S	0							✿	✿	✿			
44	Espostoopsis	C & S	5					○	✿	✿	✿	✿	✿		
45	Eulychnia	C & S	5				○	○	○	○	○	○			
	Note: rarely flowers in cultivation														
46	Euphorbia	S & grafting, (C – difficult)	10			✿	✿	○	○	○	○	○	○		
	Note: this is a summary of this large genus, there are many exceptions														
47	Ferocactus	S	5–10							○	✿	✿	✿		
48	Ficus	C & S	5–10			○	○	○	○	✿	✿	○	○		
49	Fouqueria	C & S	5				✿	✿	✿	✿	✿	✿			
50	Frailea	C & S	5						○	✿	✿	✿	✿		
51	Frerea	C & S	10				✿	✿	✿	✿	✿	✿			
52	Gasteria	C & S	5				✿	✿	✿	✿	✿	✿	✿		
53	Geohintonia	S & grafting	5–10						○	○	✿	✿	○		
54	Gibbaeum★	C & S	5	✿	✿					○	○	○	○	○	✿
55	Gymnocalycium	C & S	5					✿	✿	✿	✿	✿	✿	✿	
56	Hatiora	C	10	○	○	✿	✿	✿	✿	✿	✿	✿	✿	○	○
57	Haworthia	C & S	5				✿	✿	✿	✿	✿	✿	✿		

	GENUS	PROPAGATION	MIN TEMP °CELSIUS	Midwinter	Late winter	Early spring	Mid-spring	Late spring	Early summer	Midsummer	Late summer	Early autumn	Mid-autumn	Late autumn	Early winter
58	*Heliocereus*	C & S	10	🌿	🌿	🌿✿	🌿✿	🌿✿	🌿✿	🌿✿	🌿✿	🌿✿	🌿	🌿	🌿
59	*Hoodia*	C & S	10			🌿✿	🌿✿	🌿✿	🌿✿	🌿✿	🌿✿	🌿✿			
	Note: mist during resting period														
60	*Huernia*	C & S	10			🌿✿	🌿✿	🌿✿	🌿✿	🌿✿	🌿✿	🌿✿			
61	*Hylocereus*	C & S	12				🌿✿	🌿✿	🌿✿	🌿✿	🌿✿	🌿✿			
62	*Kalanchoe*	C	5–10												
	Note: very varied growing time														
63	*Lampranthus*	C & S	0–5						🌿✿	🌿✿	🌿✿	🌿✿	🌿✿	🌿	🌿
64	*Lepismium*	C & S	5–10	🌿✿	🌿✿	🌿✿	🌿✿	🌿✿					🌿	🌿✿	🌿✿
65	*Leuchtenbergia*	S	5–10							🌿	🌿	🌿			
66	*Lewisia*	C & S	0–5				🌿✿	🌿✿	🌿✿	🌿✿	🌿✿	🌿✿	🌿		
67	*Lithops*	S	5				🌿	🌿	🌿	🌿	🌿✿	🌿✿	🌿✿	🌿✿	
68	*Lophophora*	S	5				🌿✿	🌿✿	🌿✿	🌿✿	🌿✿	🌿✿			
69	*Maihuenia*	S & C	–10	🌿	🌿	🌿✿	🌿✿	🌿✿	🌿✿	🌿✿			🌿	🌿	🌿
70	*Mammillaria*	S & C	5			🌿✿	🌿✿	🌿✿	🌿✿	🌿✿	🌿✿	🌿✿			
	Note: this is a summary of this large genus, there are many exceptions														
71	*Matucana*	S & C	5–10							🌿✿	🌿✿	🌿✿	🌿✿		
72	*Melocactus*	S	10–15						🌿✿	🌿✿	🌿✿	🌿✿	🌿✿		
73	*Micranthocereus*★	S & C	10–15	🌿✿	🌿✿	🌿✿	🌿						🌿	🌿✿	🌿✿
74	*Monadenium*	C & S	10					🌿✿	🌿✿	🌿✿	🌿✿	🌿✿	🌿✿		
75	*Muiria*	S	5								🌿	🌿	🌿	🌿✿	🌿
	Note: rare to flower in Europe. Growing season occurs from mid- to late summer in habitat														
76	*Notocactus*	C & S	5				🌿	🌿✿	🌿✿	🌿✿	🌿✿				
77	*Obregonia*	S	5						🌿✿	🌿✿	🌿✿	🌿✿			
78	*Opuntia*	C & S	0–5					🌿✿	🌿✿	🌿✿	🌿✿	🌿✿			
79	*Oreocereus*	S	5–10				🌿	🌿	🌿	🌿✿	🌿✿	🌿✿	🌿		
80	*Orostachys*	C & S	5					🌿✿	🌿✿	🌿✿	🌿✿	🌿✿			
81	*Ortegocactus*	C & S	12–15				🌿	🌿✿	🌿✿	🌿✿	🌿✿				
82	*Othonna*★	S	10								🌿	🌿✿	🌿✿	🌿✿	🌿✿
83	*Pachycereus*	C & S	5			🌿	🌿✿	🌿✿	🌿✿	🌿	🌿	🌿			
84	*Pachyphytum*	C & S	5				🌿✿	🌿✿	🌿✿	🌿✿	🌿✿				
85	*Pachypodium*	C & S	5–10			🌿✿	🌿✿	🌿✿	🌿✿	🌿✿	🌿✿				
86	*Parodia*	C & S	5–10			🌿	🌿	🌿✿	🌿✿	🌿✿	🌿✿				
87	*Pedilanthus*	C & S	10					🌿✿	🌿✿	🌿✿	🌿✿	🌿✿			
88	*Pediocactus*	C & S	0			🌿✿	🌿✿	🌿✿					🌿	🌿	🌿
89	*Pelargonium*	C & S	5												
	Note: very varied growing time														

	GENUS	PROPAGATION	MIN TEMP °CELSIUS	Midwinter	Late winter	Early spring	Mid-spring	Late spring	Early summer	Midsummer	Late summer	Early autumn	Mid-autumn	Late autumn	Early winter
90	*Pelecyphora*	S	10				🌿✿	🌿✿	🌿✿	🌿✿	🌿✿				
91	*Peniocereus*	C & S	5												
92	*Pereskia*	C	5				🌿	🌿	🌿	🌿✿	🌿✿	🌿✿			
93	*Pereskiopsis*	C	5–10				🌿	🌿	🌿	🌿✿	🌿✿	🌿✿			
94	*Pilosocereus*	C & S	10–15				🌿	🌿	🌿	🌿✿	🌿✿				
95	*Plumeria*	C & S	15			🌿✿	🌿✿	🌿✿	🌿✿	🌿✿	🌿✿	🌿✿			
96	*Pseudolithos*	S	10						🌿	🌿✿	🌿✿	🌿✿			
97	*Pterodiscus*	C & S	10							🌿✿	🌿✿	🌿✿	🌿✿		
98	*Rebutia*	C & S	5			🌿		🌿	🌿	🌿✿	🌿✿				
99	*Rhipsalis*★	C	5–10	🌿✿	🌿✿	🌿✿	🌿✿	🌿✿				🌿	🌿✿	🌿✿	🌿✿
100	*Rhytidocaulon*	(c) & S	15					🌿	🌿	🌿✿	🌿✿	🌿✿			
101	*Sansevieria*	C	10	🌿	🌿	🌿	🌿	🌿		🌿✿	🌿✿	🌿✿	🌿	🌿	🌿
102	*Sarcocoulon*	C & S	10				🌿	🌿	🌿✿	🌿✿	🌿✿	🌿✿			
	Note: mist during dormancy to prevent leaf drop														
103	*Schlumbergera*	C	5	🌿✿	🌿✿	🌿✿	🌿	🌿	🌿	🌿	🌿	🌿		🌿✿	🌿✿
104	*Sclerocactus*	S & grafting	0				🌿✿	🌿✿	🌿✿			🌿	🌿		
105	*Sedum*	C & S	0				🌿✿	🌿✿	🌿✿	🌿✿	🌿✿	🌿✿			
106	*Selenicereus*	C	5	🌿	🌿	🌿✿	🌿✿	🌿✿	🌿✿	🌿✿		🌿			🌿
107	*Sempervivum*	C & S	0				🌿✿	🌿✿	🌿✿	🌿✿	🌿✿	🌿✿			
108	*Senecio*	C & S	10												
	Note: very varied growing time														
109	*Sesamothamnus*	S	10				🌿✿	🌿✿	🌿	🌿✿	🌿	🌿✿			
110	*Stenocactus*	S	5			🌿✿	🌿✿	🌿✿	🌿✿						
111	*Stenocereus*	C & S	10				🌿	🌿✿	🌿✿	🌿✿	🌿	🌿	🌿		
112	*Strombocactus*	S	5					🌿	🌿✿	🌿✿	🌿✿	🌿			
113	*Tacitus*	C & S	5				🌿✿	🌿✿	🌿✿	🌿✿	🌿✿	🌿✿			
114	*Tavaresia*	C & S	10				🌿✿	🌿✿	🌿✿	🌿✿	🌿✿	🌿✿			
115	*Thelocactus*	C & S	5					🌿	🌿✿	🌿✿	🌿✿	🌿✿			
116	*Trichocaulon*	C & S	10				🌿✿	🌿✿	🌿✿	🌿✿	🌿✿	🌿✿			
117	*Turbinicarpus*	C, S & grafting	5				🌿✿	🌿✿	🌿✿	🌿✿					
118	*Uebelmannia*	S & grafting	10–15			🌿	🌿✿	🌿✿	🌿✿	🌿	🌿	🌿			
119	*Uncarina*	C & S	10				🌿✿	🌿✿	🌿✿	🌿✿	🌿✿	🌿✿			
120	*Weberbauerocereus*	C & S	5			🌿	🌿	🌿	🌿✿	🌿✿	🌿✿	🌿			
121	*Weberocereus*	C & S	10	🌿	🌿	🌿✿	🌿✿	🌿✿	🌿✿	🌿✿	🌿✿	🌿✿	🌿	🌿	🌿

Appendix I *Where to See Cacti & Other Succulents*

UK

Bught Floral Hall
Inverness, Scotland

Holly Gate Cactus Garden
Ashington, West Sussex

Kew Gardens
London

USA

Anza-Borrego Desert State Park
California

Arizona Cactus & Succulent Research
Bisbee, Arizona

Arizona-Sonora Desert Botanical Garden
Tucson, Arizona

Big Bend National Park
near Marathon, Texas

Boyce Thompson Southwestern Arboretum
Superior, Arizona

Brooklyn Botanical Garden
Brooklyn, New York

Desert Botanical Garden
Phoenix, Arizona

Huntington Botanical Gardens
San Marino, Los Angeles, California

Joshua Tree National Park
California

Living Desert Reserve
Palm Desert, Palm Springs, California

Los Angeles Botanical Garden
Los Angeles, California

New York Botanical Garden
Bronx Park, Bronx, New York

Organ Pipe Cactus National Monument
Arizona

Saguaro National Park
Tucson, Arizona

Santa Barbara Botanic Garden
Palm Springs, California

AUSTRIA

Botanischer Garten der Universitat Wien
Vienna

Botanischer Garten und Arboretum der Stadt Linz
Bancalariweg, Linz

FRANCE

Jardin Exotique d'Eze-sur-Mer
Eze-sur-Mer, Alpes Maritimes

Jardin Exotique de Sanary-sur-Mer
Sanary-sur-Mer, Provence

Les Cedres
Saint Jean-Cap Ferrat, Alpes Maritimes

GERMANY

Botanischer Garten München
München

Frankfurt Botanic Garden
Palmengarten, Frankfurt am Main

Heidelberg Botanic Garden
Heidelberg

Kiel Botanic Garden
Kiel

ITALY

Hanbury Gardens
La Mortola, Ventimiglia

MONACO

Jardin Exotique de Monaco
Monte Carlo

SPAIN

Botanicactus
Ses Salines, Mallorca

Costa I Lobera
Montjuich, Barcelona

Desierto Feliz
Tenerife

Jardin Botanico
Funchal, Madeira

Jardin Canario
Gran Canaria

Jardin de Cactus
Lanzarote, Canary Islands

Marimurtra
Blanes

Pinya de Rosa
Santa Christina, Blanes

SWITZERLAND

Stadtische Sukkulentensammlung (Zurich)
Zurich

SOUTH AFRICA

Karoo National Botanic Garden
Worcester, Cape Province

Kruger Park
Transvaal

National Botanic Gardens
Kirstenbosch, Cape Province

Pretoria Botanic Garden
Pretoria, Transvaal

Appendix II *Where to Buy Cacti & Other Succulents*

UK

Brookside Nursery
Alan Butler, Elderberry Farm, Bognor
Road, Horsham, West Sussex RH12 3PS

Connoisseur Cacti
John Pilbeam, 51 Chelsfield Lane,
Orpington, Kent BR5 4HG

Kent Cacti
Doug Sizmour, 35 Rutland Way,
Orpington, Kent BR5 4DY
Note Connoisseur Cacti and Kent Cacti
nurseries both at: Woodlands Farm, Shire
Lane, Farnborough, Kent

Eau Brink Cacti
Derek Bowdery, Eau Brink Road,
Tilney All Saints, King's Lynn, Norfolk
PE34 4SQ

Holly Gate Cactus Nursery
Terry Hewitt, Billingshurst Road,
Ashington, West Sussex RH20 3BA

Plantlife
Stuart Riley, Beechwood, Friday Street,
Eastbourne, East Sussex

Doug & Viv Rowland (Seed Suppliers)
200 Spring Road, Kempston, Bedford
MK42 8ND

Toobees Exotics
Bob Potter, Blackhorse Road, Woking,
Surrey GU22 0QT

Woodside Cacti
Chapel Drove, Holbeach, Nr Spalding,
Lincolnshire PE12 0PT

USA

**Abbey Garden Cacti and
Succulents**
PO Box 2249, La Habra
CA 90632-2249

Arid Lands Greenhouses
Chuck Hanson, 3560 West Bilby Road,
Tucson AZ 85746

Bob Smoley's Gardenworld
Bob Smoley, 4038 Watters Lane,
Gibsonia PA 15044

Great Petaluma Desert
Jerry Wright Jr, 5010 Bodega Avenue,
Petaluma CA 94952

Grigsby Cactus Garden
Madelyn Lee, 2354 Bella Vista, Vista
CA 92083

Mesa Garden
Steve Brack, Greer Road, PO Box 72,
Belen NM 87002

Miles to Go
Miles Anderson, PO Box 6, Cortraro
AZ 85652

Rainbow Gardens Nursery
Jerry Williams, 1444 E. Taylor Street,
Vista CA 92084

BELGIUM

Cactussen & Vetplanten
Maurits Huygaerts, Steenweg op
Oosthoven 39, 2300 Turnhout

Kwekerij Vanbiervliet
Dirk Vanbiervliet, Dyserinck Ann,
Goedeboterstraat 42, 8460 Oudenburg

GERMANY

Exotica: Botanische Raritaten
Ernst Specks, Am Kloster 8, D-41812
Erkelenz

Kakteen Centrum Oberhausen
Flockenfeld 101, D-46049 Oberhausen

Kakteen-Haage
Blumenstrasse 68, D-99092 Erfurt

**Kakteen Sukkulenten Orchideen
& Caudex Gewachse**
Peter Momberger, Zierplanzenbau,
An der Gerbermuehle 8, D-65207
Wiesbaden-Breckenheim

G. Koehres
Wingerstrasse 32, D-64387 Erzhausen,
Darmstadt

Lausser-Kakteen
Alfons Lausser, Luisenstrasse 14,
D-92284 Trasslberg

Navajo Country
Fritz Hochstatter, PO Box 510 201,
D-68242

Jorg Piltz
Monschauer Landstrasse 162, D-5160
Duren-Birgel

Uhlig Kakteen
U. Uhlig, Postfach 1107, D-71385

ITALY

Botaniké
Lucio Russo, Casella Postale 27, Baveno
I-28831

Panarotto Cactus & Succulente
Paolo Panarotto, Via Nanon, 2-37035
S. Giovanni Ilarione

NETHERLANDS

Cactusnurserie J.v.d. Linden
J. van der Linden, Nieuweweg 18,
Honselersdijk NL-2675 BC

Frans Noltee
Rotterdamseweg 88, Zwijndrecht
NL-3332 AK

Grootscholten, Cok
Cok Grootscholten, Vijverberglaan 5,
Honselersdijk NL-2675 LC

Paul Shirley Succulents
Julianastraat 16, 2771 DX Boskoop

Plantentuin van Donkelaar
Laantje 1, Postbus 15, Werkendam
NL-4250 DA

J.F.A. Wortelboer
Meer en Vaart 360, Amsterdam
NL-1068 LH

SOUTH AFRICA

Kernkwekerij
Posbus 55, Vanrhynsdorp 8170

Selecta Succulents
PO Box 278, Klapmuts 7625

Sheilam Nursery
PO Box 157, Robertson 6705

Appendix III *National Societies & Specialist Groups*

Contact addresses for many of the societies and groups listed below are readily available on the Internet. They are conveniently accessed from the Cactus & Succulent Plant Mall website (www.cactus-mall.com) or the Amateur's Digest (www.com/~amdigest), and as membership officers may change over time we recommend that you check these sites for up-to-date information. For those not yet surfing on-line, your local specialist nursery or horticultural society should be able to provide details and application forms.

Journals produced by the societies and specialist groups listed below are given in italics.

NATIONAL SOCIETIES

UK
British Cactus and Succulent Society
British Cactus and Succulent Journal
USA
Cactus and Succulent Society of America
Canada
The Amateur's Digest
Australia
Cactus and Succulent Society of Queensland, Australia
New Zealand
Cactus and Succulent Society of New Zealand
Austria
Gesellschaft Österreichischer Kakteenfreunde
Belgium
Cactusclub 'Aylostera'
Cactussen en Vetplanten
Czech Republic
Kaktusy
Kaktusy
Society of Czech and Slovak Cacti and Succulent Growers
France
ARIDES (L'Association de Recherches et d'Informations sur les Déserts et les Succulentes)
International Cactus-Adventures
AIAPS (Association Internationale des Amateurs de Plantes Succulentes)
Germany
DKG (Deutsche Kakteen-Gesellschaft eV)
Kakteen und andere Sukkelenten
Italy
AIAS (Ássociázione Italiana Amatori della Piante Succulente)
Piante Grasse

Cactus & Co
Cactus & Co
Netherlands
Succulenta
Succulenta
Dutch-Belgian Society of Cactus and Succulent Amateurs
Scandinavia
Nordic Cactus and Succulent Society
Spain
Assocacian Amigos de los cactus y demás Suculentas
Cactus Center Club
Switzerland
Schweizerische Kakteengesellschaft
Brazil
Sociedade Brasileira de Cactos e Suculentas
India
ISOCS (Indian Society of Cacti and Succulents)
Malta
Cactus and Succulent Society of Malta
Peru
SPECS (Sociedad Peruana de Cactus y Suculentas)
Philippines
Cactus and Succulent Society of the Philippines
South Africa
Succulent Society of South Africa
Aloe

SPECIALIST GROUPS

Cacti
Echinocereus
AG Echinocereus
Der Echinocereenfreund
Gymnocalycium
Gymnos Arbeitsgruppe
Gymnos

Mammillaria
Mammillaria Society
The Mammillaria Society Journal
Arbeitskreis für Mammillarienfreunde (AfM)
Arbeitskreis für Mammillarienfreunde
Notocactus
Internoto (International Society of the Friends of Notocacti)
South American Cacti
The Chileans
The Chileans

Other Succulents
Adenium
Adenium Society
Asclepiadaceae
International Asclepiad Society
Asklepios
Conophytum
Conophytum Society of Japan
Euphorbiaceae
Euphorbiaceae Study Group
Bulletin of …
Geranium
International Geranium Society
Haworthia
Haworthia Society
Haworthiad
Hoya
Hoya Society International
Mesembryanthemaceae
Association of Mesemb Growers of Czech Republic
Mesemb Study Group
Sansevieria
Sansevieria Society
Sedum
Sedum Society
Succulents
Succulent Plant Trust

Appendix IV *Glossary of Terms*

Acauline Stemless; sometimes only appearing to be without a stem where this is hidden below soil level.

Apical At or near the apex (end) of an organ, as opposed to basal – appearing at or near the base of an organ.

Areole Axillary bud, in cacti usually the spine cluster or cushion.

Bract Modified leaf immediately below the calyx.

Caespitose Offsetting to produce many-stemmed cushions or mounds.

Callus Cells formed usually as a response to the plant being wounded. These cells are usually undifferentiated and have the ability to revert to a different form of growth, such as the cells on a callused stem cutting that become the roots when placed in moist soil or water.

Calyx Outer whorl of sepals of the perianth of a flower, often green in colour.

Cambium Layer of regenerating cell tissue.

Campanulate Bell shaped.

Caudex Massively enlarged, succulent perennial base or trunk of an otherwise herbaceous plant. The term is sometimes used for a partly submerged, large swollen taproot.

Caudiciform Plant that forms a caudex.

Cephalium Specialized growth in certain cacti, usually extra-woolly or bristly, that produces the flowers. Although usually terminal (*Discocactus*, *Melocactus*), in some genera it only covers one side of the plant stem (lateral or pseudocephalium), while in the genus *Arrojadoa* ring cephalia appear at intervals along the stem.

Ciliated Fringed with fine hairs.

Cleistogamous Flowers that do not open at the time when the pollen is ripe and the stigmas are receptive, resulting in self-pollination, as in many species of *Frailea*. The term is also used in the name *Cleistocactus*, where the flowers appear to be cleistogamous, although they do in fact open slightly to enable pollination by hummingbirds and wind.

Connate Fused or grown together.

Cristate Abnormal growth pattern where the (usually single) growing point of a stem is elongated to produce a fan-like shape.

cv. Cultivar (contracted from 'cultivated variety'). Introduced in the 1950s for varieties created in horticulture rather than those found in nature.

Cyathium (plural cyathia) Specialized inflorescence found in *Euphorbia* species, where several male flowers are reduced to a single stamen and are found alongside a single-ovary female flower. The male and female flowers together are presented with often colourful bracts and/or glandular nectaries.

Cymose In the form of a cyme, a type of inflorescence in which the relative main axis is soon terminated with a flower and subsequent growth occurs from one or several side branches.

Decumbent Creeping along the ground with tips raised.

Dehiscent Opening naturally along one or more predefined lines.

Dichotomous Branching or forking into two equal stems.

Dioecious Species that have male and female plants, ie the flowers on a particular plant will have only male or female organs and a plant of the opposite sex is required in order to produce seed.

Distichous Arrangement of branches or leaves in two opposite rows.

Diurnal Flowers that open during the day, as opposed to nocturnal flowers that open at night.

Epidermis External protective layer of cells, or 'skin', of a plant.

Epiphyte Plant that grows with its roots anchored to the branches of another plant without parasitizing the host. The roots are not usually in the soil but can obtain nutrients from accumulated leaf litter.

f. (fa.) Form (forma). Taxonomic rank below variety, used for a taxon that differs only in a single characteristic or in a group of closely interrelated characteristics.

Family In taxonomy, a group of similar plants.

Farinose Covered in flour-like or mealey white powder.

Fusiform Spindle-shaped; elongated and terete, gradually tapering at each end.

Genus In taxonomy, a category or rank of species that share a set of common characteristics.

Geophyte Herbaceous plant where the stem is wholly or partly below soil level, permanently or for short periods – for example, *Pediocactus* species that pull themselves into the soil outside the growing season to find protection from the elements, or caudiciform plants with swollen underground food-storage organs.

Glabrous Bald; devoid of hairs, bristles, glands or spines.

Glaucous Covered in a fine bloom, often caused by a fine layer of wax on the epidermis that can range from greyish white, through bluish white, to bluish green in colour.

Glochid Small spines characteristic of the subfamily Opuntioideae of the Cactaceae family. Usually very small, they are easily detached and have a barbed tip.

Hilum Part of the seed where it was attached to the fruit wall via the funicle (thread-like stalk of the ovule).

Hybrid Any organism that is the result of a cross between two different taxa. As the scope of species changes, often taking in former species as synonyms ('lumping'), so taxa that may have been regarded as hybrids may now be regarded as forms or specific populations of the species.

Hypathodium Inflorescence consisting of a flattened disk-like or vessel-like structure into which individual flowers are sunk; typical of the genus *Dorstenia*.

Inferior ovary Applies to flowers where the ovary is situated below the other flower parts.

Inflorescence Plant branch that carries the flowers.

Lanceolate Shaped like a lance.

Meristem Non-specialized plant cells that readily divide to form new cells that become specialized plant tissue.

Mitotic cell division Type of cell division where the chromosome set duplicates prior to cell division.

Monocarpic Flowering at the end of the natural life-span, when the plant dies after the fruits have ripened, such as in most species of *Agave*.

Monoecious Plants with flowers that have only male or female organs, but where both male and female flowers appear on the same plant.

Monstrose, monstrous Abnormal growth patterns due to abnormal organization of the plant's apical growing point – for example, forms of ribbed cacti species that have lost their ribs, or cacti where each areole produces an offset or an elongated growing point, giving rise to cristate forms.

Mucilaginous Slimy or jelly-like.

Obconical Inversely conical.

Obovate Inversely ovate; egg-shaped and attached at the narrow end.

Panicle Inflorescence where the raceme branches into more racemes.

Papilla Minute, nipple- or wart-like projection of epidermal cells.

Parenchyma cells Undifferentiated thin-walled cells that make up the bulk of many plant organs.

Pectinate Comb shaped, radiating along a straight line.

Peduncle Main stem of a whole inflorescence.

Perianth Protective envelope of a flower, consisting of tepals or a calyx and corolla.

Pericarp Fruit wall, often consisting of an outer exocarp and inner endocarp wall.

Pericarpel Tissue around the carpel (the female organ of a flower that is angiospermous, ie where the seeds are enclosed in an ovary).

Petal Each of the segments of a corolla, usually coloured to attract pollinators.

Pinnate Compound leaf with two or more pairs of leaflets.

Plumose Feathery.

Pollinium Waxy mass of pollen as found in the family Asclepiadaceae (and in orchids).

Porrect Stretched outward and forward.

Pruinose Covered in a fine layer of wax, giving a whitish, slightly powdery appearance, like a plum.

Pseudanthium Reduced inflorescence which as a whole appears to be a single flower – for example, the flower-heads of the family Compositae or the cyathia in species of *Euphorbia*.

Pseudocephalium False cephalium, that covers only part of the circumference of the stem.

Pubescent Downy, covered with fine hairs.

Pulverulent Covered in powder.

Raceme Inflorescence where the main flower stalk does not end in a truly terminal flower and where the flowers start to open from the bottom to the top of the stalk. May be branched or unbranched.

Ramifying Branching.

Receptacle Part of the flower stalk that carries the individual flower parts.

Rhizome Somewhat thickened, fleshy stem rooting at the nodes while continuing to grow at the tip, producing new leaves.

Rib In cacti and stem succulents, the vertically arranged ridges formed by the fusion of tubercles.

Rosulate Arranged in the form of a rosette.

Sepal Each individual part of the calyx; the leaves of the outer floral envelope.

Sessile Stalkless; without stalk, peduncle, pedicel (flower stalk) or petiole (leaf stalk).

sp. Species. In botanical classification, the basic unit or rank of closely related individuals that can interbreed and produce offspring with characteristics that also fit the description of the group. There is no precise definition of the degree to which individuals should be related in order to belong to the same species.

Stapeliad Common name used for members of the family Asclepiadaceae.

Stolon Runner or sucker – a creeping stem originating from the base of the plant, rooting at its tip and producing a bud from which a new plant grows.

Stoloniferous Producing stolons.

Stoma (plural stomata) Pore surrounded by 'guard cells' in the epidermis of the plant, through which gasses such as carbon dioxide and oxygen are exchanged with the atmosphere, thus enabling the plant to 'breathe'.

Suborbicular Almost disc shaped; flat, with a circular outline.

subsp. Subspecies. Taxonomic rank below species and above variety and form. There is no absolute definition for the term, which in recent years has been used as a synonym for and in preference to 'variety'.

Taxon Any taxonomic group or unit such as family, genus or species.

Taxonomy Study of the classification of organisms.

Tendril Slender modified branch or leaf that is sensitive to touch and coils to help a plant climb or anchor itself.

Terete Elongated-cylindrical, and circular in cross section.

Testa Outer and normally hardened protective layer of a seed; the seed coat.

Truncate Having a tip or base as if cut off.

Tubercle Conical or cylindrical outgrowth from a plant body, characteristic of some cacti such as *Mammillaria*.

Tuberculate Covered with wart-like growths.

var. Variety. Taxonomic rank below subspecies and above form. There is no absolute definition for the term, but traditionally it is used for a taxon that differs in more than one characteristic from the other components of the species. In recent years there has been a trend towards using the term 'subspecies' in preference to and instead of variety, so that it becomes a rank below species. According to some authorities, subspecies have distribution areas that are separate from the species, while varieties need not.

Vascular bundle Strand composed of phloem and xylem cells, which are specialized in transporting liquids within the plant body.

Zygomorphic With only one plane of symmetry, so will produce only two mirror images when sectioned.

Bibliography

Anderson, E.F., Arias Montes, S., & Taylor, N.P., *Threatened Cacti of Mexico*, 1994

Backeberg, Curt, *Cactus Lexicon*, 1966

Bakhuizen, B.P., *Succulents of Southern Africa*, 1978

Benson, Lyman, *Cacti of the United States and Canada*, 1982

Blum, Lange, Rischer & Rutow, *Echinocereus*, 1998

Bregman, Rob, *The Genus Matucana*, 1996

Britton & Rose, *The Cactaceae*, 1922

Charles, Graham, *Copiapoa (Cactus File Handbook 4)*, 1998

Cole, Desmond T., *Lithops*, 1998

de Wilde, W.J.J.O., *A Monograph of the Genus Adenia*, 1971

Dyer, *The Genera of South African Flowering Plants*, 1975

Eggli, Urs (compiler), *Glossary of Botanical Terms with Special Reference to Succulent Plants*, 1993

Gentry, Howard Scott, *Agaves of Continental North America*, 1982

Gibson & Nobel, *The Cactus Primer*, 1986

Hammer, Steven, *The Genus Conophytum: A Conograph*, 1993

Henrickson, James, 'The Succulent Fouquierias', *Cactus and Succulent Journal* (US) 41(4), 1969

Herre, Hans, *The Genera of the Mesembryanthemaceae*, 1971

Hunt, David (compiler), CITES *Cactaceae Checklist*, 1992

Ivimey-Cook, R.B., *Succulents – A Glossary of Terms and Descriptions*, 1974

Jacobsen, Hermann, *Lexicon of Succulent Plants*, 1970

Jonkers, Bert, 'Maihuenia – A Fascinating Cactus Genus', *British Cactus & Succulent Journal* 16 (3): 147, 1998

Kyte, Lydiane, *Plants from Test Tubes: An Introduction to Micropropagation*, 1983

Pilbeam, John, *Gymnocalycium: A Collector's Guide*, 1995
Rebutia (Cactus File Handbook 2), 1997
Sulcorebutia and Weingartia: A Collector's Guide, 1985
Thelocactus (Cactus File Handbook 1), 1996

Reynolds, G.W., *The Aloes of South Africa*, 1950

Robbins, James A., 'Lithops at 1°F (-17.2°C)', *Cactus and Succulent Journal* (US) 52(4): 270, 1980
'Mesembs that are Hardy to Cold', *Cactus and Succulent Journal* (US) 53(1): 14, 1981

Rowley, Gordon D., *Caudiciform & Pachycaul Succulents*, 1978
A History of Succulent Plants, 1997

Schulz & Kapitany, *Copiapoa in their Environment*, 1997

Stearn, William T., *Botanical Latin*, 1993

Taylor, Nigel, *The Genus Echinocereus*, 1985

White, Dyer & Sloane, *The Succulent Euphorbiae of Southern Africa*, 1941

White & Sloane, *The Stapelieae*, second edition 1937

Zappi, Daniela C., *Pilosocereus (Cactaceae) – The Genus in Brazil*, 1994

Index

ACKNOWLEDGEMENTS

One of the joys of a hobby is the close friendship that a common interest can generate. Both authors owe a vote of gratitude to Terry and Jenny Hewitt of Holly Gate Cactus Nursery in Ashington, West Sussex, England, without whose hospitality and encouragement this book would not have been produced. Many of the photographs reproduced in the book were taken in their reference collection and propagation houses, where the plants provided a valuable reference point to confirm or correct information that we have gleaned from our own collections, the available literature and trips we have made to the habitats of our favourite plants.

We want also to thank Alan Pocock and Brian Thompson who, with other members of a dedicated group of propagators, aim to make these rare and endangered plants available in sufficient numbers to meet popular demand without creating pressures on plants in habitat. Their information on micropropagation and grafting has provided us with an insight into an aspect of the hobby that usually remains a mystery.

We must also acknowledge the value of the Internet in obtaining information about our subject, and here we would like to single out Tony and Suzanne Mace, whose

Cactus and Succulent Plant Mall (www.cactus-mall.com) is the first web page to visit if you want to know more. Thank you, too, to Bob Jewett, moderator of the invaluable cacti_etc and hardycacti_etc email forums, whose contributors may recognize little snippets of information that they have shared with us and some 1,500 other enthusiasts over the last four years. We trust that they will endorse our sharing of this information with a wider audience. Thank you all.

Our thanks go also to the people at David & Charles Publishers, who made the writing and photography of this book such an enjoyable experience.

We have both learned a lot about our hobby from the research that has gone into the preparation and writing of the book, and will no doubt learn a lot more from the comments and questions that some of you may put to us after reading it.

Finally, we would like to thank the members of our respective families who, as with most hobbies, at times must feel themselves in competition with our plants and PCs. Thank you for your support, and for giving us the time to share some of our enjoyment of our hobby with others.